W9-ASB-772

John F. Kennedy
and
American Catholicism

Books by LAWRENCE H. FUCHS

POLITICAL BEHAVIOR OF AMERICAN JEWS

HAWAII PONO: A SOCIAL HISTORY

JOHN F. KENNEDY AND AMERICAN CATHOLICISM

JOHN F. KENNEDY
and
AMERICAN CATHOLICISM

by LAWRENCE H. FUCHS

PROFESSOR OF AMERICAN CIVILIZATION
AND POLITICS, BRANDEIS UNIVERSITY

Meredith Press   New York

First edition

Library of Congress Catalog Card Number: 67-11026

MANUFACTURED IN THE UNITED STATES OF AMERICA FOR MEREDITH PRESS

VAN REES PRESS • NEW YORK

To Vic and Al
for help and encouragement

PREFACE

M Y first contact with President Kennedy came in 1952 in a seminar at Harvard. I was then a graduate student and teaching fellow in government, and he was a member of the House of Representatives. Several years later, while he was convalescing from a back operation and dangerous infection, Senator Kennedy read certain portions of a book I had written and some articles of mine on ethnic factors in American politics. We began to correspond on a variety of issues, including the banning of nuclear bombing in the atmosphere. In 1957 I wrote a speech and some memoranda for him, and in 1958 he supported my successful bid for a Social Science Research Council grant to study aspects of ethnicity in American politics.

Between 1959 and 1960 we had two rather long talks, one at Brandeis and one in Hawaii; in the campaign I gave modest help to his candidacy, primarily by speaking in New England and New York. Following his election, I had no further direct contact with the President, except for a brief greeting at Hyannisport in the summer of 1961, shortly after which I left my post as Dean of Faculty at Brandeis to become Director of the Peace Corps in the Philippines.

My contacts with the President were few, and I suppose he knew at least a thousand people as he knew me. My admiration for him grew over the years as I watched his keen, incisive mind and came into contact with his free spirit. To the extent that this book is biography, it can hardly be called objective in any total sense. The more I got to know Kennedy, or know about him, the more I liked and respected him; but I hope I have been able to maintain the kind of intellectual detachment and precision that he so much admired.

For those who feel their understanding of the book will be aided by additional personal information about me, I am a Jew by birth and conviction who has long been interested in both politics and religion in America. I am a Democrat in politics, having served for many years on the Democratic town committee in my own town of Weston, Massachusetts.

I want to thank Robert W. Lutnes for persuading me to write this book. I had thought of putting these ideas into a long article, but Mr. Lutnes convinced me that they should be presented in a full-length book. I give thanks also to Stuart Jerry Brown, Professor of American Civilization at the University of Hawaii, and to John Leo, Associate Editor of *Commonweal,* for their suggestions; and especially to my brother, Dr. Victor Fuchs, Associate Director of Research at the National Bureau of Economic Research, for his tough criticisms, advice, and enthusiastic encouragement.

My appreciation goes also to Miss Barbara Duke, Mrs. Ellen Char, and Miss Lorraine Tani, each of whom helped to type this manuscript, and to the East-West Center at the University of Hawaii where I was in residence as a senior scholar on American values and character for the academic year 1965–66 and where much of this book was written.

Lawrence H. Fuchs

Weston, Massachusetts

CONTENTS

CONTENTS

INTRODUCTION

T HE psychology of each of us is shaped to a considerable extent by our religious inheritance. How could it be otherwise? Religion deals with the ways in which men approach the fundamental questions of human existence: the nature of man, the purpose of life, the meaning of death, the relationship of man to man, to nature, and to mystery.

Because in the West we have tended to agree with the psalmist that God made man "a little lower than the angels" and "put all things under his feet," we usually have seen man as an active, rational being, attempting to control his environment. There are many other essential unities in what is often called the Judaic-Christian tradition. But there are differences, too, which are more than just nuances or subtleties in emphasis. There are differences over which men have denounced their brothers, fought their fathers, and bled their neighbors. In large measure, it was because of such differences that many of the earliest settlers came to America.*

* In this book I frequently will use the term "America," meaning the United States of America. I hope this does not offend Canadian or Latin American readers who complain with considerable justice of the way in which we Americans in the United States forget the other Americans. My only defense is that the vast majority of the readers of this book will be Americans from the United States, Europeans, or Asians, and they nearly all read the word "Americans" as meaning persons who were born and educated or at least make their homes in the United States.

Out of the turbulent, familicidal warfare of the fifteenth, sixteenth, and seventeenth centuries, there developed increasingly distinctive Protestant and Catholic approaches to family life, economics, and politics. The cataclysmic rebellion called the Protestant Reformation gave birth to a new nation of Americans whose values and institutions often were based self-consciously on an explicit rejection of what was perceived to be Catholic.

Early in American history, certain Protestant principles were infused into a new culture-religion of Americanism which transcended Protestant sectarianism, but which also was felt to be under persistent and corrosive attack by the Church of Rome. During the nineteenth century, millions of Catholics from the peasant cultures of Europe came to live and work in an environment suffused with a deep suspicion of things Catholic. The clash of cultures was proclaimed in pulpits throughout the land, resounding in the main streets and back alleys of American towns and cities, and its echoes have not yet subsided. But in 1960, at a time of great national peril, a nation, born in part out of hatred for the Catholic world-view, elected to its highest office a Catholic great-grandson of Catholic immigrants.

Nineteen-sixty was a year of hope because of John F. Kennedy—a young man whose courage had been proved many times and whose ability to articulate the anguish and dreams of men gave new hope to peoples of many tongues, hope for peace, for food, for decency and human advance. In America there was fear as well as hope, because John F. Kennedy was a Catholic. Kennedy's candidacy and election brought fear to hundreds of thousands of non-Catholic Americans who believed fervently that a Catholic in the White House would do irreparable harm to them and to America. Many of them were clear-thinking, rational, and decent men, who were frightened by the prospect of a Catholic president. Later, they would mourn the death of Kennedy as a fallen leader and hero in a struggle to protect and advance the values they cherished most.

This book is about American national character, the Catholic

Church in America, and John F. Kennedy, as they relate to each other. A considerable amount of historical information precedes Kennedy's major entrance in the book, but it is necessary in my view really to understand the man and his significance as the first Catholic President in history and a culture-hero of most Americans. For me, an appreciation of Kennedy as a man, Catholic, and President is enlarged through a better understanding of American values and religion and a more sensitive appreciation of the fears and hopes that have often characterized the meetings of Catholics and non-Catholics in America.

In the first chapter, "A City upon a Hill," I explore the way and extent to which Protestant principles, transformed by the American environment, are at the heart of the culture-religion of Americanism. I attempt to provide the background for understanding, not just the fear of Kennedy as a prospective President, but the esteem and reverence of Kennedy as a President and culture-hero.

In the chapter which follows, "Defending the City," I trace the attitudes and behavior of Protestant Americans in defending their values against alleged Catholic assaults from colonial times until the defeat of Al Smith in 1928.

In the third chapter, "Hope and Fear," I describe and analyze the major responses of Catholics to the American environment and the cult of individualism. Here I try to understand the bases and nature of change within the Church in the United States in the eighteenth, nineteenth, and early twentieth centuries, in order better to understand John F. Kennedy as a symbol and catalyst of change among American Catholics in the nineteen-sixties.

In "Deepening Tensions," the fourth chapter, I depict the mounting clash of Protestant and Catholic cultures in urban politics, leading up to the election of 1960.

The campaign and election of 1960 are brought into focus in Chapter V, "Not the Catholic Candidate." In it, I try to analyze the tense battle which Kennedy fought against tradition, fear and prejudice in the primary and election campaigns.

Next, I examine in Chapter VI, "Promises to Keep" the symbolization of American values in the institution of the presidency and in presidential heroes, of whom John F. Kennedy was the latest and probably most dramatic example.

Finally, in Chapter VII, "The Value of Our Time," I speculate about the significance of the life, the presidency, and the promise of John F. Kennedy for understanding tensions and changes within contemporary American Catholicism.

Now, to begin.

John F. Kennedy
and
American Catholicism

I

A CITY UPON A HILL

IT was John F. Kennedy's finest moment. On the evening of
September 12, 1960, before three hundred Protestant ministers
in the Crystal Ballroom of the Rice Hotel in Houston, Texas, he
delivered the clearest and most eloquent statement ever made by
a presidential candidate on religion in American life. The audience, according to journalist Theodore White, was "sullen" and
"almost hostile" when he began. Later, a minister who had been
present reflected that the meeting had many of the characteristics
of an "inquisition." To that group, it made little difference that
Kennedy was a fourth-generation American, that his grandfather
had been mayor of a large city, that his father had been ambassador
to the Court of St. James, or that Kennedy himself had sworn allegiance to the American Constitution as a United States senator.
As a Catholic, Kennedy had to prove that he was American
enough to hold the presidency.

To understand fully the drama of the occasion, Kennedy and his
listeners would have had to flash back to fourteenth-century English villages where yeomen listened receptively to John Wycliffe's
criticisms of the Church of Rome. For whatever theological and
doctrinal differences existed among the ministers in Kennedy's
audience, they all were heirs to a tradition of rebellious indi-

1

vidualism which began in England more than five hundred years before. And so, of course, was John F. Kennedy.

PROTESTANTISM AND AMERICAN INDIVIDUALISM

The Protestant revolution appealed to restless men anxious to justify a break with established authority and to discover a new identity. It was not the details of the attacks by Luther, Wycliffe, or Huss—opposition to the sacraments of Penance, Baptism, or the Eucharist—which ignited anxieties and inflamed passions against the Catholic Church. It was their assault on the authority of Rome itself.

Later, Luther was to protest against the peasant rebellions he helped to inspire. His demand for spiritual freedom, he insisted, had nothing to do with political and economic reform, to say nothing of political freedom. He lamented the extremism of those who destroyed sacred images and banned music from the churches, but he was too late. To assert the primacy of man's conscience against the Pope of universal Christendom, as Luther had done, was to loosen forces for individual rebelliousness which could not be stopped.

Nowhere was that more true than in England, where in the last half of the fourteenth century John Wycliffe laid the foundation for the American dissenting tradition. Wycliffe went further than Luther or Calvin would ever dare to go in insisting that every man is a priest before God and that salvation depended on no external ceremony or church, but only upon a change of heart to which all men could be called. Although he died in the nominal communion of the Roman Church, Wycliffe led a movement of poor, lay preachers who asserted that the English Bible and individual conscience could take the place of both Pope and Church, providing the basis for a deep-seated distrust of established authority in first the Roman Church and later the Church of England.

It was out of this tradition of dissent that the earliest American

Churches outside of Virginia derived. As Edmund Burke later saw, all of Protestantism "is a sort of dissent," but the Protestantism of North America is "a dissidence of dissent, and the Protestantism of the Protestant religion."

The central Protestant principle of justification or salvation by faith and faith alone has encouraged dissent and individual rebelliousness wherever social and economic conditions were favorable. Although Protestants have differed among themselves with respect to the central issue of all Western religions—how does one give meaning to life, justify, sanctify, and save one's soul?—the dominant Protestant response has been that salvation can be achieved only through the operation of grace in the heart. Each man can reach God only through the purity and depth of his own faith. Cast out was the Catholic emphasis on good works, the sacraments and the Church itself. With salvation bestowed by operation of grace in the heart, the whole fabric of organized religion was implicitly threatened. To threaten organized religion was to undermine the foundations of any established authority.

The idea of a priesthood of believers in which all men stood on the same footing toward God did not necessarily mean that all stood on the same footing with respect to each other or that men could achieve salvation through personal effort—the earliest leaders in the Massachusetts Bay Colony and at Plymouth were horrified at such thoughts—but it did provide the psychological impetus for the assertion of personal independence later on. By insisting on the capacity of the individual to experience God directly, checked only by conscience and Scriptures, Protestantism provided the ideological seed which fostered a cult of personal independence—the desire for self-sufficiency in the exercise of free choice—that swept eighteenth-century America.

The principles of dissent and independence imply doctrinal differences as well as stylistic unity. The Anabaptists rose in protest against the Lutherans, Puritans against the Anglicans, Quakers and Independents against Presbyterian Puritans, and Evangelical and Republican Methodists against the formalism of the Episcopal Methodist Church. Yet, despite their differences, each of the Protestant movements—as contrasted with Catholicism—has emphasized personal responsibility for salvation and individual regeneration and mission. Whatever direction Protestantism took, whether a God-centered Puritanism, a Bible-centered pietistic Evangelicalism, or a person-centered Deism, the central principle of justification by faith promoted individualism, the assertion of the individual personality in opposition to *established* tradition or authority.

The Calvinists who settled the Massachusetts Bay Colony had rebelled against the middle way of Anglicanism, but they did not believe in personal independence. They sought to free the individual in relationship to God but subject him to strict rules in relationship to others precisely in order to liberate the spirit and save the soul. High seriousness, thrift, asceticism, and diligence were to be linked to a total dedication to God for which only the individual could finally account; but a rigidly governed corporate commonwealth was to help through unstinting enforcement of laws against sloth and lechery.

When John Winthrop led the Puritans into the wilderness of Massachusetts, he envisioned close-knit families and communities which would "delight in each other; make others' conditions our own; rejoice together, mourn together, labor and suffer together." Each man was to live in a state of mutual dependency, governed by a hierarchy of rights and duties because "God Almighty in His most Holy and wise Providence has so disposed of the condition of mankind, as in all times, some must be rich, some poor, some high and eminent in power and dignity, others mean and in subjection."

This was the English way and the way of all Europe, but it was not to be the American way. Within two decades after his arrival, Winthrop was complaining that neither women nor servants knew their proper places. A hired man threatened to put his employer to work for him, and a gentlewoman was meddling in things as were only proper for men. The Calvinistic commonwealth envisioned by Winthrop had already begun to disintegrate because the germinal concept of independence inherent in the central Protestant idea of salvation on one's own did not brook distinctions between classes or sexes; and open, sparsely settled land which yielded to hard work promoted a spirit of self-reliance which subverted authority and undermined hierarchy.

OPEN AND ABUNDANT LAND

The psychological individualism implicit in Protestantism was stimulated by open and abundant lands. Frederick Jackson Turner and other historians have called the moving frontier the main spur to personal independence in America. Regardless of how much Turner may have ignored other factors, there is no question that the frontier appealed to the adventurous spirit and rewarded self-sufficiency. The tendency of the frontier, Turner wrote, "is anti-social. It produces an antipathy to control, and particularly to any direct control." It was in "the atomic conditions of the backwoods society, that the individual was exalted and given free play. . . . He fashioned a formula for social regeneration—the freedom of the individual to seek his own."

Protestant principles supplied the religious and ideological justification for the cult of personal independence, but open land and abundance made it possible. Sumner Chilton Powell has traced the process of land settlement in Watertown, Sudbury, and Marlborough, Massachusetts, showing the effect of open land in promoting individualism and equality. The original settlers to Watertown, about ten miles west of Boston, had been granted twenty-five to fifty acres of uncleared land, but newcomers were given nothing; the smaller, less desirable parcels available had to be purchased. Looking longingly and covetously to the open lands to the west, they complained of "want of meadow" and petitioned the General Court to establish the new town of Sudbury. There, land distribution was based on English rank according to feudal custom. Soon the poorest among the settlers began to ask why they should accept limited acreage when vast fields awaited a man's labor to the west. What was the point of knowing one's place when there was a better place to go? One of the farmers told Sudbury's minister and largest holder of meadowland, "Setting aside your office, I regard you no more than another man." Again, settlers decided to move. "Some of us have taken pains to view the country," said a petition to the General Court requesting the establishment of a new township, "and we have found a place which lyeth westward."

The petitioners wished to realize not only their own independence, but that of their children too. "God has been pleased to increase our children which are grown to manhood," they said, and we "should be glad to see them settled before the Lord take us away." Their independence was encouraged by prosperity. "God has given us some considerable cattle," the petitioners said, putting God in a position of helper to man. The never-ending spiral of rising American expectations had begun. "God has given us some considerable cattle," they said, "so that we are so confined that we cannot live as comfortable as could be desired."

A new town of Marlborough, larger than Sudbury, was ample enough to accommodate thirty-eight settlers, two thirds of whom had owned no land in Sudbury. Now every man received some land, and the gap between the largest landowner and the least was much narrower than it had been in Watertown or Sudbury. It was also decided for the first time that men would run their farms independently with no common-field system. Landholdings were more equal; farming was more individualistic than it had been before. The future was predictable. The sons of the original settlers would grow to manhood, desire land of their own, and move on.

Available land encouraged a spirit of personal independence in the separatist Pilgrim colony of Plymouth, too. During the early years of settlement, land was held in common, a condition which Governor William Bradford found "to breed much confusion and discontent" and to impede initiative. According to Bradford, the young men most able to work complained about laboring for other men's wives and children without pay. Under common ownership, a strong man who worked hard received the same amount of food as a weak man who worked little. Wives thought it a kind of slavery to be commanded to work for other men in dressing their meats and washing their clothes.

Concluding that settlers could raise more and better corn if each man set his own crop, Bradford assigned a portion of land to each family according to the number in the family. By the governor's testimony, the women now went willingly into the field to work; they took their children with them to plant corn, where before they had often argued weakness and inability. They were motivated to help their husbands increase their stocks of corn and cattle. Men, able to sell their surplus, wanted more land for cattle and for plowing and tilling. As Bradford put it, "... no man thought he could now live except he had cattle and a great deal of ground to keep them." Soon men were scattered over the bay leaving Plymouth town "very thin, with few people." Bradford brooded: settlers wanted more land, thinking themselves constantly crowded. They would break away "under one pretense or other, thinking their own need and the example of others as sufficient warrant." Americans, as the governor correctly but remorsefully perceived, would make decisions for themselves. They would not be bound by the corporate interests of the Church or by obligations to authority. Despite the hardships involved in clearing new land and fighting Indians, they were determined to be independent.

In Virginia, settlements were not in towns as in New England, and plantations concentrated on the cash crop of tobacco, but land was available at low cost to anyone who could pay the quitrent, build a house, keep stock one year, and tend one acre of ground. The availability of large tracts of land encouraged the independence of farmers, and soon men pushed beyond the tidewater land into the Piedmont, to the hills and beyond on America's moving frontier.

The frontier was hard, especially in New England, but water was plentiful and a variety of crops could be raised. Disease and Indian raids sometimes ravaged frontier settlements. But there was a sweetness in the earth which yielded to hard work and tempted men to hope for the independence of themselves and their children. Seventeenth-century reports from Virginia to the Colonial Board of Trade in London described many rivers and creeks and an abundance of fowl, timber, fruits, and minerals. Many farmers and their wives looked on a new valley recently cleared of Indians and saw soil "so rich, a clime so pure," where "plenty spreads her gen'rous board" that, as one Kentuckian concluded, "poverty must stay behind."

Independence—the right and ability to choose one's God, domicile, mate, friends, pastors, and rulers—was possible in such a land. The blessings of the earth invited activity and made achievement a realistic standard of judging human worth. And in the beneficence of the earth and the spread of personal freedom prideful men saw the hand of God. In 1797, a Methodist minister who moved from southern Ohio to Virginia wrote in his journal, "Oh, what a country will this be. . . ! What a field of delight! What a garden of spices!" Here, he predicted, the gospel would spread "unshackled by the power of kings and religious oppression."

Personal independence was also encouraged by the political relationships which the colonies had with the mother country. The earliest royal charters virtually placed the colonists on their own. Although the king began to furnish the colonies with royal governors of his choosing toward the end of the seventeenth century, their authority was nearly always uncertain. The colonists constantly asserted their independence through popularly elected general assemblies, which—much more than the English House of Commons—were made up of ordinary men who had been sent to the capitol by their neighbors, not just as consultants to royal governors, but to be governors themselves. With the passing of time, the assemblies, backed by the vast majority of the colonists, gained in strength and prestige. The king and his Privy Council were three thousand miles away. "Seas roll and the months pass between the order and the execution," exclaimed Edmund Burke. It was extremely difficult to enforce unpopular laws which colonists found it profitable to violate.

HERETICAL PROTESTANTISM BECOMES ORTHODOX AMERICANISM

The corporate Puritan commonwealth of men and women linked together by a hierarchy of rights and duties was smashed by American conditions and so was Puritan theology. What remained of Calvinism one hundred years after the founding of the Massachusetts Bay Colony—in addition to a legacy of asceticism and self-righteousness—was its insistence that each man's relationship to God was his own responsibility. On this central issue orthodox Calvinism did not differ from its most important seventeenth-century heresies, Antinomianism (meaning "against the law") and Arminianism (named after a dissident Calvinist in Holland who believed in the basic goodness of men and their ability to choose between right and wrong).

Massachusetts Bay Calvinism and its heresies had in common an insistence on pure faith as the only road to salvation. Where they differed—and Antinomians and Arminians attacked orthodox Puritans from completely opposite poles—was on the Antinomian insistence that a man's conduct could not testify to his redeemed condition and the Arminian emphasis that a man had it within his power to choose redemption.

When considered against its Hebraic origins, Protestantism as a whole is essentially Antinomian. Judaism even today emphasizes subservience to the law. It is how a man behaves, and not what he says he believes, that matters to God. By contrast to the Jews and the Puritan leaders of the Massachusetts Bay Colony, Anne Hutchinson and the first important Antinomians maintained that the experience of communion with God could not be cheapened by identification with sanctification through good works. By arguing for direct inspiration against the usual Puritan teaching that no revelations had been made since the age of the apostles, Anne Hutchinson was a precursor of the Evangelical revivalists of the 1730's who insisted that the only way a regenerate person could be known was through an emotional declaration of feeling.

The main message of the Antinomians—that religion was an entirely personal, subjective experience not dependent on a life of sanctification or good works—was similar to Roger Williams' view that the law and the gospel were unrelated. The gospel promised spiritual and even moral liberation from the impediments of the Mosaic law. Any man might be possessed of personal godliness. That was a matter between him and God only. Divine truth could not be proclaimed by a Calvinist or any other corporate entity.

The Arminian heretics attacked from a completely different direction in emphasizing the importance of human effort in the scale of eternity. The Quakers, a major Arminian group, asserted that the ultimate responsibility for salvation rested with each individual. The children of God were not indelibly stained by Adam's fall but sinned by their own actions.

Orthodox Puritans tried to steer a middle course between the Antinomian and the Arminian heretics, many of whom were hanged in the seventeenth century, but by the early eighteenth century the Puritan commonwealth was virtually dead, and Antinomianism and Arminianism were the dominant competing, yet converging, theological views of salvation. Although it is often thought that Arminianism, with its emphasis on the possibilities of human action, triumphed completely, those elements of both heresies most congenial to the American environment infused as powerful forces in the shaping of American values and character.

Arminianism provided the ideological underpinnings for the emerging American emphasis on personal independence and achievement, but Antinomianism suffused both with a sense of mission or crusading zeal with its stress on the principle of witness. The American environment took from Antinomianism, not its belief in human helplessness, but its emphasis on individual intuitive experience as opposed to authority and tradition. From a psychological point of view, despite their antithetical theological tenets, Antinomianism and Arminianism converged to produce the effect of pronounced aloneness which observers from de Tocqueville to Reisman have seen as a major feature of the American psyche.

Obviously, it is one thing to say, as the Antinomians did, that there can be no proof of salvation through leading a sanctified life or performing good works, and that renewal is entirely a matter of divine inspiration directly from God. It is quite another to insist that all men have the power of self-determination, as the Arminians maintained, and that evil and good spring from man's free choice. In simpler terms, neither success nor propriety is a proof of virtue (an Antinomian emphasis) and only each of us can nurture and exercise the good within us (an Arminian thesis). Thus, while Antinomianism and Arminianism were ostensibly apart, one stressing man's helplessness, the other his goodness and capacity to choose, they both emphasized his aloneness and the desperate importance of personal salvation.

One hundred years after Anne Hutchinson arrived in Boston, the revivalism implicit in her position—demonstration of salvation through fervor and devotional exercises (a decision for Christ)—burst forth among the Dutch Reformed congregations of the Raritan Valley in New Jersey, the Presbyterians of the middle colonies, and throughout the Connecticut River Valley. Ever since, revivalism has been an endemic characteristic of American religious life.

The Great Awakening of the 1730's was undoubtedly a reflection of the changing class structure of America; but it was also a cause. The recurrent stress on direct inspiration in the Antinomian heresy of the seventeenth century gave emotional support to the growing sense of personal independence which relatively open and abundant land made possible. The revivalists yelled and shrieked and rolled in their churches in witness to their salvation to the utter disgust of the respectable theological faculty of Harvard. In the theology of the Puritan founders, man had been conceived as standing alone, struggling with his sins. Only after revelation in solitude could he walk into the church and give witness to prove his right to the covenant. Now there was communal testimony, with revivals providing not only a way to witness one's faith but to relieve the affliction of its loneliness.

Throughout American history there have been recurrent religious movements emphasizing the importance of personal regeneration through direct inspiration and the millennialism of the second coming of Christ. At the time of the Revolution, the Freewill Baptists, the Schismatics on the southern end of the frontier line in eastern Kentucky and southern Ohio, and the Shakers, who began near Albany, New York, but who spread into New England and even into Kentucky and Ohio, attacked any authority that presumed to stand between man and God; and expressed their union with Christ in spontaneously intense exhortations, dancing, singing, and uncontrolled seizures.

Later the Antinomian emphasis on intuitive, subjective truth found its way into transcendentalism. Men became feeling beings, not just in the revival meetings of the Second Great Awakening led by Methodist and Baptist preachers in the early nineteenth century, but among the Congregationalist and Unitarian New England divines too. Intuition was judged by them to be at least the equal of rational knowledge. James Marsh at the University of Vermont thought in 1828 that truth could be found "by those immutable laws of the understanding which belong in common to all men" but that one must "try the conclusions by one's consciousness" as a final proof. Sylvester Judd at the Harvard Divinity School wrote in the 1830's that man found truth only in "the . . . boundless, authoritative depths of *his own nature*." Philosopher Caleb Sprague Henry discovered that "the instantaneous but real fact of spontaneous apperception of truth" was found only "in the intimacy of consciousness." Historian George Bancroft, writing in 1835, defined reason as "an internal sense . . . not that faculty which deduces inferences from the experiences of the senses, but that higher faculty which from the infinite treasures of its own consciousness, originates truth, and ascends to it by the force of intuitive evidence." And one of America's most characteristic painters, Washington Allston, wrote that aesthetic truth, "having its own evidence in itself, can neither be proved nor disproved by anything out of itself; whatever then, impresses the mind *as* truth *is* truth, until it can be shown to be false."

THE TRIUMPH OF INDIVIDUALISM

Great heresies never die in their entirety. The Antinomian emphasis on helplessness largely faded because it had little meaning in the American experience; the stress on subjective truth and personal witness lived because it interacted with and reinforced the condition of Americans. Vitally alive long after the banishment of Anne Hutchinson, it lived in the transcendentalism of Emerson, the revivalism of Billy Sunday and Billy Graham, the emphasis on feeling as opposed to reason in certain modern American psychotherapies, and even in the campaign slogan of Barry Goldwater, "In your heart you know he's right."

Elements of Antinomianism lived, but Arminianism triumphed. That greatest of seventeenth-century sectarian heresies became the basis for the secular orthodoxy of Americanism in the eighteenth century. One hundred years after the first Great Awakening, the enormous energy released by the Protestant emphasis on self could

be found mainly on the farms and in the small shops and legislative halls of expanding America. Although belief in an afterlife
was everywhere formally asserted in the years before the American
Revolution, most Americans were completely absorbed in the
affairs of this life and believed in the extraordinary capacity of
man to manipulate his natural environment for greater comfort
and happiness. Sectarian Protestantism remained, but it was rapidly being subordinated to a new culture-religion based in part on
Protestant principles which had been transmogrified by the American environment. Transmogrification—the process of transforming
with bizarre effects—had made the spiritual freedom which sectarian Protestantism had emphasized contingent upon freedom
from social restraints. The independent (free from authority), active, and purposeful man was at the center of the new religion of
Americanism. Corporate institutions which stood in the way—
standing armies, powerful governments, political parties and factions, and established churches—were the enemies of the new
culture-religion which would soon be sanctified by success in revolution against England.

By the end of the Revolution, the elements of the new religion
were clear. Its major components were personal independence
(the right to choose without restraint); individual achievement
based on equality of opportunity (self-reliance, standing on one's
own two feet); a belief in the mission of the United States to spread
the gospel of personal independence and achievement; and confidence that a benign God favors the secular American values of
independence, achievement, and mission. The culture-religion was
a creature of the interaction of Protestant principles with a situation of open and abundant land where every man's labor was
needed and where every man was judged by what he could do.

From the Revolution on, Americans believed that their experiment in government was no less holy than the Puritan vision of
a new Canaan in Massachusetts where John Winthrop had written: "You'll find that the God of Israel is among us . . . when He

shall make us a praise and glory that men shall say of succeeding plantations: 'the Lord make it like that of New England.' For we must consider that we shall be as a city upon a hill, the eyes of all people are upon us." The version of the new Zion in America had changed, but Americans believed with the early Puritans that God had "sifted a whole nation" in order to "plant his choice grain in the New World." Even ten years before the Battle of Lexington, John Adams had written that he considered the settlement of the American colonies "as the opening of a grand scene and design in Providence for the illumination of the ignorant and the emancipation of the slavish part of mankind all over the earth."

INDIVIDUALISM BLESSED BY GOD

As early as the Marlborough petition, Americans began to see the unfolding of God's plan for Zion in a society of self-reliant and independent farmers who were free to choose not just mates and land, but churches and governments too. The growing sense of individual utopianism based on the power of independent choice, which had replaced the sense of corporate mission exuded by Puritan leaders in the early seventeenth century, was joined through revolution with a sense of national mission blessed by God.

When it came time to justify America's break with England, Jefferson wrote in the first draft of the Declaration of Independence that it was "sacred and undeniable" (not just true or desirable) "... that all men are created equal and independent." Equality in the sight of God and independence in relationship to Him constituted no strictly logical basis for rebellion, as Martin Luther would have been the first to acknowledge. Equality of opportunity for independent men to shape their own destinies was something else again, and it was that in which Jefferson believed. The glorious task which Providence had assigned was to protect individual liberty, not merely to assert American sovereignty. Liberty meant more than freedom from restraint to Americans. It signified the exercise of choice, doing, and accomplishing. God wanted men to be independent in order to choose and achieve and would judge them accordingly. As a minister in Georgia put it in 1775: "We are not to imagine that because the Gospel is the law of liberty, therefore men will not be judged; on the contrary judgment will be more severe against those who have heard and professed the Gospel, and yet walk contrary to its precepts and doctrines."

Protestant ministers commonly reminded Americans that defense of American liberty was also defense of the gospel. As one sermonized on the eve of the Revolution to a militia battalion: "... if we cultivate the spirit of Liberty among our children; if we guard against the snares of luxury, venality and corruption; the genius of America will still rise triumphant.... The country will be free—nay, for ages to come a chosen seat of Freedom, Arts and Heavenly Knowledge." A New England Methodist prophesied that "if we may judge the designs of Providence ... we shall be led to think that the perfection and happiness of all mankind is to be carried further in America, than it has ever yet been in any place." The Reverend Samuel West of Dartmouth, New Hampshire, undoubtedly spoke the thoughts of many in a sermon when he juxtaposed personal liberty and true religion in a way that made them barely distinguishable, and asserted that Providence had designed America to be the asylum of both.

Franklin called the Revolution "a glorious task assigned to us by Providence," and John Adams, writing of the Declaration of Independence, remarked that it was "the will of Heaven that the two countries should be sundered." The quintessential prophet of the American Zion, Thomas Jefferson, wrote in the Preamble to the Declaration that "Nature's God" had given Americans the authority to declare their independence.

The Continental Congress changed Jefferson's draft of the Declaration to make even more clear their belief that the American mission was or should be favored by God. The Congress amended

Jefferson's first draft which read: "We hold these truths as self-evident, that all men are created equal and independent; that from the equal creation, they derive rights inherent and unalienable, among them are the preservation of life, liberty and the pursuit of happiness." The final version read: "We hold these truths to be self-evident, that all men are created equal, that *they are endowed by their Creator* with certain unalienable Rights, that among these are Life, Liberty and the pursuit of Happiness." [italics mine]

The Continental Congress also amended Jefferson in two other places in order to show their trust in God as they made a revolution. Jefferson had written: "We, therefore, the representatives of the United States of America, in the name and by the authority of the good people of these states. . . ." Congress changed the language to read: "We, therefore, the Representatives of the United States of America, in General Congress, Assembled, appealing to the *Supreme Judge* of the world for the rectitude of our intentions, do, in the Name, and by Authority of the good People of these Colonies. . . ." [italics mine]

The Congress also rewrote that portion of Jefferson's draft which read: "And for the support of the Declaration, we mutually pledge to each other, our lives, our fortunes, and our sacred honor." The final text was changed to read: "And for the support of this Declaration, with *a firm reliance on the protection of divine Providence,* we mutually pledge to each other our Lives, our Fortunes, and our sacred Honor." [italics mine]

Success in revolution against the mighty power of England convinced many that America truly was intended by the Creator to be as a city upon a hill. It was unthinkable to thousands of colonists that they could have won against insurmountable odds unless they had been chosen by God. As Samuel Cooper declared in 1780 upon the inauguration of the new Massachusetts Constitution, America was a new Israel, designed as "a theater for the display of some of the most astounding dispensations of His Providence." The new constitution was a thing of beauty and godliness,

maintained Cooper, because the powers of government were so
intricately balanced as to let man do only good. The president of
Yale College, Ezra Stiles, preached before the General Assembly
of Connecticut in 1783, singing hosannas to the new Zion: "This
will be a great, a very great nation ... before the millennium the
English settlements in America may become more numerous millions than the greatest dominion on earth, the Chinese Empire.
Should this prove a future fact, how applicable would be the text,
when the Lord should have made His American Israel high above
all nations which He has made, in numbers, and in praise, and in
name, and in honor!"

The content of mission in the New World was no longer the
triumph of a Puritan commonwealth; it had become the celebration of the individual through the success of the American nation.
As Jefferson wrote to a friend in 1787 during the writing of the
Constitution: "Our experiment will be that men may be trusted to
govern themselves without a master. Could the contrary of this be
proved, I should conclude, either that there is no God, or that He
is a malevolent being."

Few, even among the Deists, would have gone as far as Jefferson
in reversing the positions of man and God and presume to judge
Him, but most leading Americans—politicians, theologians, edu-
cators—shared Jefferson's conviction that men could be trusted to
make decisions for themselves as God had intended. Even when
they tended to consider human nature untrustworthy, at least
when given power over others, Americans still maintained a strong
faith in progress based upon the actions of self-sufficient individuals. Conservatives such as John Adams and George Washington
agreed with James Wilson of Pennsylvania, who wrote that "we
have more and better things before us than all we have yet ac-
quired or enjoyed." Others shared Jefferson's hopeful, euphoric
view that "no definite limits could be assigned to the improvability
of the human race." Franklin, struck by "the growing felicity of
manhood, the improvement in philosophy, morale, politics, and

even the conveniences of common living," wished it would fall to his lot "to be born two or three centuries hence." Dr. Benjamin Rush exclaimed "that it is possible to produce such a change in the moral character of man, as shall raise him to a resemblance of angels—nay more, to the likeness of God Himself." A generation later, Unitarian leader William Ellery Channing said, "If there be one striking feature in human nature, it is the susceptibleness of improvement."

Men of all classes and denominations tended to agree with the assertion of Andrew Jackson in his 1829 inaugural address: "Man can become more and more endowed with Divinity and as he does he becomes more God-like in his character and capable of governing himself." God did not disappear from the cosmology of the new religion. His presence gave the American experiment a transcendental significance: to enable men to prove, without the restraints of orthodoxies, hierarchies, and rigid restrictions that they were in truth only a little less than the angels.

PSYCHOLOGICAL AND CULTURAL EXPRESSIONS OF INDIVIDUALISM

The culture-religion was a complex of ideals, beliefs, symbols, and rituals based on a fundamental conviction that the salvation of man was possible if only he could be loosened from the grip of rigid hierarchies and orthodoxies. The central value of the new Zion—belief in the worthwhileness of personal independence—was so powerful as to mold a new and distinctive American personality. Foreign visitors to the United States in the eighteenth century and early nineteenth century commented with astounding unanimity on the outstanding character traits of Americans—self-reliant, active, inductive and intuitive, gregarious and conformist, frank, and optimistic—all of which stemmed at least in part from the value of personal independence.

To be able to choose on one's own, one must know how to

choose (self-reliant). When status is no longer prescriptive, it must be won by ceaseless labor (active). When authority and tradition are eliminated as guides for reason, experience (inductive or intuitive) takes their place. When men are psychologically on their own and physically mobile too, they seek the superficial fellowship of others outside of the family circle partly to find out how they are doing and partly to discover what others are doing (gregarious and conformist). When men are judged by qualities of independence, they feel a compulsion to express disagreement with authority and tradition (frank). When they are confident of the possibilities of change through personal choice and achievement, they look to and plan for the future (optimistic).

From the end of the eighteenth century on, the culture-religion of Americanism has provided the cement which enabled America to conquer a continent and absorb millions of immigrants from traditional cultures. For more than two hundred years a belief in the value of personal independence has permeated our language, literature, drama, music, art, philosophy, and science, and has molded our political, economic, and religious systems.

American culture-heroes have been honored for their qualities of independence and achievement: the independent pioneers, always on the move, performing feats of daring; the lonesome cowboys, unencumbered even by family ties, who protect the widows and kill the bad men; the Horatio Algers who rise from one suspender through their own efforts; and the athletes whose gargantuan heroics can be measured in the latest recorded percentages.

The dominant theme of our most characteristic poets—Emerson, Longfellow, Whittier, Lowell, Dickinson, Robinson, Frost—has been the independence and often the loneliness of man. Our important literature—from Cooper and the Leatherstocking novels of independent heroes in the West to Mark Twain and independent boys who are up and doing, to Hawthorne and Melville and the agonizing struggle for self, to Hemingway and Faulkner pitting man against nature or social restraints—deals with the American search for self-sufficiency. American artists, particularly those of the eighteenth and nineteenth centuries such as Copley, Sargent, Eakins, and Homer, emphasized individual portraiture and activity. Americans who have written popular philosophy, including Jefferson, Emerson, Thoreau, William James, and John Dewey, each have seen a vision of a perfect society of independent men and women, infinitely mutable, plastic, and capable of change from within.

Those secular philosophies which have had the most impact on American thought—transcendentalism, social Darwinism, and pragmatism (despite their differences)—have stressed the sovereignty of the individual in developing his highest moral, intellectual, and emotional capacities without the interference of the state, clergy, family, or even history.

American science and scholarship have emphasized the testing of truth against experience or feeling as opposed to theory. The radical empiricism in the American approach to knowledge as compared to the European can be seen in any field of scholarship from physics to psychology.

Confidence in the capacity of independent men to govern themselves has shaped our political institutions. Governments and churches threatened free men as did extended, authoritarian families. Governments, at least, could be restricted by ingenious constitution-making in order to leave individuals free to determine their own lives in the race for personal achievement. Thus, in politics Americans have insisted on splitting power in as many ingenious ways as they can devise: federalism, separation of powers, checks and balances, bicameralism, multiplicity of local governments, rotation in office, frequent elections, long ballots, and resistance to civil service.

Americans have usually agreed with Jefferson and Emerson that the least government is best, but that has not kept every group—farmers, merchants, industrialists, laborers, and others—from wanting to exercise as much power as possible or from wheedling special favors and benefits when they could. Such behavior comes under the heading of self-help within the framework of existing power. Americans have wanted government to leave men alone to run their race in their own way, but that has included competition in the arena of power.

In economics, Americans have cherished the principle of the open market which lets man make decisions for himself. They speak of free enterprise for the individual as a sacred right. Even as they built public parks, public schools, and manage giant public corporations such as the TVA, they have resisted terms like "planning" and "socialism" as completely alien to the American way of life.

THE AMERICANIZATION OF
SECTARIAN PROTESTANTISM

The powerful culture-religion of Americanism transformed Protestant sectarianism itself. A half-dozen God-centered, theologically obsessed sects, whose pastors were divinely commissioned and whose members believed in a close union of church and state, soon became a multiplicity of theologically vague, humanistically oriented denominations whose members believed in the subordination of clergy to laity and the separation of church and state.

Even the important Protestant revivals which took place between the end of the Revolution and the middle of the nineteenth century drew strength from a culture-religion which was highly individualistic, active, and messianic. In turn, the evangelical and revivalist emphasis in Protestantism, emphasizing a democracy of feeling and scorning elites and aristocracies, rekindled the egalitarian and individualistic emphasis in the culture-religion.

More than any other people, Americans have insisted that religion is a personal matter. Few have gone as far as Jefferson ("I am a sect by myself") or Paine ("My mind is my own church"), but the most influential Protestant ministers and public figures of all periods since the Revolution have tended to agree that a man's religion is a matter between his conscience and God. While not usually accepting all the theological implications of Deism, most Americans have agreed with the Deists concerning man's God-given capacity to choose between right and wrong. Benjamin Franklin explained in his autobiography that any man could strengthen his sense of right and wrong with a list of rules for living comparable to his own. After all, God had given men that faculty to choose; it was up to men to use it well. Washington, Jefferson, Paine, Barlow, Franklin, Madison—Arminians all—agreed with Samuel West, who told his parishioners that the Deity had given them "moral powers and faculties by which we are enabled to discern the difference between right and wrong, truth and falsehood, good and evil."

Arminian extremism was opposed by leading ministers of all denominations. But who remembers Bishop Watson, Timothy Dwight, or Thomas Fessenden except the historians of the period? It is Jefferson, Franklin, and Jackson who interpreted and enlarged the dominant American point of view. Without forgetting God, most Americans have shared William Ellery Channing's opinion that the powers of spiritual regeneration were already in human nature and man must rely on himself to exercise them. Those religious groups which flourished in the United States in the first half of the nineteenth century—Unitarians, Universalists, and especially Methodists and Baptists—all emphasized free will. Only in the South with the emergence of the slavery issue did theological orthodoxy gain and did the people turn toward fundamentalism. By the Civil War most Protestant churches of the North accepted a humanistic, individualistic metaphysics exemplified by Phillips Brooks's advice to Americans to "believe in yourselves and reverence your own human nature."

Far from destroying God, the culture-religion of Americanism needed Him as much as any sectarian religion, as is shown in the Declaration of Independence. How else could one justify the excessive Arminian faith in man's nature except by accepting Jackson's view that God had invested man with Godlike attributes? How else could one defend the radical experiment of democracy in America except by seeing it as a mission ordained by God? Without belief in God, how dare one fly in the face of history and tradition by proclaiming personal independence and the American way of life as moral truths?

In America, humanistic liberalism has not been an enemy of religion. The idea of liberty drew strength from belief in a benevolent God, and belief in God has been seen as justification for the ideal of liberty in nearly all our great historic documents beginning with the Declaration. Willard Sperry has written of the symbolism on the American ten-cent piece. One side of the coin shows the head of the Greek god Mercury, encircled by the single word "Liberty." At the lower left in a less important but supporting position, is the motto "In God We Trust."

Americans have felt another need for God, too. Bereft of ancestry, tradition, and an authoritative church, a general belief in God is thought to be important as a restraint on man's baser instincts. Those who profess atheism usually have been suspect as libertines who promote the sinfulness of pleasure. They also are frequently thought to harbor an *alien* orthodoxy which denies the individual's right to independence. At different periods, atheism has been associated with French Jacobinism, German socialism, Russian communism, and other utopian orthodoxies which deny the primacy of the individual.

Thus, the culture-religion encourages a belief in God at public meetings which usually open with a prayer and conclude with a benediction. The speeches of politicians and statesmen require allusions to God's will and benign concern. Chaplains are a part of the armed services, church property is tax exempt, and it is widely assumed that a "good American" will have some religious faith.

While the culture-religion of Americanism encourages a belief in God—"I do not know how a man can be an American, and not

get something with regard to God's purpose as to this great land,"
said Phillips Brooks—its proponents have judged sectarianism
largely in terms of its ability to perfect a way of life in which
individuals would be free to choose and achieve. By exalting the
potentialities of man's nature, the culture-religion blunted the
Protestant concept of original sin, making the God of Americans
more bland and benign than righteous and wrathful. By valuing
individual decision, it elevated the importance of individual conscience.

The assertion of the primacy of conscience meant a proliferation
of Protestant sects. Madison argued at the Constitutional Convention that "in a free government the security for religious rights
consists in a multiplicity of sects." But the culture-religion, while
permitting every man to be his own sect, required that doctrinal
differences be subordinated to the needs of civic unity. Small
pockets of orthodox resistance such as the Amish could be tolerated, but vital differences between large groups were threatening. While anyone not committed at least to a belief in God has
been suspect as un-American, anyone committed to a particular
set of beliefs which threatens fundamental articles of the American
faith has been viewed as ungodly.

The pressure toward unity has blurred dogmatic and theological
differences ever since the eighteenth century when it became difficult for foreign visitors to tell Presbyterians and Congregationalists
apart. Even Baptists and Presbyterians seemed to converge in organizational and doctrinal matters. Baptists became more central-
ized; Presbyterians were looser in structure than in Scotland.
"Baptists are Presbyterians in all other respects, differing only in
the point of infant baptism," exaggerated the famous colonial
Presbyterian leader, John Witherspoon, at the close of the Revolution.

Most Americans at the time of the Revolution took doctrinal
differences lightly, moving from one church easily into another.
Theological questions were no longer burning issues. In fact, they

were suspicious of theological preoccupation and ritual. At a time when doctrine and theology were less complicated than ever before, as staunch a Calvinist as John Adams expressed irritation at "the ecclesiastical synods, conventions, councils, decrees, confessions, oaths, subscriptions, and whole cartloads of trumpery that we find religion encumbered with these days." Benjamin Franklin was even more indifferent. "As to Jesus of Nazareth," wrote Franklin, "I have . . . some doubts as to his divinity tho' it is a question I do not dogmatize upon, having never studied it, and think it needless to busy myself with it now, when I expect soon an opportunity of knowing the truth with less trouble." Washington was an Episcopalian, but there is no record of his ever having taken Communion, and Jefferson belonged to no Christian body even though he attended church regularly.

Those who differed on theological issues sometimes formed their own churches. By the time of the Revolution, there were several miscellaneous evangelical churches in addition to nine major Protestant denominations (there were six times as many Quaker meetinghouses as Roman Catholic churches in the United States in 1775). A Protestant church was like a private society that might convene and dissolve. That was the understanding of the majority of the Deists, nominal Anglicans, and Baptists, who wrote the Constitution and who later supported the First Amendment separating church and state by preventing Congress from prohibiting the free exercise of religion or respecting the establishment of any church. A culture-religion which exalted the capacity of man to make choices required the separation of church and state, although state churches remained in Massachusetts and Connecticut well into the nineteenth century.

Although Protestants originally favored a sectarian state, they had asserted earlier the limitations of ecclesiastical authority in relationship to the laity. Congregationalists and Baptists enunciated antiauthoritarian principles during the English Civil War in the middle of the seventeenth century, and later Presbyterians explicitly limited ecclesiastical discipline. In America, independent men meant independent and self-governing churches. The principle of congregational control became preeminent everywhere. In Virginia, the control of the Anglican churches soon went into the hands of lay vestries which had the power to hire the minister and determine his salary. In Congregational New England, the laity assumed increasing control until ministers virtually were at the beck and call of their congregations. Even Presbyterian congregations found they could successfully defy control from above when determined to have their own way.

All these developments—a spreading but bland humanistic religiosity, a dilution of doctrinal orthodoxy, the proliferation of sects, the separation of church and state, and the blurring of distinctions between laity and clergy—owed much to the secular ideal of voluntary choice, which had in part stemmed from the Protestant principle of justification by faith. In America, that ideal was accorded divine significance, raising it and its corollary, the principle of personal activity, to the status of a culture-religion.

AMERICANISM FOR WHITE PROTESTANTS

The culture-religion of Americanism was clearly not just the result of the Enlightenment, since it was viewed with contempt by many of the best-educated Europeans of the eighteenth and nineteenth centuries. Nor was it a consequence of urbanization, since Europe had dozens of cities far larger than any in the United States, and since men genuflected to its principles more sincerely in the American hinterland than anywhere else. Nor was it just the religion of the educated and well-to-do. It captured the small farmers of seventeenth-century Massachusetts, Vermont, and New Hampshire no less than the merchants of Boston and Philadelphia. It was the culture-religion of all white men in America, both North and South, despite the institution of slavery. Thomas Jefferson, in a letter to a French friend comparing Northerners to

Southerners, found eight personality differences (for example, Americans in the North were "cool," in the South, "fiery") and one similarity: Americans everywhere, he said, were "independent."

Obviously he did not include black Americans. Whereas free Americans were probably more independent than any other people in history, slaves, imported from Africa against their will, were treated as beasts of burden. Slavery, by the time of the Revolution, was vital to the economy of the South (in South Carolina more than half the population were slaves; in Virginia almost half), and was even rationalized as fitting into America's culture-religion. Whites of every section managed to compartmentalize their thinking surgically. While the churches of the South rang with denunciations of British tyranny, American slavery was justified when applied to Africans whose "nature" made them slothful, improvident, and incapable of being independent. Then and in subsequent decades many Americans were able to rationalize their maltreatment of Negroes (and Indians and some foreigners too) because they were seen as nonbelievers in the American creed of self-reliance.

Most Americans appear to have been little troubled by the co-existence of slavery and the ideology of personal independence. Ordinary men and women were not as self-conscious as either John Winthrop or Thomas Paine in proclaiming their versions of a city upon a hill. For every Winthrop who settled in America there were dozens without ideological pretensions. For them, America did not mean "a new Jerusalem"; it was a plot of land, a cow or two, or escape from debt, the jailer, poverty, or a memory. Their eighteenth-century descendants could live with the anomaly of slavery for blacks and independence for whites because both increasingly were taken for granted. When Thomas Paine proclaimed in *Common Sense* that "the birthday of a new world is at hand," he was speaking of a new world for white men. White

Americans contrasted their own condition with that of Europeans, not Negro slaves.

Even those Americans who felt loyal to the British Crown up to the time of revolution tended to regard Europe and its institutions as—if not iniquitous—poor soil for the growth of personal liberty. Even many of the earliest settlers explicitly rejected European decadence. "There never was a generation that did so perfectly shake off the dust of Babylon, both as to ecclesiastical and civil constitution, as the first generation of Christians that came into this land for the Gospel's sake," wrote Increase Mather in 1677. William Penn later said of America, "Oh, how sweet ... freed from the troubles and perplexities of woeful Europe." Foremost among the troubles and perplexities was the Roman Catholic Church. Regardless of differences among Congregationalists, Presbyterians, Anglicans, Quakers, and the nonchurched (a large majority), Catholicism was universally disliked. One of the primary reasons advanced for settling the New World by Sir Walter Raleigh's chief entrepreneur and public relations man, Richard Hakluyt, in 1584 was to prevent Catholic missionaries from winning Indian souls and colonizing the territory between Florida and Canada. Anti-Catholicism was a feeling shared by all classes as well as denominations. Even those who were not usually religious or ideological, such as sailors on merchant vessels, expressed strong hostility toward papists. William Warren Sweet has written that the Elizabethan seamen who came to the New World "were Protestants of the Protestants when it came to hating Roman Catholicism ... to the Pope, whom they named the Turk and the Devil, they wished destruction."

From a strictly theological point of view seventeenth- and eighteenth-century Catholics and Protestants, when compared to non-Christians, shared a great deal. They agreed that men were stained by original sin, and that the purpose of life on this earth was to redeem their souls. They believed that men could achieve salvation only through the mediation of Jesus Christ the Savior, and that the Church's task was to assist in Christ's mission. They differed primarily in respect to how a Church goes about assisting the faithful in their search for salvation. Out of this difference and those which flowed from it came the great religious wars of the sixteenth century and the aftermath of bitter persecution and hatred on both sides.

To the vast majority of Americans in the seventeenth and eighteenth centuries, Catholicism was not just another Christian denomination, another way of interpreting God and Christ, but a mélange of decadence, superstition, corruption, and authoritarianism. In their eyes, popery was despotism pure and simple. The papacy stifled liberty and made independence impossible. Moreover, it was a foreign despotism in alliance with the kings of France and Spain, who also resisted tenaciously the spread of liberty. Furthermore, the Church was a conspiracy whose plans were made in secrecy, and its hierarchy was inscrutable and devious. Romanism, when in power, brooked no opposition. Its distinctions between priests and ordinary men bred corruption among cardinals, bishops, in the religious orders, and in the papal kingdom itself. Even Popes were only men and were led easily to debauchery and lechery when unchecked by the restraint of individual conscience. These were the beliefs of nearly all eighteenth-century Americans.

With the rejection of Europe went the rejection of Catholicism. Where Rome held sway, Americans tended to believe, men and women were made dependent and craven, fatalistic and superstitious, vulgar and poor. It was these conditions—associated with feudalism and Catholicism—which Americans were determined to cast off forever.

II

DEFENDING THE CITY

IT was in the spring of 1959. John F. Kennedy had come to Hawaii in search of that new state's votes in the 1960 Democratic National Convention. I was in the Islands completing research for a book on the social and political history of Hawaii. Kennedy knew me slightly, but he knew my politics well. I was a liberal, with political friends in New York City and New England.

We talked animatedly for more than a half hour in the senator's hotel room. He sat hunched over the edge of his bed, occasionally getting up to attend to a packing chore. He thrust questions at me like rifle shots. Why was so-and-so opposed to his candidacy? Why was a certain newspaper critical? What did the liberals want? Wasn't his voting record good enough? Didn't they believe his words? Did they think that because he was a Catholic, he was like (and here he named another politician)? Not satisfied with my demurs, he concluded (in an oversimplification, I think), "Why, that's prejudice!"

Kennedy wanted to be judged not as a Catholic or as the son of Joe Kennedy or by any label, but for himself only. He wanted to accomplish the impossible by eliminating historic memories of fear and distrust from the minds of Americans. Before his death, and perhaps even prior to his election, he was to do more to blunt the ancient mutual hatred of Catholics and non-Catholics than any

31

American had ever done. But on that sunny afternoon in the Royal Hawaiian Hotel his characteristic impatience betrayed his own deeper understanding (to be proved later many times over) of the complexity of emotions that lay behind the historic American fear of a Catholic in the White House.

THE SOURCES OF ANTI-CATHOLICISM

Like any other prejudice, anti-Catholicism is based largely on fear. Where prejudice is widespread and persistent, it is important to discover what it is that people fear. Any group prejudice has its social bases; but in the United States ethnic and religious prejudice is frequently stimulated by personal anxieties growing out of the demands of the culture.

Almost from the very beginning of our history Americans have felt the pressure of a success ethic based on achievement. The desire to succeed and fear of failure are ever-present in a society in which success is possible. In a land of promise which makes the admission of failure unbearable, explanations must be given for promises unfulfilled. Where status is measured by achievement and where upward and downward mobility are facts of life, anxiety is ever-present. Where it is disastrous to admit failure, real or imagined, even to oneself, anxiety breeds fear and scapegoating.

Personal insecurity feeds the sources of group prejudice, which in the case of anti-Catholicism have been sectarian (fear of the antichrist), ethnic (fear of the unfamiliar), economic (fear of class), and ideological (fear of values). Underlying them all has been the political fear of power: the apprehension that Catholics would capture the city on the hill through foreign conquest or internal subversion.

The parents of America's earliest settlers lived during England's struggles with Catholic France, and during their own lifetime they knew the threat of the Spanish Armada and the Gunpowder Plot. For them, Rome was more than a theological heresy. It was a foreign conspiracy in alliance with other nations to restore papal authority in England and destroy English liberties.

Although Catholics were almost as scarce as Hindus in seventeenth-century America, anti-Catholic feeling was unquestionably stronger than in the mother country itself. The leading colonists had been trained in the intolerance of early seventeenth-century England, and as dissenters or left-wing Protestants (except in Virginia) they wished to move as far from Rome as possible in organization, style, and dogma. The reforms asked by Puritans of the Church of England had been intended to take Anglicans even farther away from Catholicism by doing away with the bishops, ecclesiastical courts, sacraments, and such Catholic relics as kneeling, priestly robes, and extravagant altars. Congregationalists and other Protestant denominations had their own definitions of religious orthodoxy, and dissenting Protestants in Massachusetts were persecuted as ruthlessly as Roman Catholics. Anne Hutchinson was excommunicated by the Calvinists of the Massachusetts Bay Colony who in the 1660's also branded Quakers with the letter "R" and had them "stripped naked from the middle upwards, tied to a cart's tail and whipped through the town." A few heretics were even sold as slaves under the authority of the General Court of Boston and four of them were hanged, including the saintly Quaker, Mary Dyer.

In colonial America, Protestant sectarianism resulted in established Churches. The separation of church and state would come later with the rise of America's culture-religion; but in seventeenth-century Virginia, Anglicanism was established and supported by taxes; and in Connecticut, New Hampshire, and Massachusetts, Congregationalism remained the state church for many years after the Revolution. In South Carolina, the Anglican clergy shared a major part of the colony's budget for seven decades up to the Revolution. Among the overwhelmingly Protestant colonies, religious toleration was often espoused only in Quaker-influenced

Pennsylvania, that "swamp of sectarianism," and Baptist Rhode Island.

COLONIAL PREJUDICE

Most seventeenth-century Catholics clustered in Maryland because of the charter granted in 1632 to Catholic Sir George Calvert, Lord Baltimore, which had made him a patron of all the Churches in the colony. Despite the efforts of his son, Cecilius, to induce Catholic emigration, Protestants were in the majority in Maryland from the beginning. Realizing that Protestants could control the legislature, Cecilius won passage of the Toleration Act of 1649. But as soon as Maryland Protestants were in charge, they banished him from his own province, repealed the act, and passed a law providing that "none who profess to exercise the popish religion, commonly known by the name of Roman Catholic religion, can be protected in this province."

Virginia had few Catholics, but the House of Burgesses decided in 1641 that no popish followers could hold office in the colony or even vote, and that priests could not enter its borders. There were even fewer Catholics in Massachusetts, but the General Court of 1647 ruled that priests entering the colony were to be banished or, if they failed to leave, be executed. In New York, a successful Protestant insurrection was staged against a Catholic governor who had been sent by James II; and a new governor, chosen by a Protestant assembly, drove Catholics from the colony.

After the outbreak of the French and Spanish wars in 1690, antipapist laws were strengthened. In Virginia, rumors spread that Catholics and Indians were plotting to kill Protestants in their beds. Only thirty years before the Declaration of Independence, the House of Burgesses passed laws preventing Catholics from acting as guardians, serving as witnesses, congregating in large groups, carrying arms, or even keeping a horse valued at more than five pounds. Catholics in Maryland were forbidden to join the militia companies in the 1740's. Any priest in that colony who attempted to proselytize was declared guilty of treason. In 1754, legislation provided for the confiscation of all property belonging to any priest; and in 1775, Catholics were obliged to pay a double land tax. Pennsylvanians also passed rumors of French and popish plots to overthrow the government, and even the usually tolerant Quakers forbade services by Catholics in the militia, imposed extra taxes, and made a list of Catholics living in the colony, as was done in Maryland, to closely scrutinize their whereabouts.

The fear that Catholic activity among Indians was directed against the Americans was not entirely without foundation, since Maine Indians who had been converted by French Catholics began a series of raids against Massachusetts settlements in 1718. But fear of internal Catholic subversion was unrealistic. Anti-Catholic legislation in the mid-eighteenth century was a reflection of the growing belief of Protestant farmers, merchants, mechanics, and workingmen that Rome was the greatest single threat to American (and English) liberties. Catholicism signified "damnable heresies, fatal errors, abominable superstitions," as Harvard's Paul Dudley stated in establishing a lecture series to combat the Roman religion, but to judge from the pamphlets, sermons, and letters of the day, it was not mainly superstition or heresy which plunged the colonists into fear and fantasy. Fear of Catholicism was based mainly on fear of Roman tyranny. To most Americans, Catholicism meant an authoritative, dominating, repressive clergy, led by a foreign Pope who destroyed liberty.

After the passage of the Quebec Act by Parliament in 1774, extending toleration to Catholics in Quebec and to the French settlers of the Ohio Valley, new waves of antipapist feeling swept America. John Jay, Patrick Henry, Alexander Hamilton, Richard Henry Lee, and even John Adams repeated the common antipapist sentiments of the time. Hamilton warned that "they may as well establish popery in New York," and Jay was astonished that "a British Parliament should ever consent to establish in that country

[Canada] a religion that has deluged your island in blood, and dispersed impiety, bigotry, persecution, murder, and rebellion through every part of the world." To the Protestants of the Ohio Valley, the Quebec Act signified an alliance between an autocratic king and a dictatorial Pope to crush the liberties of colonists. Even in South Carolina an effigy of the Pope was burned in a bonfire of English tea, and Boston (where Paul Revere produced anti-Catholic engravings) and other New England towns revived the popular American holiday, Pope Day, which featured a large parade ending in the burning of an effigy of the Pope.

Popery, according to one Protestant minister, was the religion "most favorable to arbitrary power." Kings and Popes were linked together as destroyers of liberty. It was not just the liberty of Englishmen but of Americans that was at stake. The new Jerusalem under siege was neither John Winthrop's Puritan commonwealth nor King George's colonial outpost. It was a new Zion imbued with the nascent culture-religion of Americanism.

SUCCESS IN REVOLUTION:
AN ERA OF CONFIDENCE AND ACCEPTANCE

When Catholics in America and France united in the war for independence against Great Britain, the strident anti-Catholicism of a decade before diminished, revealing the extent to which hostility toward the Roman religion had become nationalistic rather than sectarian. Although public celebrations in behalf of freedom preceding and during the Revolution often included diatribes against the Pope, the virtually unanimous support given by Catholic leaders to the cause of independence and the assistance of the French ally against England resulted in a marked decline in anti-Catholic attacks. American patriots could no longer cry that Jesuits were advance agents of the Pope conspiring to destroy American liberties. Now it was the loyalist newspapers, reflecting the anxieties born of vanished privileges and lowered status, who denounced "the scarlet whore of Rome."

The war for independence was a dulling influence on Catholic-Protestant antipathies. Because Catholics always provide their share of fighting men and heroes in defense of the city on the hill, the anti-Catholic ideological fears of Americans are largely dissolved in the passion of wars to defend Americanism. Between the Revolution and the early 1830's, goodwill toward Catholics was the rule. Although seven state constitutions forbade Catholics from holding office, and others imposed additional penalties, the federal Constitution prohibited the imposition of any religious test on officeholders in the new government. The first American Congress, in passing a Bill of Rights, made it unconstitutional for Congress to make any law "respecting an establishment of religion, or prohibiting the free exercise thereof." It was acknowledged that Catholics had fought bravely in the Revolution; two distinguished Romanists had signed the Constitution; and Catholics worked their farms and prospered as did other Americans. George Washington and John Adams contributed to funds for the erection of Catholic churches, and although relatively few Catholic immigrants arrived in the country during the first two decades of the nineteenth century, most American writers and statesmen agreed, that the new Jerusalem could absorb whoever came, of whatever religious persuasion.

A wave of euphoric self-confidence swept America. After success in war and the creation of a new nation, the institutions of Europe seemed even more prejudiced, superstitious, and oppressive than before when contrasted with the reality of freedom in America. Feeling even more certain of their moral superiority, Americans were prepared not just to reject Europe but to accept its refugees. "We are the heirs of all time, and with all nations we divide our inheritance," wrote Herman Melville. "On this western hemisphere all tribes and peoples are forming into one federated whole; and there is a future which shall see the estranged children of

Adam restored as to the old hearthstone in an [American] Eden
. . . the seed is sown and the harvest must come."

The widespread confidence in the salvific powers of the new
Zion—not shared only by the most conservative remnants of the
Federalist Party—applied to Catholic as well as Protestant immigrants. But it would only be a short time before that most persistent and oldest hostility—fear and hatred of the Catholic Church
—would be revived by the arrival of Catholics from Ireland by the
tens and then hundreds of thousands. Soon some of the most ar-
dent proponents of Americanism would feel as threatened by the
Roman Church as did their Protestant ancestors in seventeenth-
century England. But for the last two decades of the eighteenth
century and first three of the nineteenth, confidence in the assimilative power of Americanism was pervasive.

A transplanted French-American farmer on the Pennsylvania
frontier wrote shortly after the revolution on the assimilative
power of American values. De Crèvecoeur (J. Hector St. John) gave
an idyllic picture of a Catholic farmer living next to a Lutheran
who lived near a low Dutchman, each indifferent to the religious
principles of the other, comfortable in his own beliefs, and without
religious pride and the desire to persecute. Differences were
washed out because what each man cared about most—regardless
of his sectarian religion—was his independence: his own land,
horses, and produce. The main thing was to raise good crops and
take care of one's own house and family. "How does it concern the
welfare of the country, or of the province at large, what this man's
religious sentiments are, or really whether he has any at all?"
wrote Crèvecoeur. He confidently predicted that religious indifference and toleration would grow from generation to generation.

> The very perceptible indifference even in the first genera-
> tion, will become apparent; and it may happen that the
> daughter of the Catholic will marry the son of the Seceder,
> and settle by themselves at a distance from their parents. . . .
> If there happens to be in the neighborhood any place of wor-

ship, we will suppose a Quakers Meeting; rather than not show their fine clothes, they will go to it, and some of them may perhaps attach themselves to that society. Others will remain in a perfect state of indifference; the children of these zealous parents will not be able to tell what their religious principles are, and their grandchildren still less.

The perceptive Crèvecoeur did not foresee the immigration of huge numbers of Irish Catholics to the growing cities of America, or the Second Great Awakening, which generated a sense of militant Protestant renewal and anti-Catholicism throughout the country. When he wrote, there were probably no more than seven thousand Catholics in western Pennsylvania. The number in other states was infinitesimal (only about two hundred in Virginia). Even in Maryland, Catholics were a decided minority. Protestant church membership probably was no higher than 10 percent; but within a few decades the Second Great Awakening burst forth in the revivalism of the frontier.

REVIVALISM AND ANTI-CATHOLICISM

The evangelical emphasis in Protestantism, demanding a conversion experience as the beginning point of Christian life, stimulated antagonism to the Church of Rome. The Anglicans, the denomination closest to Catholicism in ritual and style, suffered a sharp decline because Anglican leaders had been associated with England in the Revolution. They broke away from the Church of England and formed the Protestant Episcopal Church in the United States of America and conformed to the American pattern of participation by the laity in the enactment of all ecclesiastical legislation. The hyperindividualistic Baptist and Methodist Churches emerged as the most aggressive and actively growing denominations in America. They drew Protestantism further away from Catholicism with a stronger emphasis on salvation through direct experience with God, witnessing for Christ in group meetings, and reliance on the New Testament as the only source of moral truth. Native lay preachers took the place of departed English Methodist ministers John Wesley had sent to the colonies, and by 1784, a wholly independent church had emerged, whose theology had eliminated the sacraments from a crucial role. Even further removed from the Church of Rome were the various sects that made up the so-called "Christian" movement. The Christians, or Disciples of Christ, another important denomination by the 1830's, were left-wing Baptists, Presbyterians, and Methodists who emphasized the original unity and purity of New Testament Christianity.

The sectarian Protestant offensive was carried by new schools, academies, colleges, charitable causes, cheap tracts, religious periodicals, and missionary organizations. The American Education Society and the American Bible Society were formed in 1816, the American Sunday School Union in 1824, the American Tract Society in 1825, and the American Home Missionary Society in 1826. Missionaries were sent to the West to organize theological seminaries and publish millions of pages of Bibles and tracts. Popular evangelicalism was fired by declericalized Baptist farmer-preachers, Methodist circuit riders, and at camp meetings.

At the very time of Protestant renewal, Roman Catholic immigrants were beginning to arrive in the United States in substantially larger numbers than ever before. In 1790, eight years after Crèvecoeur's prophecy, there were approximately 35,000 Catholics in America ministered to by 40 priests. Fifteen years later there were about 70,000 Catholics and 70 priests; at the end of the next fifteen years, in 1820, there were 200,000 Catholics in the United States; and anti-Catholicism was beginning to rise again. By 1827, several religious newspapers appeared which were consistently anti-Catholic. Ministerial exhortations to read the Bible, discover the gospel of good news, and witness for Christ were frequently interlocked with attacks on the papacy as a symbol of tyrannical power.

But there was still considerable religious peace in America in the early 1830's as was observed by Alexis de Tocqueville, the most insightful of all writers on America. De Tocqueville found Americans full of fervor respecting the duties of religion, but differing on insignificant matters of detail. His informants, including Catholics, usually described a peaceful coexistence among religious groups, attributed to separation of church and state. The Frenchman noticed that even Catholic priests in the United States show less concern for forms, figures, and observances than they do in Europe. "There are no Roman Catholic priests who show less taste for . . . extraordinary or peculiar means of salvation, or who cling more to the spirit and less to the letter of the law than the Roman Catholic priests of the United States." Most Protestants—probably no more than 15 percent were churchgoers—were prepared to accept Catholics as good Americans. John Quincy Adams, who had visited Catholic churches in Baltimore during the campaign of 1828, appointed several Catholics to high office when President. De Tocqueville made no mention of the growing agitation against popery, despite the fact that while he was in New England the Reverend Lyman Beecher, pastor of the Park Street Church in Boston, delivered a series of fiery anti-Catholic sermons charging that Catholicism and tyranny were allied in opposition to Americanism. Perhaps de Tocqueville's strong conviction that Catholicism and democracy were compatible prevented his hearing vitriolic opinions to the contrary; or perhaps he thought such outbursts were not significant against the background of religious peace which prevailed.

Soon after his return to Europe, coinciding with the growth of both Protestant evangelicalism and Catholic immigration, new attacks were mounted against the Church as inimical to American freedom. At the very time that de Tocqueville was preparing his final draft of *Democracy in America* for the publisher, the American artist and inventor Samuel F. B. Morse, recently returned from a trip to Europe, wrote a series of newspaper articles against the tyrannical tendencies of Rome. Observing the operation of the Church on the continent, Morse concluded that Catholicism was not agreeable to a society of independent men and women. The Morse articles were extremely popular, and led to a call by the Protestant Association of New York for a meeting to discuss the question "Is popery compatible with civil liberty?"

De Tocqueville maintained that Catholicism was perfectly compatible with democracy because it was congenial "to equality of condition among men." But it was not *equality* of condition which was at the heart of the culture-religion of Americanism. It was *independence* of condition. It was precisely because Catholicism appeared to many Protestant leaders to level the spirit and economic condition of Catholic laymen while elevating the clergy to the position of a privileged class, that Catholicism was seen as un-American. De Tocqueville himself had written that while Catholicism does not prepare men for inequality, it predisposes the faithful to obedience, while Protestantism "generally tends to make men independent more than to render them equal. Catholicism is like an absolute monarchy; if the sovereign be removed, all other classes of society are more equal than in Republics." That was exactly the essence of the ideological conflict as seen by Morse, Beecher, and leaders of the Protestant Association. Protestant militants cared not one whit for equality; their passion was for liberty, freedom, and independence to think, write, choose, and to rise above the crowd.

DEFENDING THE FAITH

As Catholic immigrants from Europe arrived in unprecedented numbers, the city on the hill seemed threatened. There was no one Protestant reception to Catholics as they grew from 200,000 in 1820 to 2,000,000 by 1850 with 1,000 priests serving nearly 1,500 churches and mass stations of various kinds ruled by a hierarchy of 35 bishops. Although Catholics constituted only about 8 percent of the population, they were much more visible, especially in the growing cities of the Northeast. Tens of thousands of Protestants found nothing sinister in their presence, but at least an equal number viewed Catholicism as an alien conspiracy attempting to subvert the American way of life. The hostility expressed against Irish Catholics was not directed against Protestant Irishmen from Ulster who were welcomed and quickly absorbed into Protestant churches. Only the Catholic Church did not accept the American ideal of churches as voluntary associations in competition with each other; only the Catholic Church did not indicate that individual conscience was the virtually exclusively trustworthy way of knowing God; only the Catholic Church could not claim to be free from the authority and dictation of foreigners; and only the Catholic Church was seen as an enemy of personal liberty and the, institutions which had been designed to protect and extend it.

Not everyone agreed with Beecher's attacks against the Catholics. The *Boston Courier* and the Boston Debating Society, both non-Catholic, denounced him; and Boston had no counterpart to the New York Protestant Association, at least not in the early 1830's. But the tide of hostility was rising, particularly after the first Provincial Council of Catholic Bishops in 1829 urged the establishment of Catholic schools in each community to be supported, as were the Protestant inspired common schools, by public funds. In 1840, the *American Protestant Vindicator* warned that Catholics "demand of republicans to give them funds to train their children to worship a ghostly monarchy of vicars, bishops, archbishops, cardinals, and popes! They demand of us to take away our children's funds and bestow them on the subjects of Rome, the creatures of a foreign hierarchy!"

From a non-Catholic point of view, there was stubborn evidence that Catholic immigrants would not adapt to American individualism. They clustered like tribes in the cities rather than showing the initiative to move west. For Jeffersonians and Jacksonians who believed in the moral primacy of the yeoman farmer as the archetypal independent man, the urban tendencies of the Catholics, particularly the Irish, made them suspect. There was no individualism in the fierce loyalty which they gave the family and clan. To Americans long imbued with a sense of individualism, such loyalty amounted to corruption. The rituals of Catholicism, such as the Latin mass, seemed like so much mumbo jumbo designed to keep laymen from thinking for themselves. The sacrament of Penance, or confession, performed with foreign priests, kept them from taking responsibility for their own actions.

The anti-Catholic agitation which spread between 1830 and 1860, while often couched in patriotic slogans about the defense of Americanism, was obviously a mixture of xenophobic, sectarian, and economic, as well as ideological, fears. With hundreds of thousands of foreign Catholics—nearly two million Irish Catholic immigrants arrived in the United States between 1830 and 1860—voting as Americans, it was no longer possible to say, as John Jay had in defending the Constitution, that God had blessed Americans as "a people descended from the same ancestors, speaking the same language, professing the same religion, attached to the same principles of government, very similar in their manners and customs." Foreigners had taken over whole sections of cities where one heard a medley of foreign accents and even languages. Strange holidays which had nothing to do with American independence were celebrated with gusto. While there was nothing comparable to the racism which would develop in the late nineteenth century —few voices were heard to suggest that Anglo-Saxons were inherently superior to others—there was a growing tendency toward nostalgia for the familiar bygone days when what were now burgeoning cities crowded with foreigners had been simple villages "very similar in their manners and customs," whose inhabitants also shared the memory of fathers and grandfathers, again in Jay's words, "fighting side by side throughout the long and bloody war, having nobly established their general Liberty and Independence." The poet James Russell Lowell, then a strong believer in the Arminian idea of man's capacity for choice and the transcendental vision of man's natural divinity, saw two Irishmen looking at George Washington's statue, and was shocked when one asked whom the figure represented. In the memory of many Bostonian Protestants, the city on the hill had been more than an ideal. It had been a fact.

The continued rapid growth of the most individualistic and evangelical Protestant denominations also stimulated anti-Catholic feeling, not just by contributing to the idea that Americanism was under attack, but by casting the Roman Church in the role of Antichrist, whose presence threatened the souls of good citizens. In 1850, Methodists constituted the largest denomination with a reported membership of more than one and a quarter million. Baptists were next with more than 800,000 members, and Presbyterians third with nearly half a million. The new Disciples of Christ already had 118,000 members, whereas the Congregationalists, who in colonial days had been dominant, had slipped in influence and power to 197,000 members. Smaller rapidly growing denominations such as the United Brethren, Free-will Baptists, and the Evangelical Church shared with Methodists, Baptists, and even many of the sophisticated Unitarians of New England (whose growth resulted from a schism with the Congregational Church between 1815 and 1820) a strong suspicion of Catholic doctrines and a profound conviction that the Church had rejected Christ.

The ways of the foreigners were unfamiliar; the dogmas of their Church seemed idolatrous. *And* they were poor. They came down from Canada or arrived with little more than the clothes on their backs in miserable ships whose captains had charged as little as five dollars per person. They crowded into wretched tenements or shacks in the marshlands or outlying districts and were plagued by disease and drink. Many entered almshouses, mental institutions, and prisons (by mid-century, more than half of the criminal offenses recorded in the United States were committed by immigrants). Often willing to work for lower wages at carrying hods,

cleaning stables, and sweeping streets, they would have provoked
the antagonism of native workers even if they had not worshiped
a "foreign" religion with its statues, crucifixes, and ornate vest-
ments. It would be several decades before poor Catholics would
constitute a threat to the upper classes through their control of
the ballot box. In the meantime they supplied cheap labor which
was badly needed to man the growing factories, build the bridges,
and serve the wives of businessmen, merchants, and professional
men.

VIOLENCE AND PSYCHOPATHOLOGY

It was the poor Protestants who felt the economic pressure of
the newcomers in the competition for jobs. The street fighting of
the 1830's and 1840's invariably was between Catholics and Protestants of the lower classes. Much has been written about the burning of churches, the stoning of homes, and crowds of ruffians
thrashing in the streets, and the history of violence between Catholics and Protestants in this country often seems shocking to Americans in retrospect. But compared to bloodlettings between Hindus
and Moslems in India or Catholics and Protestants in Europe,
violence between Catholics and non-Catholics in America actually
has been mild.

In 1830, a group of drunken Irishmen beat a native American
citizen to death and a mob burned houses in retaliation in Charlestown, Massachusetts, near Boston. Three years later in Boston, a
crowd of toughs burned and smashed several Irish homes following
a rumor that a band of Irishmen had beaten a native American.
In 1834, a new rumor swept Charlestown concerning the Ursuline
sisters, whose convent school enrolled many upper-class girls from
Boston whose Unitarian fathers had rebelled against Congregationalist influence in the public schools. A so-called "escaped nun,"
Rebecca Theresa Reed, known as a girl of loose virtue around
Charlestown, spread wild stories of debauchery in the convent.

Soon after, a real nun who taught music in the school did run away as a result of strain from overwork, but she returned to the sisters the following morning. Feelings against the Ursuline convent, already running high, were exacerbated further by three vitriolic anti-Catholic sermons delivered by Lyman Beecher on the hot Sunday night of August 10. Twenty-four hours later in Charlestown a group of forty or fifty truckmen and some New Hampshire Scotch-Irish brickmakers burst into the doors of the convent building a little before midnight and set fire to the school and a neighboring farmhouse belonging to the sisters. Fortunately, the dozen sisters and sixty pupils escaped without injury.

Most Boston leaders publicly disapproved of the gutting of the convent building. Some expressed horror. The press generally rallied to the defense of Catholics as loyal Americans, and a mass meeting at Faneuil Hall expressed sympathy with the victims of mob action. As has usually been the case, violence between America's large-city ethnic and racial groups came in the summer, and, as usual, Americans recoiled at the sickness of it. Although historians of the episode are in dispute as to the extent to which the prominent citizens of Boston shared responsibility for, and enjoyed vicarious participation in, the destruction of the convent school, there was a general reaction of shock, based in part perhaps on a deep, inner recognition of the darker, twisted side of man's nature.

Whatever ideological or even economic rationalizations may have been employed to justify violence against Catholics, such outbursts (and there were more to come) appear to have been more a manifestation of psychopathology than a defense of either liberty or theology. The extraordinary preoccupation of anti-Catholic sermons, tracts, and books with the alleged sexual proclivities of nuns and priests appealed to a widespread pathologically prurient interest in Americans. Almost any work dealing with the supposedly lurid life of the nuns in the Ursuline convent of Charlestown was assured popularity. One book sold forty thousand copies in the first week of publication and went through five editions. To judge by the runaway sales of such works, nothing interested Protestant America so much as so-called "popish brothels or priests' harems."

A rash of books purported to be written by ex-nuns and priests found a ready market for their shocking revelations of the details of confessional and monastic life. Probably the most mischievous was Maria Monk's *Awful Disclosures of the Hôtel Dieu Nunnery of Montreal,* first published in 1836 and reprinted frequently thereafter. Maria told a story of nuns being forced to have sexual intercourse with priests and to strangle the baptized infants born of such unions. Rather than strangle her own baby, Maria escaped to tell the world her story of lust and foul murder. Backed by a half-dozen evangelical ministers, her book was widely accepted by the Protestant press. Although the details of her story were later disproved, and Maria died in prison in 1849 after picking the pockets of a client in a house of prostitution in New York City, Americans were so anxious to know her story that 300,000 copies of the *Awful Disclosures* were sold before the Civil War.

The popularity of such works continued into the 1850's when anti-Catholic hysteria often seemed paranoid. A plethora of books appeared by so-called escapees from nunneries. One best seller was actually written by a young woman who had been a novice in a convent for ten months, but many books were complete fabrications. The very frequency of female testimony on the licentiousness of nuns and priests made even the wildest charges believable. Many of the stories probably were based on hallucination and fantasy and were believed by the young women themselves. News stories of girls lured to nunneries and forced to take the veil gave further credence to blatantly untrue documentaries. As a consequence of such stimulation, mobs stormed convents in New Orleans, Galveston, and Charleston, South Carolina, shouting insults at the nuns, and were prevented from committing serious destruction only by the police.

Street fighting became more common in the major cities of the

Northeast during the 1840's and 1850's. In Philadelphia in 1844, nativists and foreigners clashed in a series of bloody fights comparable in American history only to the horrible race riots of New York, Detroit, and Los Angeles in the twentieth century. The ostensible issue was the question of Bible reading in the schools. (Bishop Francis Patrick Kenrick had won permission for Catholic children to read their own Bibles in the schools.) The underlying reasons were economic and psychological. The slogans of battle, as usual, were ideological.

The major fight took place in the suburb of Kensington, an industrial section of Philadelphia where Irish laborers worked and lived in large numbers. Following a day of skirmishes in which several men were killed, mobs of anti-Catholic natives crowded the streets of Kensington to demand vengeance for the "Americans" who had been killed forty-eight hours earlier. Protestant Irish and natives in the suburb protected themselves by putting signs on the doors of their houses—"Native American"—which were respected. The Hibernia Hose Company (an Irish fire company) was stormed and demolished and more than thirty houses belonging to Irishmen were burned to the ground.

The militia which had been called out to protect the citizens of Kensington seemed powerless to stop the rioters who set a torch to St. Michael's Church and seminary and fired St. Augustine's Church the next day. The priests of Kensington fled for their lives and many laymen left with what belongings they could carry to safer sections of the city. Violence erupted again following an Independence Day celebration when an editor of a nativist paper called on his fellow citizens to fight for their liberties. Gangs of armed men roamed the streets and thousands of Catholic families left the city entirely. This time military assistance was called to quell the riots, but not until the three days of mob rule had resulted in thirteen killed and more than fifty wounded.

Again leading citizens and officials were shocked at the excesses of ruffians, but a city investigating committee, and later a grand jury, blamed the riots entirely on the Irish for having disturbed a peaceful procession of American citizens before the first outbreak of violence.

At its worst, the anti-Catholic activity of the 1840's was similar to the vigilantism of the Minute Men and White Citizens' Councils of the 1960's. Frightened men saw the Catholic immigrants as responsible for growing licentiousness in the cities and the general decline of moral fiber in America. Tens of thousands of Protestants believed they were embarked on a holy crusade to save Americanism from an enemy which was represented as a medley of saloon-sotted Irishmen, lecherous priests, corrupt politicians, and an authoritarian Pope.

As the Irish became more numerous and active in big-city politics, conflicts over ideals and power became inextricably confused. It became unclear whether Catholicism was an enemy of the culture-religion of Americanism or of city hall. In the minds of the vigilantes, the answer was both. Interests as well as ideals were threatened.

The potato blight of 1845–47 left hundreds of thousands dead and starving in Ireland. After several years of hopelessness for Irish peasants beset by mortgage foreclosures and convictions, huge migrations made their way to the New World. Between 1848 and 1864 at least one million came on the New Brunswick lumber ships to America. By 1850, some 42 percent of the foreign-born inhabitants of the United States were Irish and 26 percent German. The vast majority of the Irish and a considerable number of Germans, impossible to estimate accurately, were Catholic. A large proportion of the Germans moved to the Middle West, where they were not as visible as the Irish in the big cities of the Northeast. To many Americans, Catholic became almost synonymous with Irish. So intractably Catholic were the Irish considered to be, that the Protestant Reformation Society later concentrated its missionary efforts among the Portuguese fishermen and French farmers of New England and the German settlers in the Middle West.

THE ENEMY WITHIN

Anti-Catholic idealism remained the primary motive power—at least ostensibly—of almost every criticism leveled at the Church or the Irish. That was especially true for sectarian Protestant groups such as the American Protestant Union formed in 1841 to protect Americanism against the "subjugation of our country to the control of the Pope of Rome and his adherents and for the preservation of our civil and religious institutions." One year later, sixty-one Protestant clergymen of Philadelphia, representing most of the evangelical sects, formed an American Protestant Association pledged to defend the United States against Romanism. The danger to American liberties was internal, argued militant Protestant leaders. Not foreign bayonets, but internal subversion was the Catholic weapon for conquest of America. To many Protestants it was obvious that a grand conspiratorial design dictated by Rome was at work. They wildly imagined that poor noneducated immigrants were sent to sap the vitality of America. The Jesuits were subjected to special attacks for being so devilishly clever that even when they appeared to agree with American principles it was only for the purpose of deceiving true Americans. The source of the most strident anti-Catholic attacks was often Methodist or Baptist, partly because those two denominations accounted for two thirds of all the affiliated Protestants in the United States by 1850, but also because their members combined a militant ideological equalitarianism with a lower middle-class interest to defend against the newcomers. Those Protestant denominations which had been longest identified with new Zion—Congregationalist, Presbyterian, and Quaker—supplied the early leadership for the general morality, temperance, and antislavery movements of the 1830's. One decade later, the evangelical sects also turned against the sin of drink and the abolitionist movement began to draw considerable strength from areas which had been "burned over" by successful revivalist campaigns. Wherever religiously inspired temperance sentiment and abolitionist feeling were keen, anti-Catholicism was rife. The individual rebelliousness, asceticism, and moral righteousness which characterized the Protestant mentality since Puritan times now associated Catholics with the sins of intemperance and slavery.

The ideological basis of anti-Catholic attacks transcended Protestant sectarianism since approximately two thirds of the American people belonged to no church at all. These included Deists, freethinkers, and agnostics, who were as strongly committed to faith in Americanism as churchgoers. Newspaper readers of any religious persuasion or none learned of the implacable opposition of Rome to the liberal revolutions of Europe. Wherever the principles of the American Revolution were applied, the Catholic Church seemed to be in opposition. They also found evidence of Catholic authoritarianism in the recurrent struggles between Catholic laymen and clerics over the legal ownership of church property. In 1849, Monsignor Gaetano Bedini, who had helped squelch the Italian uprisings of 1848 and 1849 and was associated with the death of Italian liberals and the resurgence of monarchy in that country, was appointed Papal Nuncio to the United States to settle controversies within the Catholic communities of Buffalo and Philadelphia as to whether church property should be legally held in trusteeship by the laity or the clergy. Here was Bedini, an official of the Roman Catholic Church, telling American citizens what they should do. He was burned in effigy in Boston and Baltimore, manhandled as he entered the bishop's carriage in Pittsburgh, and saved from assassination in Wheeling, West Virginia, only by the action of several hundred armed Irishmen who guarded him and the churches of the city. To thousands, Bedini was a symbol of Popes and kings united in the destruction of freedom, and of the utter impossibility of Catholics becoming independent of the authority of Rome.

The ideological battle was focused on education. Non-Catholic parents who would not permit their children to play near the marshes and shanties lest they become contaminated by the Irish riffraff, objected to Catholic sectarian schools as un-American, and especially opposed Catholic attempts to obtain public support for their schools. The earliest battles took place in New York City in the 1830's when Catholics objected to the fact that a Protestant sectarian organization, the Public School Society, ran the common schools of New York City and used books with an anti-Catholic slant. Protestants saw in Catholic opposition to the common schools an unwillingness to let their children become Americanized. In 1840, Catholics petitioned for a share of the school funds to support their own sectarian schools, but Protestants, controlling both the Whig and Democratic parties, rebuffed the effort.

Unable to win support for his position from the major parties, Bishop John Hughes led Irish-Catholics in advancing their own candidates for the state assembly and senate. Although badly beaten in the election, the Catholic party received enough votes to frighten the Democrats (who were trounced by the Whigs because of Catholic defections) into realizing how much they depended on the foreign vote. Upstate Democrats were impressed also when Hughes presented a petition to the legislature bearing the names of thirteen thousand Catholics in support of a bill to put New York schools under the jurisdiction of the state rather than the Public School Society.

Not all non-Catholics were insensible to the arguments of the newcomers. Democratic Governor William H. Seward thought it unreasonable that twenty thousand Catholic children should be kept from public schools because of their Protestant sectarian bias and supported the bill which passed the Democratic-controlled legislature. To the Catholics, secular schools were definitely preferred to those with a Protestant slant. An important victory had been achieved for school secularization, and by 1844 Bible reading was excluded from thirty-one of the city schools.

AMERICANISM AS NATIVISM

The organization of Bishop Hughes's Catholic party provided a shocking demonstration of Catholic separatism to many Protestants. It brought the issue of political control out into the open as never before. Some nativists had already argued that the defense of Americanism would have to be made in the voting booth. Native American political parties had been formed in New York City, Brooklyn, Paterson, New Jersey, New Orleans, and Cincinnati as early as 1835. The nativist party in New York, which published a newspaper entitled the *Spirit of '76,* elected a mayor and a complete common council in 1837. It provided the genesis of the American Republican party, which was swept into office in New York City in 1844 on an explicitly anti-Catholic platform. Soon after, branches were established in every county of New York State and New Jersey and in the cities of Boston and Charleston, South Carolina. The party song revealed the main nativist concern: "To defend the free and happy land inspired by the heroes of '76 against priestly politics."

Following an early alliance with the Whigs, the American Republicans changed their name to the Native American party, embracing a program of positive reform as well as antiforeignism and anti-Catholicism. The trouble with foreigners, the party's literature maintained, was that they were so long used to despotic government that they did not know how to exercise personal independence even after arriving in the United States. They had so little experience with civil and religious liberty that they could not hope to become Americanized (and should not be naturalized as citizens) without living in the United States for at least twenty-one years. There was considerable truth in charges of political corruption in the cities as an 1845 congressional investigation revealed. Fraudulent citizenship papers were obtained through party manipulation; judges and court officials violated their oaths of office; and in some cities foreign paupers were led from the alms-houses to the polls by party workers. Mainly, nativists saw their hostility toward the Irish not as prejudice but as the desire for reform.

The 1850's saw the rise of the Know-Nothing party, the only xenophobic, nativist party in American history to win substantial power in national and state politics. The organization, officially called the Order of the Star-Spangled Banner, and appearing on the ballot as the American party, had its own elaborate hierarchy and ritual. Believing that Catholicism was a foreign conspiracy bent on destroying American institutions, its members were sworn to exclude all immigrants "and Roman Catholics in particular" from places of trust, profit, or honor. No one who was a Catholic or even married to a Catholic could join. Secret grips, passwords, and signs appealed to adolescent and paranoid mentalities. Since Rome would stop at nothing to destroy civil and religious liberty in America, the Order of the Star-Spangled Banner promised to retaliate in kind.

The success of the Know-Nothings was phenomenal partly because the major parties—Whigs, Free-Soilers, and Democrats—were rent with dissension over the issue of slavery, but also because many American Protestants of the 1850's had been trained for almost twenty years to believe that Roman Catholicism constituted a vital threat to American freedom. In 1854, the new party carried Massachusetts and Delaware, and, in alliance with the Whigs, captured Pennsylvania. In Massachusetts, the governor and all state officers were Know-Nothings. The state Senate was entirely in the hands of the new party and all but two of 378 members of the state House of Representatives were Know-Nothings. In the fall congressional elections, about seventy-five members of the party were sent to Washington pledged to carry on the fight against popery. In the next year, Rhode Island, New Hampshire, and Connecticut were won by the nativists. Maryland and Kentucky went solidly Know-Nothing and party members were elected to key state offices in New York, Pennsylvania, and California. By 1856, seven governors, eight senators, and 104 national representatives were elected after campaigning on anti-Catholic sentiments. Talk of a Know-Nothing President became commonplace.

Not every Know-Nothing leader was anti-Catholic and the program of the party in Boston—largely executed—called for a true public school system (among other things, eliminating separate schools for Negroes), the abolition of imprisonment for debt, the extension of the power of juries, compulsory vaccination, and a personal liberty law to assure the safety of fugitive slaves. Irish military companies were disbanded and foreigners were fired from the police force and state agencies; but no punitive action was taken to limit the voting power of immigrants, as had been demanded earlier by many leaders.

Despite limited success in Massachusetts, the Know-Nothings failed to carry out important aspects of their program in other states and in the national legislature. In Congress, they had to trade with Whigs and Democrats on a variety of measures. Their one-track view of Catholicism and immigration had little appeal to men whose election was based on the broadest possible consensus among factions and interest groups. In addition, the First Amendment stood in the way of legislation against the Catholic religion.

Know-Nothings usually botched their chances in the state legislatures. Even in the Massachusetts legislature there was considerable bungling. A nunnery committee appointed by the General Court to investigate Catholic theological seminaries, boarding schools, and nunneries was discredited by stupidity and extravagance. The excessive secrecy of the Know-Nothings and their encouragement of violence were probably factors in the rapid demise of the American party; but the most important reason for its quick disintegration was the reemergence of the slavery issue. Like the other parties, the American party was torn by sectional strife. Millard Fillmore, its nominee for the presidency in 1856, was viewed in the North as a champion of slaveocracy for having signed the Fugitive Slave Law in 1850 when he was President. The nativists of New England, perhaps already discouraged by the excesses of some leaders, were disgusted by the nomination of Fillmore. Although the American party polled about 25 percent of the votes, it won a majority only in Maryland. As the irrepressible conflict over slavery drew near, religious passions gave way to feelings on the race question, and the American party disappeared.

Irish Catholics seemed mainly unsympathetic to the abolitionist cause even during the war. In New York City in July, 1863, they protested the draft by burning the draft headquarters, destroying a Negro home for orphans, raiding homes, and beating and hanging several Negroes. Because they were vulnerable to the draft (unable to purchase exemptions or obtain substitutes) and because many enlisted, probably a disproportionate number fought on the side of the North despite their anti-Negro feelings. When the war was over, the riots were largely forgotten and remembered were the heroes of General Thomas Meagher's Irish Brigade, two thirds of whom had been killed in the Battle of Fredericksburg, and the thousands of Catholic soldiers who fought in the Union Army and lived to celebrate their patriotism. Americans had been so preoccupied with the terrible years of war that they hardly took notice when Pope Pius IX issued a series of eighty condemned propositions in 1864 as the Syllabus of Errors. Among the errors denounced as tending to undermine religion was the assumption that "the Pope may and must reconcile himself with and adapt himself to progress, liberalism, and modern civilization."

AFTER THE CIVIL WAR: QUIET AND STORM

With the ending of carnage, Americans set themselves to the tasks at hand: Reconstruction of the South; conquering the West; and industrial expansion. For the latter, there was an unquench-

able need for immigrants from the ould sod to do the backbreak-
ing labor of building railroads and canals and to fill the factories
of the Northeast.

In this atmosphere, indifference to the alleged papal threat grew
and tens of thousands of friendships begun in war or at work between Catholics and non-Catholics made the Syllabus of Errors
seem relatively unimportant. Even the Vatican Council of 1870,
a gathering including forty-five bishops from the United States,
which not only reaffirmed the Syllabus but which promised excommunication for all who held such erroneous views and which
proclaimed the new doctrine of papal infallibility, went largely
unnoticed. Some Americans were shocked. The honored historian,
George Bancroft, warned that the Roman system would force civilization back. "No band of conspirators was ever more closely
welded together" than the Roman Catholic Church, he argued.
"The one will of the Pope rules the creed, the politics, the conduct
of all." Most Protestants probably saw nothing new in the doctrine
of papal infallibility, perhaps believing that it had been operative
long before its official pronouncement. Whatever the reasons, the
1870's was not the time for a new crusade against popery.

Because Irish Catholics constituted one of the core elements in
the coalition which made up the Democratic party, Republican
candidates periodically warned against the insidious influence of
Rome. Rutherford B. Hayes, when a candidate for governor in
Ohio in 1875, warned that the Catholic menace had infiltrated the
Democratic party. Another future President, James A. Garfield,
denounced the trinity of rebellion, Catholicism, and whiskey,
warning ". . . what the future of our country will be no one can
tell." President Ulysses S. Grant told a veterans' reunion that the
public schools must be kept free from Catholic influence if the
nation was not to face a new civil war; but by the time Grant
spoke, most Catholic leaders had backed away from their demands
for state support of parochial schools. By the late 1870's, Catholics
had served the nation in high positions—the Supreme Court, the

Cabinet, and in Congress—and one of them, Charles O'Conor, a prominent New York trial lawyer and counsel to Jefferson Davis in his treason trial, was nominated for President in 1872 on a states' rights Democratic ticket. Nothing in the 1870's approached the vitriolic attacks of the American party and its affiliates in the 1840's and 1850's.

By 1884, a half-million Irish Catholic votes were at stake in the presidential election. When a Protestant minister supporting James G. Blaine (whose mother was a Catholic) told the Republican candidate before a public meeting of ministers that they would not vote for his opponent, Grover Cleveland, because the Democrats were "the party whose antecedents are rum, Romanism, and rebellion," enough Catholics in New York were incensed by the insult to cost Blaine that state and the election. Henceforth, it would be perilous to insult American Catholics in presidential contests.

Anti-Catholicism was quiet but far from dead. Rapid economic and social change in the 1880's brought forth a number of fraternal orders to defend American individualism against anarchists, socialists, and Catholics. When Catholics began building a spectacular number of parish schools following the Third Plenary Council of Bishops in 1884, a widespread fear developed that they might gain control over education in America. Once again, fear that the new Zion was being undermined from within by subtle, conspiratorial forces reached paranoid proportions. A large number of secret, anti-Catholic societies cropped up throughout the country with such names as the Minutemen, the United Order of Native Americans, the American Patriotic League, and the Loyal Men of American Liberty. One popular book, devoted to the alleged papal plot against the American school system, argued that James Cardinal Gibbons, a strong friend of American institutions, had already taken over control of the United States. An organization called the National League for the Protection of American Institutions revived the movement for a constitutional amendment against the use of public funds for sectarian purposes and worked to end the system of federal grants to Indian mission schools, which were going to Catholic as well as Protestant missions.

The most important secret order against Catholicism was the American Protective Association (APA) formed in 1887 in Clinton, Iowa, by Henry F. Bowers, an extremely religious but somewhat hysterical foe of Catholicism. He traveled widely throughout the Middle West to form citizens' councils whose members took an oath never to vote for a Catholic, employ one when a Protestant was available, or to go out on strike with them. The APA drew heavily from farmers, railroad men, and laborers who were opposed to unions and threatened by Irish competition, but the appeal which seemed to unify most members was the call to defend the public schools and free institutions against the Catholic conspiracy.

Despite the efforts of American prelates such as Cardinal Gibbons and Archbishop John Ireland, who did everything they possibly could to break down Catholic separatism, APA leaders saw in the expansion of unions, the growth of churches and parochial schools, and the control of Democratic organizations in the North and West ample proof that their city on the hill was under siege. In 1893, the APA, previously concentrated in the Middle West, surged eastward and westward, growing rapidly from a membership of approximately seventy thousand to perhaps a half million. With its elaborate rituals and paraphernalia of uniforms and insignia and its promise to save American civilization, it appealed, as did the Know-Nothings and the Ku Klux Klan, to anxious, frustrated, and drab people with a desperate need to feel important.

But the APA, like the Know-Nothing movement, was much more than a projection of, and an appeal to, personal insecurity in America. Pointing to the Syllabus of Errors, which had warned against too much freedom and the separation of church and state, and to the doctrine of papal infallibility, its leaders apparently believed that Americanism was locked in a life-and-death struggle with the Roman Catholic Church. When a bogus encyclical alleged to have been sent by Pope Leo XIII, purporting to absolve American Catholics from any oath of loyalty to the United States and instructing them "to exterminate all heretics," appeared in a Detroit newspaper, panic seized many APA members in the Middle West. The city officials of Toledo, Ohio, bought Winchester rifles to prepare for an invasion. Farmers in Illinois were afraid to leave their homes, and a large part of the population in some of the smaller towns in Ohio was terrorized by reports that Catholics in Columbus were preparing for war.

The APA never achieved the political power of the Know-Nothings. Its members boycotted Catholic merchants and discriminated against Catholic labor; they supported Republican candidates in the Middle West, and in some states—Michigan, Kentucky, and Nebraska—were especially influential. But the two-party system was firmly entrenched and not split into a dozen minor parties as in the 1850's, and a single-track anti-Catholic platform was not enough to attract a majority of voters in any state.

The vast majority of Americans were not preoccupied with the Catholic menace. Perhaps a majority were only remotely aware of the existence of the APA. It required a colossal leap of the imagination to believe that the Roman Catholic neighbor on the workbench was planning an insurrection, or that the Catholic farmer from the next town whose bull won a prize at the county fair was a subversive, or that Cardinal Gibbons—friend of Presidents and Cabinet ministers—was secretly plotting to destroy the United States. Many Catholics in the Middle West were particularly well assimilated and many Catholics in every section held positions of trust in business and government where silent friendships with non-Catholics, if limited to the working day and rarely cultivated in society, became increasingly common.

For every APA hysteric, there were probably fifty Protestants who were indifferent to, or even friendly with, Catholics. Many

non-Catholics abandoned or at least eased their traditional prejudice toward papists. In New Hampshire in 1902, the protection
theretofore given only to Protestants in the state constitution's
bill of rights was changed to include all Christians. The following
year, the Presbyterian Church in the U.S.A. deleted from the
Westminster Confession of faith, written in 1643, an explicit reference to the Pope as "anti-Christ."

In the 1890's, threats to new Zion were seen mainly in racial
rather than religious terms. To the reformers of New York City,
the Irish, not the Church of Rome, were the enemy. The problem
of the "average Catholic Irishman" from their point of view was
not that he believed in the doctrine of papal infallibility but, as
Theodore Roosevelt wrote in his legislative diary in 1882, that he
"is a low, venal, corrupt, and unintelligent brute." The problem,
Roosevelt might have added, was that the Irish Catholics were in
city hall, and Roosevelt's friends were out.

Theories of racial superiority and inferiority were becoming
widely accepted. Social Darwinism—belief in the moral superiority
of technologically successful societies—justified the growing conviction that the so-called "Nordic" race, having demonstrated its
capacity for self-government, was suited to govern others. Fear of
the ideology of the Roman Catholic Church as such was far from
dead, but anxiety about the pollution of the race through contamination with hordes of immigrant Poles, Italians, Irish, Jews,
and Orientals swarming into the United States in unprecedented
numbers was more prevalent. Leading American nativists saw the
citadel of freedom under assault not so much from Rome as from
the Asian and Eastern and Southern European peasants who
flooded American shores.

During the first quarter of the twentieth century, most Americans were indifferent to charges of an alleged Catholic conspiracy.
Catholics fought bravely in World War I, were national heroes in
the boxing ring, on the football field, and the baseball diamond.
It was hard to believe that Knute Rockne and his teams at Notre

Dame were conspiring to anything more subversive than a victory over Army. Cooperation in war, sports, business, and labor unions brought non-Catholics into close contact with flesh and blood Romanists who seemed pretty much like everyone else. Intermarriage became more common, and thousands in New York audiences applauded *Abie's Irish Rose.* Irish Catholic Joe Tumulty was at the right hand of Woodrow Wilson, and Associate Justice Pierce Butler sat on the Supreme Court. While probably believing that the Pope was a reactionary tyrant, an increasing number of Americans in the Northeast were not frightened that the Catholic children who shared lunches and textbooks with their own youngsters constituted a menace to American liberty; and Yankee reformers railed at boozing Irish politicians and Italian racketeers much more than at the doctrine of papal infallibility.

Only in the rural Middle West, and especially in the South, where Catholics were few in number and where the Know-Nothings and even the APA had relatively little success, were Catholics portrayed as advance agents of the Vatican's plan to destroy American freedom. Insecure and anxious in a changing America, small-town Babbitts of the Middle West and the South blamed the Jews, Negroes, Catholics, or all of them, for lost status or other threatening changes.

In 1910, the persuasive Populist rabble-rouser, Tom Watson, turned his personal magazine toward incessant attacks on Catholicism. Another "patriotic" weekly called the *Menace* built a circulation of one million in three years. Like *Watson's* magazine, this one was published in a small country town and appealed primarily to a rural audience in the Middle West, border states, and the South, where Americanism was still associated with rural, Protestant virtue.

In the 1920's, a torrent of anti-Catholic books and pamphlets flooded the South and Middle West accompanying the rise of the Ku Klux Klan. As the paranoid postwar Red scare faded (the Bolshevik bomb throwers seemed to disappear) antipopery and anti-

Semitism stirred again. In 1920, Alabama set up a convent-inspecting commission to protect Protestant maidens (presumably vulnerable to kidnapping or seduction) against the alleged sexual aggressions of priests. Tom Watson of Georgia campaigned successfully for a seat in the United States Senate, claiming that President Wilson had become a tool of the Pope. The governor of Florida warned that the Pope planned to invade the Sunshine State and to transfer the Vatican there. Itinerant preachers for the Klan warned against a Roman plot to destroy the only true Christian nation.

The Klan touched a raw nerve in Americans throughout the South and the Middle West, where rural virtue was trying to defend itself against the predatory industrial power of the Northeast. America was changing, but its apocalyptic promise of a new Zion had not been fulfilled. The war to make the world safe for democracy seemed in retrospect only to have promoted anarchism, crime, moral disintegration, the rise of the cities, and the growing power of industrial capital. The new Jerusalem had been betrayed. Some found the Jews responsible; others damned the Socialists.

The Klan appealed to resurgent fundamental Protestantism. Its brew of Americanism consisted of a heavy dose of moral regulations (women of doubtful virtue were flogged and had their hair cut off; men who gambled too much were taken for a midnight ride), Bible reading in the schools, and anti-Catholicism. By the end of 1923, the Klan had a membership of close to 3 million, and its power was felt in Indiana—where it could organize meetings of 75,000 people—Arkansas, Oklahoma, Ohio, Colorado, Pennsylvania, upstate New York, and Oregon, as well as throughout the South.

While the power of anti-Catholics grew in the South, Catholics were gaining increased power in the industrial states of the Northeast. The Catholic population in the United States had more than doubled from a little more than 8 million to nearly 20 million between 1891 and 1928. The largest jump was in New York, New

Jersey, Pennsylvania, and New England, where non-Catholics were long used to having Catholic mayors and even governors.

BATTLE FOR THE PRESIDENCY

In American presidential politics since the Civil War, any popular and reasonably successful Democratic governor of New York becomes a potential candidate for the Democratic presidential nomination. That is because the national Democratic party until the Eisenhower years has been mainly an alliance between the solid Democratic South and the Democratic city machines of the industrial Northeast. To win the presidency, it was essential to be victorious in the South and the Northeast. Samuel Tilden and Grover Cleveland, both popular and effective governors of New York, were nominated. Tilden was counted out in two southern states because of a deal made between Republicans and southern Democrats to end reconstruction in 1876. Cleveland defeated Blaine in 1884 by carrying New York State, with a large enough plurality from the city to outweigh Republican gains in the rural areas. At the turn of the century, the southern wing of the Democratic party made its alliance with the Populists of the Middle West and nominated William Jennings Bryan, the fundamentalist free-silver advocate from Nebraska, who was defeated three times. Woodrow Wilson, the reform governor of New Jersey whom the bosses thought could be controlled, a Virginian by birth with southern predilections on the race question, defeated a badly divided Republican party in 1912. James Cox, an Ohio newspaper publisher, a compromise candidate in 1920, was not particularly satisfactory to either the Northeast or the South. Neither he nor his aristocratic vice presidential candidate, Franklin D. Roosevelt, could claim to represent the immigrants and their children who increasingly constituted the core voting strength of the Democratic party in the North.

There was one man who could make such a claim and be believed. He was Alfred E. Smith, born of Irish Catholic parents in a third-floor tenement of New York's lower East Side. By 1924, Smith had served four years as a brilliant governor of New York State, home of Democratic Presidents, and was the logical candidate against Coolidge in 1924; but Smith lost the nomination in a bitter convention struggle due to opposition from the South. After a West Virginian, John W. Davis, carried the Democratic standard to defeat, it was not possible to deny the New York governor again in 1928.

Smith's nomination roused anti-Catholic crusaders from a period of relative quiet. The usual pathological appeals, made through an estimated ten million handbills, leaflets, and posters with familiar titles as "Popery in the Public Schools," "Convent Life Unveiled," "Convent Horrors," and "Crimes of the Pope," were rushed into circulation within one week. But the attacks against Smith and Catholicism were more than a mix of xenophobic claptrap and projections of pathological sexuality. Underlying the more hysterical attacks was the widespread and sincere conviction that Americanism itself was threatened. Hundreds of thousands of non-Catholics—increasingly aware that America was no longer a nation of independent, ascetic, thrifty, hard-working Protestant farmers—believed that Smith's election would end the dream of a new Jerusalem forever. Of course Al Smith had been as thrifty, hard-working, and self-reliant as most American frontiersmen; but the brown-derbied, cigar-chewing New York governor represented other qualities in the new America which were frightening to old-stock Americans. Smith was a son of the Bowery in New York, Tammany-trained, and a Roman Catholic. The Kansas editor, William Allen White, saw in his candidacy a threat to "the whole Puritan civilization, which has built a sturdy, orderly nation." To thousands of farmers and small-town merchants, fundamentalists and prohibitionists, Smith was a stranger to the American dream. What they imagined to be his world of gambling, prostitution, saloons, and foreign accents caused them to lament over a lost Eden which had never existed. The *Christian Century,* a nondenominational journal, summed up Protestant fears in more pretentious language than that used by White: "They [Protestants] cannot look with unconcern upon the seating of the representative of an alien culture, of a medieval Latin mentality, of an undemocratic hierarchy, and of a foreign potentate in the great office of the President of the United States."

Racism, fear of and hostility toward big cities, and anti-Catholicism overlapped in the crusade of the Ku Klux Klan against Smith. Its Imperial Wizard wrote in the *North American Review* that a Catholic in the White House was unthinkable because "America was Protestant from birth," and "must remain Protestant if the Nordic stock is to finish its destiny." But the Klan's leader denied charges of bigotry, maintaining that he was fighting for the American values of "freedom and achievement" against the "theocratic autocracy" of Rome which was "at odds with Americanism."

Al Smith was bewildered by the attacks. He was an Irishman and a city boy. These were facts that could not be denied. He was also a Catholic, but he was an American Catholic who believed in personal liberty and separation of church and state just as much as the next fellow. Why hold him accountable for papal bulls and encyclicals which he had never even read? He had been going to Mass, saying his beads, and making his confessions all his life, but that never prevented him from living up to his oath of office or from being a superb governor in New York.

Although he was convinced that most of the attacks came from bigots and lunatics, he tried to answer honest doubts about the compatibility of Americanism with Catholicism in a letter to the *Atlantic Monthly* in May, 1927. He disclaimed expert theological and legal knowledge, but he made it plain that he felt no conflict between his Catholicism and his responsibility as a public official. Quoting from Bishop John England, Archbishop John Ireland, and James Cardinal Gibbons, three dead and honored spokesmen for the American Church, Smith asserted that he believed in the absolute separation of church and state and recognized no power of his Church to interfere with his responsibilities under the Constitution. "I stand," he said, "squarely in support of the provisions of the Constitution which guarantee religious freedom and equality."

Many Protestant churchmen were satisfied and joined Herbert Hoover in denouncing bigotry. The *Christian Century* repeatedly stressed that many Catholics believed as strongly in the separation of church and state as Protestants. Others were not convinced. They relied heavily on relatively recent pronouncements of Popes in 1864, 1870, 1888, 1895, and again in 1907 which questioned the desirability of the American formula of church-state separation. They maintained that because the Church of Rome demands absolute allegiance in faith and morals, and because it is virtually impossible to separate politics from questions of morals, Catholics could not be unswervingly loyal to American institutions.

Years after his defeat, Smith was convinced that religious bigotry had beaten him, but the evidence now seems abundant that no Democrat could have won in 1928. "You can't lick this prosperity thing," said Will Rogers. In addition, Smith undoubtedly lost many votes because of his out-and-out opposition to the "noble experiment" of prohibition. It is often forgotten that Hoover typified the Horatio Alger story at least as effectively as Smith and in a much more familiar format. Born to poor parents, orphaned early, he became a great mining engineer, leader of a successful relief expedition to Belgium following World War I, a strong Secretary of Commerce, and was thought to be above narrow, petty partisan politics.

In retrospect, it is obvious that Smith would have lost even if he had been a Protestant. The astounding thing about the 1928 election was that Smith, with his New York accent, Irish-Tammany upbringing, and unpopular, uncompromising stand against prohibition actually won 15,000,000 votes or 41 percent of the national two-party vote, more than any other Democratic candidate in the twentieth century with the exception of Wilson in 1916. Smith did extremely well in the cities where the sons and daughters of millions of immigrants who arrived in America between 1880 and 1914 voted in increasingly large numbers. Four years before, the Republicans had won the twelve largest cities in the nation by approximately 1,500,000 votes. Smith carried those cities by a plurality of 38,000. Even in the rural Middle West, Smith did better than Cox had done eight years before. Only in the South, where Hoover won two hundred counties, and in the smaller cities and towns of the Middle West were the attacks on Smith's background and religion converted into a substantial number of votes.

Still, Smith blamed his loss on the vicious personal attacks against him and his faith. He could never understand what seemed to him to be the pure prejudice of millions. No one had told him that there were hundreds of thousands of Americans for whom the promised land of America was to have been a new Zion for the fulfillment of Protestant principles infused into the culture-religion of Americanism. No one had warned him of the belief of millions that America's city on the hill was to have been the antithesis of Rome, first as a biblical commonwealth and rapidly thereafter as a secular Jerusalem whose transmogrified Protestantism gave primacy to independent choice in human and not just spiritual relations. Fears which Protestants had imbibed with their mother's milk and which surged forth at moments of peril—following the passage of the Quebec Act, again in the 1840's and 1850's when Catholic immigrants pressed into the cities, and in the 1880's and 1890's at a time of drastic social change—were touched off once more by Smith's nomination as hundreds of thousands felt personally threatened by the possible election of a papist.

That Smith won as many votes as he did was testimony to his extraordinary ability. He belonged to the Church which had long been identified in the minds of American Protestants with persecution, superstition, and control over the minds and behavior of its communicants. Many voters undoubtedly were able to see in

Smith an able and archetypal representative of American values. Others were imprisoned by the conviction that no Romanist— regardless of what he said or did—could be free from conflict between the designs of the Church and the values of Americanism.

Smith made the mistake of largely dismissing such fears as the fantasies of diseased minds. But some of the most creative minds in America had shared such fears, from Jefferson to William Ellery Channing and from Theodore Parker to William Allen White. For more than 150 years, their views reflected those of millions of Americans who saw in the Church of Rome an instrument of despotism at war with the value of personal independence. However mistaken they may have been, they believed themselves to be the watchmen of freedom defending the city against its most formidable and implacable enemy.

III

HOPE AND FEAR

THE soul of America was torn by civil war in 1862 and 1863 when John F. Kennedy's grandfathers were born in the city of Boston. In Boston, home of reform and hotbed of abolitionism, the war was considered the supreme test of Americanism by the Congregationalist and Unitarian men and women who had made the city a center of intellectual, literary, and political activity. But Patrick J. Kennedy and John F. Fitzgerald, their red and wrinkled skin properly spanked and dried, bellowed their way into an Irish Boston more concerned about food and jobs than slavery. In the rough-and-tumble Irish enclave of East Boston, they scrambled to manhood and success. For them and hundreds of thousands from the ould sod, ideological reform was not worth bothering one's head about. There were mouths to feed, backs to clothe, deals to be made, and interests to defend.

But John Kennedy's people were not afraid of encounter with the world outside of East Boston. Patrick Kennedy and "Honey Fitz" were optimistic, hopeful Irishmen whose success justified their disposition. In 1910, Fitzgerald became the first native-born son of Irish parents to be elected mayor of Boston. He even bought a home in the historic town of Concord, where he lived for a while near places made famous by the Minutemen and later by Emerson and Thoreau. Patrick Kennedy sent his boy, Joe, on a ferry ride every school day across Boston Harbor to Boston Latin School (America's most distinguished public school, once attended by Cotton Mather, Samuel Adams, Ralph Waldo Emerson, and Henry Ward Beecher) from the seventh grade on, and later, when he had made enough money from his East Boston saloon and other deals, he entered him at Harvard College.

AMERICAN CATHOLIC OPTIMISM

From the earliest days of the Republic, there have always been Catholics who welcomed the American emphasis on personal freedom without yielding in their commitment to the Church of Rome. These men and women have been hopeful, even confident, that American values were compatible with Catholicism. Other Catholics, doubting that the United States—child of the Enlightenment and Protestantism—was a hospitable home for their faith, have defended themselves against every attack, real or imagined, by separating themselves further socially and psychologically from non-Catholic Americans. Sometimes they saw Protestants, if not Americanists, as allied with Masons, Jews, and infidels against the Church.

The state of mind of those who were hopeful about Catholicism in America was optimistic and adventuresome; those who were afraid were pessimistic and conservative. The tendency to hope resulted in a desire for encounter; the tendency to fear in wanting to protect one's separateness. Those who were optimistic saw in the growth of Catholic wealth and power and in the millions of silent friendships between Catholics and non-Catholics confirmation of their hopes. The pessimistic saw in the successes of the Know-Nothings, the vigilantism of the APA and Ku Klux Klan, and the defeat of Al Smith proof that their fears were justified.

Up to 1820, the small, poor, and badly organized Catholic Church lost at least 250,000 followers to indifference or conversion, leaving no more than 200,000 practicing Catholics in the country. The leakage was understandable. Most Catholics were of English descent, with a sprinkling of Irish and some Germans in Pennsylvania, whose reasons for leaving the home country were comparable to those of Protestant immigrants: personal freedom, a piece of land, and a chance to rise. The decision to emigrate frequently was based at least as much on attraction to America as rejection of the home country. That decision often signified a willingness to do without the extended family and close relationships between community and church. In the New World, Catholics lived on farms far from each other largely unattended by priests, some of whom had to ride as much as three hundred miles a week in order to say Mass. America was a place where everyone was religious in a general way, but where few belonged to a church; and many Catholics fell into the general pattern.

Those who remained Catholic were usually more staunch in support of religious freedom and the separation of church and state than their Protestant neighbors. The first proprietor of Maryland, Catholic Cecilius Calvert, urged his appointed governor to treat Protestants with as much mildness and favor as possible. Perhaps Calvert was no more than prudent, since the majority of the population even in Maryland were Protestants, and he knew his colony was a Catholic island in a sea of almost total antipapist sentiment.

Throughout the colonial period, Catholics had everything to gain and nothing to lose from religious toleration. They appear to have given consistent and overwhelming support to every action to promote religious freedom, including the Revolution itself. They knew that the antiestablishment liberalism of Thomas Jefferson, Samuel Adams, and Benjamin Franklin was the best guarantee of their safety and prosperity. Never before and not again until the 1960's was there such harmony of friendship and interests between Deists such as Thomas Paine and Jefferson and Catholic religious leaders. No one was more enthusiastic about the passage of the First Amendment to the Constitution than these two groups, whose theological predilections were so far apart. Even after the passage of the amendment, Catholics had equality in civil affairs in only five of the thirteen states, but the process of disestablishment was well under way and would be completed in Massachusetts in 1833.

The spirit of toleration which prevailed following the Revolution encouraged Catholics to hope that their religion was safe in the new nation. Increasingly secure and respected, they shared in the dream of the city of freedom, and were anxious to encounter non-Catholics in fulfilling it. Father John Carroll, named by the Holy See as superior of American Catholic Missions in 1784, recognized that certain fundamental conditions in the New World were different from anything Catholics had experienced before. Not only was the United States removed from centers of Catholic power and culture, but it had never gone through an agonizing struggle to overturn the influence of a feudal church. Never torn by religious civil wars, most Americans, while suspicious of the Church of Rome, were prepared to let their neighbors practice their religion in peace as long as they obeyed the laws and were devoted to the ideals and interests of their country. Because Americans gave "free circulation to fair argument" and because Carroll believed in the truth of Catholicism, he welcomed encounter with non-Catholics.

Encounter is the response of self-confident men who are aware of the possibilities of influencing others; but it is a dynamic two-way process involving the risk of change as well as the opportunity of changing others. Encounter meant constant exposure to the culture-religion of Americanism—that religion which in de Tocqueville's words found each American "in most of the operations of the mind" appealing "only to the individual efforts of his own understanding"—including the pressure to adopt typically American forms of church organization and practice. The American system of putting local churches under the control of laymen who were not only responsible for church property but for the choice of their local pastors stemmed from the value of personal independence and implied hostility to episcopacies of any kind. Carroll and the twenty-five priests under his jurisdiction obviously did not oppose the principle of episcopacy but they wanted to adapt it, at least for a while, to American conditions. At first they opposed having a Catholic bishop on American soil until they could be more certain of his reception, and when it was suggested that the Bishop of Quebec visit Maryland and Pennsylvania to administer confirmation in 1784, they preferred to forgo that sacrament rather than affront their Protestant neighbors. Later that year the American priests sent letters to Rome urging that a foreign bishop was not necessary in America and threatened that he would not be entitled to the support of the clergy if sent against their wishes. They wanted someone who knew American conditions; but when the Anglicans talked of appointing a bishop for themselves, Carroll realized it might be possible for Catholics to have a bishop in America too, and advised the Holy See that it would be wise to give the American clergy the right to elect a bishop for themselves in order to frustrate the idea of foreign control of American Catholics. He was consecrated Bishop of Baltimore in 1790, and later became the first Archbishop of Baltimore.

Rome permitted local choice in the selection of the first three bishops, acknowledging and unintentionally encouraging the existing tendency within American Catholicism to adopt some kind of Presbyterian form of government in which the laity had the right to hire and fire their pastors without interference from the bishop, just as the clergy exercised the choice of their own bishop. American Catholics had lived for generations without effective ecclesiastical control, and many parishioners believed that they had the right to appoint pastors and even to withhold salaries.

CONGREGATIONAL TENDENCIES

The Anglicans could not succeed in America until they broke away from the Church of England and became Episcopalians. Presbyterians and Methodists had to develop an American organizational structure free from binding ties to the mother churches of Europe. For a while it appeared as if Catholics would follow the same course.

But John Carroll's belief in American freedom, his willingness to encounter non-Catholics, and his support of the priests in their desire to choose their own bishop did not mean that he shared the Protestant view on the subject of the control of church property and the selection of ministers. Carroll had no choice but to accept trusteeism—the laity serving as trustees of church property rather than the clergy—since state laws were made to accommodate the Protestant pattern of incorporating church property under the names of vestrymen, deacons, or elders. He could understand the view which many Catholics shared with their Protestant countrymen, that since they built their churches, owned them, and since the law upheld them, the bishop had no right to interfere in the control of property. He would not have objected to trusteeism as such had it been merely a partnership between priest and people in the administration of property; but he could not abandon the Catholic view that such property was a gift to God which made the Catholic Church its real owner. Nor could he acquiesce in the notion that trustees were immune from episcopal control in the selection of pastors simply because they held the moneybags. While he and his successors often yielded on the right of the laity to control ecclesiastical finances, they insisted on their authority to appoint pastors.

Catholic parishioners muttered about freedom, liberty, and rights as only Americans did in the nineteenth century. During the first half of that century, canon law and the regulations of bishops were openly derided, and schisms lasted for years in congregations in New Orleans, Charleston, Norfolk, and Buffalo, which were usually led by lay trustees in cooperation with individualistic foreign priests who had caught the American independence fever. In 1819, the board of trustees of the church for Catholics in Norfolk and Portsmouth, Virginia, rejected a summons issued by Archbishop Ambrose Marechal, and called his action "a most glaring violation of their civil rights and religious liberties and in direct opposition to the state laws of Virginia."

The most notorious attempt to challenge the authority of the episcopacy took place in Philadelphia in 1821, where the board of trustees of St. Mary's Cathedral had controlled church property and named their own pastors in typically Protestant fashion since the formation of the church in 1808, despite the opposition of the clergy. When Bishop Henry Conwell assumed responsibility for the diocese, he attacked the trustees by withdrawing the privileges of the cathedral from the Reverend William Hogan, the pastor who had been chosen by the congregation, and who was later to win fame as a strongly anti-Catholic apostate. The trustees of St. Mary's defied their bishop, whereupon Conwell told Hogan that he either had to resign or be excommunicated. The trustees stood firm; Hogan was excommunicated; and the congregation attempted a compromise. But the Pope would have none of it, and the new bishop, Francis Patrick Kenrick, who took charge in 1830, placed the church under an interdict, dispersing the congregation.

Gradually the episcopacy reasserted its control over church property and the appointment of local pastors. When struggles over trusteeism led to a rash of schisms, the first Provincial Council of bishops, meeting in Baltimore in 1829, decided not to consecrate any church unless the deed was made in trust to them. The laws of the states were often on the side of rebellious trustees, as in Pennsylvania where an 1855 statute forbade episcopal control of church property and in New York where trustees were given the right to overrule their bishop. But regardless of the laws, most bishops found that reasonable discussions with rebellious trustees

could resolve their differences. Some of the bishops were terrified
by trusteeism as being incompatible with the good of the Church
and did everything they could within the law to crush it, while
others, refusing to yield on the principle of episcopal authority,
recognized certain aspects of it as a healthy manifestation of lay
interest in church matters.

When Archbishop Carroll died in 1815, the control of the
Church passed temporarily to French clerics who were much less
enthusiastic than Carroll about the liberal, Protestantized American environment. In alliance with the Irish-born bishops appointed to the sees of Philadelphia, New York, and Richmond,
they saw every tendency toward trusteeism as a threat to the
Church. A quite different approach was taken by Bishop John
England, appointed to Charleston in 1820 following demands by
Charleston laymen that their bishop be a man who understood
American conditions and who they hoped would have the merit
of being obnoxious to the un-American French bishops nicknamed
"the Baltimore junta." Charleston Catholics had not gone as far
as their coreligionists in Norfolk, Virginia, who asked Rome in
1817 if they could elect their bishop in consequence of what they
called "our inalienable right of patronage," and who even suggested their own candidate. The Pope, of course, recognized no
such right, but he also realized that the Catholic lay leaders of Virginia and Charleston had to be accommodated at least partly.
Since the appointment of Frenchmen would have infuriated them,
he chose two Irishmen, Patrick Kelly for Norfolk and John England for Charleston. Kelly was ineffectual and the Virginians
forced his resignation within a year, but England became the first
significant clerical spokesman for an American church since Carroll. Although England warned against Irish priests who became
"intoxicated with the spirit of liberty" as soon as they set foot on
American soil, he strongly believed in the institutions and the
values of America, and his French colleagues annoyed him because
of their inability to understand why Catholicism "should be . . .

assimilated to American principles." He accepted the principle of separation of church and state, because a self-confident religion, he reasoned, did not need the support of the state.

Although he took extremely prompt and decisive action to check rebellious trustees in North Carolina, Georgia, and South Carolina, he welcomed the active participation of the laity in the management of church affairs while stoutly defending the prerogatives of the episcopacy. England embodied his ideas for cooperation between the laity and the clergy in an elaborate constitution written in 1823, which authorized an annual convention of lay and clerical delegates to advise the bishop in his vast responsibilities. But other bishops, particularly those in New York and Philadelphia, recoiled against extending the influence of the laity any further and neither they nor any of their successors ever adopted a comparable constitution. Although England's constitution was rejected, his repeated pleas for a Provincial Council (really a National Council of Bishops) to issue uniform regulations for all the dioceses was finally acted on in 1829 when the first council met in Baltimore. Its meeting made conservative bishops in the United States and in Rome even more nervous than the Charleston constitution, since it raised the specter of a national legislative council which might grow in power and become independent of the Holy Father. But England saw the council as a simple way of dealing with national problems, including the absorption of the rapidly growing number of immigrants which raised the Catholic population from approximately 24,000 in 1790 to about 361,000 in 1830.

THE IRISH INHERITANCE

The problems of the Church in America in 1829 were minuscule compared to what lay ahead. The 700,000 immigrants who arrived in the 1840's practically tripled the Catholic population. More significantly, they completely altered its ethnic composition. Out of Ireland they came by the tens of thousands, fleeing from the misery and death which followed the great potato famine of 1845–47. More than a half-million persons had starved to death or had been eaten away by disease. The land of mists and valleys, of devils and spirits, had become a country of poverty and despair.

Of the differences between the Irish immigrants of the 1850's and the English settlers of the 1630's—religious, political, familial —probably none was as significant as their reasons for coming. There were no adventurous proprietors among the Irish; few were merchants; they had no illusions about owning their own land, and no vision of building a city on the hill. They were driven out of Ireland by sheer, stark poverty. The census of 1841 showed that nearly half of the families of the rural population of Ireland were living in windowless, mud cabins of a single room. Then came the horror of the potato blight. For hundreds of thousands emigration was the only escape from famine, typhus, or cholera.

Fiercely Catholic, they were driven to a Protestant land. Doggedly Irish despite centuries of Danish, Norman, and English invasions, they were forced to a country dominated by the descendants of hated Englishmen. For more than three hundred years the English had tried to destroy Irish nationalism. Henry VIII, responsible for leading England away from the Church, deprived Catholic Irish noblemen of their property in an attempt to drive the Irish off the land. The Irish were stubborn; and Henry and his successors repeatedly tried to smash them. By 1652, all Ireland had been devastated, and one third (about 616,000 persons) of the population had died in wars, plague, and famine during the preceding ten years. Then came the Cromwellian terror. The hated Puritan, whose name would be likened to the black death for generations after, sold thousands of Irishmen as slaves to the West Indies and divided two thirds of the land in Ireland to give to his own violently anti-Catholic soldiers and supporters. Although Cromwell's Puritan commonwealth could not stifle Catholicism, the English succeeded in making local farmers into landless peasants with no legal rights to the soil. English landlords and merchants, soon owning three fourths of the land and controlling two thirds of the trade, forced the passage of a new penal code in 1691 to subjugate the Irish further.

For the next 125 years, the Irish, already mired in economic hardship, were humiliated through brutally discriminatory laws intended to make plain the message that English Protestants were better than Irish Catholics. The penal laws, which were only sporadically enforced by destroying cottages and seizing cattle, forbade the Irish language and subjected priests to arrest and deportation. No Irish Catholic was permitted to enter a university, become a lawyer, or work for the government; and every Irishman was obliged to pay tithes for the support of the established Church of England. None were to serve on juries, vote, enter the army or navy, or teach school. No Irish Catholic craftsman or tradesman could have more than two apprentices, and it was forbidden for any Catholic to buy land from a Protestant in Ireland. Those few Irish who retained large landholdings did so at the price of allegiance to the English Church.

The English could never completely subdue the Irish. Bloody massacres, penal laws, and rack renting only made them more stubborn. Rents were raised at will since the Irish farmers had no long-term contracts and no fixed rights to work the land, putting the peasant figuratively on a rack, since the more he improved his land or livestock, the more likely he was to have his rent increased. Secret organizations such as the Hearts of Steel Boys, the Molly Maguires, the Black Feet, and the White Boys sometimes burned the landlords' crops or terrorized Irishmen who cooperated with the hated English.

English domination eventually gave Ireland and England a common language; but despite their shared tongue, differences in geography, history, and economics kept the two peoples far apart psychologically. Of all the countries of Europe, Ireland was farthest removed from the seats of ancient civilization. It had no grand pre-Christian civilization of its own, and its major contacts with foreigners had meant only oppression, destruction, and death. Lacking in natural resources, battered by Atlantic storms, worn down by long rain-chilling winters, and kept even from the pride of owning their own land, the Irish developed a pervasive, brooding fatalism.

The land was lonely and hard, and death was often a familiar friend. Escape also came in religion, first in a primitive cosmology ruled by pagan gods and holy spirits, and later in the universal Church of Rome. Nourishing food was scarce but fermented potatoes were not. To overcome a sense of failure and futility, of weakness and lost masculinity, the Irish often took comfort in the release of alcohol. One bore the unchangeable burdens of this world as best as one could, and drink as well as talk often became a substitute for action.

The fatalism of the Irish was encouraged by the influence of Jansenistic priests from France who staffed the seminary at Maynooth in the decades following the French Revolution. Jansenism, later declared a heresy by Rome, stressed the depravity of natural human instincts, especially the sexual. Although the Church later saw Jansenism as underestimating the importance of free will and depriving the quest for salvation of its moral complexity, it was a significant factor in the Irish Church in the late eighteenth and early nineteenth centuries. To this day the Irish of Boston appear to be more puritanical than the descendants of Calvinists regarding sex. Ironically, although Arminianism had triumphed over orthodox Calvinism in America before the beginning of the nineteenth century, Jansenism, officially declared a heresy by the Catholic Church, persisted as an important force in Ireland and was carried with immigrants to the United States at the height of its influence.

IRISH REACTIONS

Cursing the English or forgetting one's misery in drink brought no lasting peace, and religion increasingly provided the only real solace which hundreds of thousands of Irish peasants knew. In the salving rite of Communion, in the sharing of blood and flesh through wafers and wine, Irish peasants were united in Christ beyond the reach of the English.* The penal laws which had been designed to destroy Catholicism made the Irish depend on their Church more than ever. Could there be better proof of the truth of Catholicism than in the cruelty of Protestant landlords, tax collectors, and soldiers? Parish priests were—more than ever before —protectors of the people as well as guardians of the faith.

Over three million Irish came to the United States between 1845, the first year of the famine, and 1890 when the number of Irish-born in the United States was at its peak. Each year the youngest and healthiest of farmers and laborers left behind the more bleak and desolate. Imprisoned by their own poverty, the immigrants remained in the cities where they landed or moved to those close by on rivers and railways, where work was available. In America, the Irish became more Irish and Catholic than in Ireland. It was their way of defending against the harshness and hostility of the cities, and the strangeness of America's ways.

Although a minority of immigrants were attracted to the American cult of personal independence, most of the Irish, already fiercely tribalistic, were repelled. If the Irish had learned anything throughout their history, it was first, not to trust outsiders; and second, that the individual could do and was nothing outside of his own family and clan. The concept of independent man celebrated by Emerson and Thoreau was an absurdity to the Irish. It was a trick to make them believe in English and Yankee concepts of abstract justice. There was no such thing. It was horrifying to have to testify against a relative or neighbor in an impersonal court of law. Oaths of fealty were one thing, but oaths to tell the truth even against one's friend or relative were plainly absurd.

Everyone takes care of his own. To pretend otherwise is to prac-

* Only the priest actually sipped the wine, but the communion was shared.

tice deceit. The familiar phrase in the advertisement or store window, "No Irish Need Apply," was ample proof of the hypocrisy in the Yankee boast of impersonal justice. Hypocrisy, after all, was no different in new than in old England. What Protestant reformers saw as Irish Catholic corruption in politics was simply a matter of following the laws of survival. What the Yankees saw as a want of self-reliance was simply recognition that if your brothers, sisters, and cousins could not take care of you, no one else would.

The American Protestants prattled about personal responsibility. Another abstraction! What a horrible way to bury man in his own misery and guilt! No confession and no penance. What would keep a man from committing mortal sins? He either must live with fearful guilt, bury it, or succumb to the devil. To whom are these Protestants loyal? Do abstractions breathe or suffer or bleed? Loyalty can be given only to flesh-and-blood men and women with dreams and miseries to be shared. The sentiments of village loyalty and emotions of family love were reinforced in the ghettos of the cities as Irishmen defended themselves against an alien environment.

The tribalism of Irish peasant culture was at one with the authoritarianism of the Church in opposing the American creed of independence. Catholic newspapers in the 1840's and 1850's warned their readers against the contagious idea that "every tinker and plowboy" could "interpret the Scripture as he thought proper." Freedom of religion definitely did not mean that every man was at liberty to do what he pleased. No man had a moral right to follow any but the true religion, Catholicism.

So-called American freedom was often seen as Protestant license. Such independence had enabled Luther to repudiate his vow of celibacy and to marry a nun, had permitted Henry VIII to get a divorce and to destroy universal Christendom and had allowed his earls and barons to seize church lands in wanton selfishness. In America, Protestant license facilitated the whims and idiosyncrasies of self-seeking or lecherous men, permitting group marriage in the Oneida community, polygamy among the Mormons, and a high divorce rate. Protestant license, it was widely alleged, could even mean immorality at camp meetings and frontier revivals.

Catholic critics pointed out that American freedom permitted every kind of wild idea to be organized into a so-called Christian sect. Under the umbrella of Protestantism, Americans claimed to find truth as Jehovah's Witnesses, Mormons, Unitarians, Shakers, Seventh-day Adventists, Quakers, and Dunkers. Independence in America clearly meant chaos. Surely God did not intend his truths to be spoken in so many contradictory voices.

In America, getting ahead was a way of demonstrating independence and reforming humanity was the way of justifying it. To the Irish Catholic mind, developed in the elemental world of peasant villages, humans were often seen as the victims of uncontrollable malevolent forces. Getting ahead, achieving, reforming the world were strange slogans to men and women wedded to the virtues of obedience, loyalty, and devotion. Irish literature revealed a deep fear that children might rise beyond their parents and embarrass them. A person should accept his lot in life, which, after all, was only a prelude to something much more important. Distinctions between class, race, and sex were inevitable. Pre-Civil War Catholic journals and newspapers uniformly warned against efforts to change them. Reformers seemed to be wild Protestants in favor of change for its own sake, espousing every proposal from vegetarianism to communal marriage. Woman's rights and compulsory public education usually were opposed by the Irish as threats to the family which, in Irish culture and Catholic theology, constituted the prime regulator of morality.

Public education was particularly frightening because it weakened the hold of parents and Church over the children. It asserted the supremacy of a secular state whose schools were often infiltrated by Protestant principles. The abolition of slavery was usually advocated by the very zealots who preached woman's rights, public education, and temperance. If the abolitionists had their way, freed slaves would crowd the job market of the northern cities. Negroes were already competitors as the hewers of wood and drawers of water and were feared and hated by tens of thousands of Irish immigrants who fought them for jobs. Irish hostility toward the Negroes would persist on through the Civil War and into the twentieth century. Large numbers resented being drafted to fight for Negro freedom. "Who's fighting for my freedom?" they would ask. In New York, on the Monday morning following the publication of the first draft list, which seemed to fall more heavily on the Irish than others, where Negroes had been used as strike-breakers on the docks, sullen crowds commenced four days of rioting, including the burning of a Negro orphan asylum, the beating of helpless older men and women, and the hanging of several Negroes. A large proportion of the police who tried to keep order were Irishmen too, and Archbishop John Hughes effectively used his great prestige to quiet the rioting on the fourth day, but Irish hostility toward the black man was strong and widespread.

THE SEPARATIST RESPONSE

Archbishop Hughes was the most powerful Catholic leader in a period that covered the great immigrations, the rise of the Know-Nothings, and the Civil War. Where Carroll and England had represented the tendency in American Catholicism to encounter the American environment on its own terms, John Hughes promoted and defended the separatist Catholic response to the culture-religion of Americanism. Hughes, who believed vaguely in the principle of separation of church and state, served the government in many connections, most notably on a mission for Lincoln during the Civil War to persuade the government of Emperor Napoleon III to maintain its neutrality in the American struggle. He was respected by many leading Americans; but the total effect of his leadership at mid-century was to intensify Catholic suspicions and fear of encounter and to sharply curtail the influence of the laity within the American Church.

Catholic historians have argued that Hughes had no other real choice. Under the pressure of economic discrimination, religious prejudice, and especially poverty, the formation of Catholic ghettos in the large cities of the eastern seaboard seemed almost an economic and psychological necessity. Hughes and his fellow clerics were faced with overwhelming numbers of immigrants for whom churches and schools had to be built, hospitals and orphanages opened, teachers and pastors found. American public institutions—schools, hospitals, charities—usually had been formed under Protestant auspices. Catholics who were dying sometimes were refused the last rites at public almshouses and Catholic children often were obliged to read Protestant attacks on the papacy in textbooks. To Hughes, separatism was the only answer.

As much as any other man, Hughes was responsible for smashing the control of lay trustees over church property. As a newly appointed bishop of the New York diocese in 1838, he inherited a 1784 statute which provided that lay trustees chosen by the congregation should control all church property. By steadily applying pressure to local congregations to deliver their property to him, he defeated the intention of the law except in the case of St. Louis' Church in Buffalo, whose wardens refused to give up control. Following a long and indecisive struggle, Hughes, by then an archbishop, had the church placed under interdict in 1851. The St. Louis trustees defied the interdict and were excommunicated three years later. The state legislature, in a wave of resentment against Hughes, passed a law to make clerical ownership illegal under any circumstances, but officials made no attempt to enforce it, and it was finally repealed in 1863.

For forty years, between 1830 and 1870, Hughes and other bishops did little to encourage England's point of view concerning the role of the laity in church affairs. Since the bishops could receive no support from the state against refractory priests, they made their will the law of the Church. Dealing with an overwhelmingly lower-class, immigrant population, they were able to reassert and maintain clerical control.

Episcopal control was facilitated by the creation of parochial schools. Hughes's paper, the *Freeman's Journal*, urged Catholics to demand public money for the support of their schools or, second best, passage of laws forbidding the reading of Protestant Bibles in the public schools. When his campaign resulted in an 1842 state law forbidding the teaching or practice of any religious sectarian doctrine in the common schools, Hughes remained unsatisfied. He continued to build Catholic schools, and by 1850 he was leading New York and other major cities into the establishment of a vast private school system. Probably no decision has had more profound consequences for separating Catholics from other Americans. Hughes and other bishops seemed to think they had no alternative but to take Catholic children away from an increasingly secular, even if less Protestant-influenced, public school system.

The archbishop was at one with Rome in viewing the Church as under attack from liberalism and secularism in Europe and the United States. He warned against the "republicanism of Europe," as he called the liberal revolutions of 1848, and vigorously attacked such enemies of Catholicism as the popular liberal Hungarian Kossuth. Defending the Church not only meant separate institutions of charity and schools but it also meant defending them by force if necessary. With nativist feeling running high in New York following a mass meeting, Hughes urged Catholics to take every measure necessary, including force, to protect Catholic institutions should public authorities fail in their responsibilities. He probably prevented riots in New York comparable to those in Philadelphia by stationing thousands of men around the churches in his city. In that instance, and in others, his courage and decisiveness were admired by many, but his militant separatism on all occasions undoubtedly deepened and exacerbated tensions between Catholics and non-Catholics. Only twenty-four years before, Bishop John

England had been applauded by an enthusiastic Congress following his explanation of the principles of Catholicism. Now, in 1850, Hughes boasted of the Catholic Church: "Everybody should know that we have for our mission to convert the world—including the inhabitants of the United States—the people of the cities and the people of the country, the officers of the navy, and the marines, commanders of the army, Legislatures, the Senate, the Cabinet, the President, and all!"

DESIRE FOR ENCOUNTER

Although Hughes was the most formidable separatist leader in America, Irish Catholic separatism prevailed in the other major cities too. Perhaps in Boston the Irish felt their difference more than anywhere else. If Boston was not the hub of the universe, Massachusetts was certainly the center of the Americanist faith. Cradle of liberty, source of revivals, home of transcendentalism, here the Yankees were in complete control, and the Irish felt obliged to act apart until they would be able, by sheer force of numbers, to capture Boston for their own. In 1854, at the zenith of Know-Nothing power, the Catholic Boston *Pilot* concluded that "cooperation for any length of time in important matters between *true* Catholics and *real* Protestants is morally impossible."

A small group of Catholics, led by native-born converts, opposed the separatism of their coreligionists. The converts, the best known of whom were Orestes Brownson and Isaac Hecker, had shown independence and courage in converting to the Church. Brownson, a close friend of transcendentalists, had found in Catholicism significant answers to anguished questions he had been asking all his adult life. Through the distinguished journal, *Brownson's Quarterly Review,* he attempted to reconcile the Church with American ideals. His response to the Know-Nothing crusade was the opposite of that given by Hughes. The archbishop saw bigoted Protestants who must be beaten. Brownson saw misguided Americans who needed to be persuaded. Beginning in 1854, he began to preach the doctrine of Americanization. He attacked slavery and supported the Republican party. Although the *Pilot,* formerly a friend and champion, angrily opposed his ideas, Brownson continued to oppose separatism. It was a mistake, he said, to believe that Catholic children could be removed from harm's way "by keeping them in ignorance of the world around them." Neither parental nor sacerdotal authority would suffice to protect Catholics from secular American influences. The only safety was to confront danger boldly rather than to run from it. "In the world in which we live it is no less important that our young men should feel their freedom, and be encouraged to use it, than it is that they should feel and discharge their obligations to authority." The New England editor believed that the American emphasis on personal independence was perfectly compatible with obedience to God and his Church. He attacked what he called "blind obedience," arguing that "blind obedience even to the authority of the Church cannot be expected of a people reared under the American system." In this country, he maintained, the Church would prosper by dealing with people as freemen. He wanted the Church to promote "an intelligent, free willing obedience, yielded from personal conviction" after seeing the reasonableness and logic of Catholic dogma. Such an obedience, he insisted, "is far more consonant to the spirit of the Church, and far more acceptable to God, than simple blind obedience."

Brownson, a Yankee to the core, was more at home with the New England divines of Cambridge and Concord than with the Irish immigrants of Boston. Isaac Hecker had been born in America too, but of German ancestry. He made the priesthood his vocation and with three other convert priests evolved a plan for a missionary society to be named after the great apostle, St. Paul. Their intention was to obtain a fair hearing for Catholicism by writing books, articles, religious tracts and letters, and by giving lectures in answer to every reasonable question or doubt in the

minds of Americans. Hecker argued that error could not be prevented through the use of force or legal compulsion. He believed
in the values of Americanism, and wanted to blend them with the
wisdom of Catholicism. Several viewpoints with which he was associated later became extremely controversial and were repudiated
by Rome as a so-called "Americanist heresy." But at mid-century
neither Hecker nor Brownson, while causing Archbishop Hughes
some discomfort, were significant enough to be widely controversial. Even if the bishops had joined in Brownson's plea for the laity
to take a more active role within the Church, it is doubtful if they
would have responded. Possessing none of the self-confidence of
Brownson or Hecker, it was more comfortable for immigrants to
avoid encounter with non-Catholics and to accept the leadership
of the trusted episcopacy.

THE DEFENSE OF ROME

The hostility of nativists obliged most of the Irish to fall back
on their Irishness as well as their Catholicism. Under the impact
of Know-Nothingism they developed a strong sense of identity
with revolutionary nationalist movements in the home country.
Although Archbishop Hughes did not like the liberal smell of
Ireland's young revolutionaries, some of whom attacked the temporal claims of the papacy, they were heroes to many of the American Irish who were less submissive to the clergy on this issue than
on others. Shortly after Hughes's death, the Fenian Brotherhood,
begun in 1858 as the first significant Irish nationalist organization
known later for its abortive raid against Canada in 1867, soared in
popularity. Over 100,000 persons gathered at the picnic grounds
in Jones Woods, New York City, in March, 1866, to applaud a
Fenian rally, despite the opposition of Archbishop John McCloskey, Hughes's successor. The sacraments provided spiritual food;
they calmed anxiety and brought inner peace, at least for a while.

Irish nationalism provided an outlet for resentment and anger, stirring the passions and bringing a measure of self-esteem.

In their opposition to the revolutionaries of Ireland, a majority of the bishops were following the leadership of Rome, where Pope Pius IX defended the Church against the nationalism, republicanism, revolution, and rationalism of nineteenth-century Europe. The Pope tried to protect Catholics against the spirit of the times by emphasizing new devotions, clarifying Catholic dogma, and reasserting papal prerogatives. The Virgin Mary especially became the primary object of new devotions with the promulgation of the doctrine of the Immaculate Conception in 1854. In the years that followed, dozens of devotional histories and biographies of saints were published to emphasize the mysterious, spiritual essence of Catholicism as contrasted with the materialistic, secular spirit of rationalism.

Even more than the new emphasis on devotions, the Pope's warnings to the minority of Catholic scholars and clerics in Europe who advocated new ideas in politics and science were evidence of his intention not to compromise with liberalism in any way. In December, 1864, his position was made plain with the publication of the Syllabus of Errors. The Syllabus, aimed primarily as a contribution to the ideological warfare being waged in Europe, branded as false some of the basic beliefs of most Americans, probably including a large proportion of American Catholics. Among other things, it was an error to believe that "the Church ought to be separated from the State and the State from the Church," or that the Catholic religion should not be recognized by the state "to the exclusion of all other modes of worship." In error, too, was the belief that "each man is free to embrace and profess the religion he shall believe true guided by the light of reason."

Five years later, Pius convened the Vatican Council of 1869–70, which ratified two dogmatic constitutions aimed at protecting the Church against the dynamic changes sweeping the Western World. The first, *Dei filius,* denounced the rationalism and materialism of the age, attributing perversions of truth to the influence of Protestantism. The second, *De ecclesia,* asserted that the Pope was infallible when teaching ex cathedra on questions of faith and morals.

A group of American bishops, led by Archbishop Peter Kenrick of St. Louis, spoke several times in opposition to both constitutions, and many of the Americans left Rome rather than accede to the final definition of papal infallibility. Bishop Edward Fitzgerald of Little Rock, Arkansas, remaining to the end, cast one of the two "no" votes in the final balloting. Probably the American bishops accurately anticipated that the doctrine of papal infallibility would be widely misinterpreted in the United States, where infallibility with respect to faith and morals would be thought to include everything and be construed as an assault on human freedom. But the views of the small and uninfluential American episcopacy did not prevail. They were unable to blunt the edge of the majority's sharpest attacks on the so-called errors of the age or to qualify the doctrine of infallibility to make it more acceptable at home.

Pius was probably not particularly concerned with the reactions of the Americans. He had once pointed out that the American people showed little interest in things spiritual. That the Church prospered in America where liberals and secularists were stronger than in any country in Europe may have perplexed him, but it certainly did not lead him to conclude that compromises could be made with such forces in Europe. There, the Church appeared to be losing. The council itself was closed when Italian troops seized Rome and ended the temporal power of the Popes until Mussolini restored papal sovereignty over Vatican City. From Pius' point of view, the center of the struggle to defend Catholicism was Europe, where Gladstone asserted that Catholics could not be good citizens, Bismarck waged war on the Church in Germany, Gambetta favored anticlericalism in France, and church-state relations were deteriorating in Spain, Italy, and Austria. America was still technically missionary country and would remain so until 1908.

THE ASCENDANCY OF THE AMERICANIZERS

The opposition of the American bishops to the doctrine of papal infallibility was a reflection of the extent to which the Church in the United States was becoming Americanized despite the attacks of nativists, the separatism of Archbishop Hughes, the parochialism of ghetto life, and the Syllabus of Errors. In the decade following the Civil War, while the Church and its enemies fought bitterly in Europe, the vast majority of Catholics and Protestants in America cooperated in business, labor, and politics. The Catholic laity was not yet vitally active in Church affairs, but an increasing number of Catholic prelates were abandoning the extreme defensiveness exemplified by Archbishop Hughes and returning to the approach of encounter advocated by Carroll and England. In the 1870's, the influence of Hecker and Brownson began to be widely felt, and during the next thirty years, the points of view they espoused gained in strength within the American Church.

Among the laity, the two best-known newspapers, Patrick Ford's the *Irish World,* and John Boyle O'Reilly's Boston *Pilot* revealed the growing power of American ideas on the Irish community. In the *Irish World,* the most popular Irish-American paper in the country during the 1870's and 1880's, Ford pushed social reform, temperance, and Irish national freedom. He fought many battles with the clergy and was barred from at least two dioceses but continued his advocacy of radical democracy. O'Reilly changed the *Pilot* from its strident hostility toward Protestants of Know-Nothing days to advocacy of toleration and fair play as required by a multiethnic society. Many in the laity like Ford and O'Reilly saw no inconsistency between Americanism and Irish nationalism. A growing number of priests and bishops felt no conflict between the American emphasis on freedom and activity and Roman Catholicism despite the Syllabus of Errors and the doctrine of papal infallibility.

Chief among those who believed that the Church would be no less Catholic by being more American—emphasizing activity of the laity, welcoming secular education, and asserting the importance of the individual—was Archbishop James Gibbons of Baltimore, who was elevated to the cardinalate in 1886. Probably no other Catholic in history except John F. Kennedy has made as significant an ecumenical impact on non-Catholics. Gibbons reached out to the non-Catholic world as a public speaker, consultant to Presidents, and friend of Protestant and Jewish causes. Citizens of all faiths, including President William H. Taft and former President Theodore Roosevelt honored him at the jubilee of his cardinalate in 1911. Before being awarded a red hat, Gibbons had been vicar apostolic of North Carolina, then still mission territory, and bishop of Richmond, Virginia, where Catholics were in a small minority. Baltimore, his archdiocesan see from 1877 onward, had a large Catholic community, but they were not in the majority as in Boston and New York, and the Irish and the Germans were divided almost equally. American pluralism was an ever-present reality to Gibbons, who over the years became convinced that Catholics would gain more than they would lose by cooperating with Protestants, Jews, secularists, and liberals rather than by trying to protect themselves from their influence.

Gibbons had been influenced to become a priest by reading articles in Orestes Brownson's *Review,* and by attending a retreat led by three Redemptorist Fathers who later joined with Isaac Hecker in founding the Paulist order. Urbane, competent, and thorough, he was the perfect diplomat who became the prime spokesman of American Catholics to Rome during the papacy of Leo XIII, and that influential Pontiff's interpreter in the United States.

Gibbons' personality was complemented by his chief lieutenant, the blunt, argumentative Archbishop John Ireland of St. Paul, Minnesota. Ireland had been a chaplain of the Fifth Minnesota Regiment in the Civil War and vicar apostolic of Nebraska, and he also knew the diversity of American life. His personality, a mixture of energy, ambition, and eloquence, made him the foremost spokesman of Gibbons' policy of encounter and an uncompromising advocate of America's culture-religion. Ireland usually went beyond Gibbons and others in defending Americanism and arguing that the mission of America was "to show nations that men are capable of the highest civil and political liberty." Although the Third Plenary Council of Baltimore in 1884 had made parochial schools almost mandatory for Catholics, Archbishop Ireland told the National Education Association in St. Paul only six years later that the parochial school was an unnecessary burden and should be abolished. He saw no need to teach religion and believed that the state had the right and obligation to educate children according to its standards. Going even beyond advocacy of Americanism, the Archbishop of St. Paul occasionally made disparaging remarks about pilgrimages and penitential practices in his own Church. He even defended many Protestants who were called bigots by Catholics, arguing that they were not really prejudiced but simply were misguided. They imagined the Catholic Church to be tyrannical and hypocritical. It was the task of the episcopacy in America to persuade non-Catholics that Catholics hated those qualities too.

Gibbons and Ireland found a superb collaborator in the lofty, intellectual bishop of Peoria, Illinois, John L. Spalding. Born in a small village in Kentucky in 1840, Spalding ranked as the most scholarly American Catholic bishop of his time. Although he is remembered primarily for the inspiration he gave to founding the Catholic University of America, he also served for many years as chairman of the Irish Catholic Colonization Society (1878–91), an imaginative but largely unsuccessful effort to relocate slum dwellers from the cities to the prairies of the West.

Like Ireland, the Peoria bishop consistently praised American liberty, seeing no threat in it to Catholicism. He warned Catholics that "there is no subject of thought, no sphere of action, no interest which is possible to fence about and shut in from the all-searching breath of Liberty." Spalding agreed that liberty favored Catholicism in America, and that Catholics should encounter non-Catholics whenever they could. At the height of the ugly APA agitation against Catholics, he refused to answer back, maintaining that "it is not necessary for us to hold the flag in our hands when we walk the streets [or] to wave it when we speak."

The team of Americanists—Gibbons the administrator and diplomat, Ireland the eloquent and vigorous man of action, and Spalding the intellectual—were supported by hundreds of priests and laymen who believed that, whatever the conditions of Europe, religious liberty and personal freedom were well mated with Catholicism in the United States. Their point of view was a mixture of many things: a belief that non-Catholics and Catholics could work and live harmoniously together (Bishop Spalding thought that even the agnostic Robert Ingersoll was well intentioned); a skepticism of Pope Pius' emphasis on devotionals (Archbishop Ireland equated passivity with defeat, and wanted "steam and electricity" in religion as well as divine grace); a belief that the American Church should have a considerable amount of autonomy in dealing with its national problems, which were thought to be different from Europe's (the Americanists hoped that the promulgation of the doctrine of papal infallibility would keep Rome from exercising its authority too often, and that their own committee of archbishops established by the Third Plenary Council could act on a variety of questions independently of Rome); a belief that Catholics should participate in public ceremonies with other Americans, regardless of their religious convictions, and willingly explain Catholicism in open forum (in North Carolina, where he had been vicar apostolic, Gibbons had been welcomed by non-Catholics as a preacher of mission sermons at courthouses, in

Protestant churches, and even occasionally in Masonic lodges; and Bishop John J. Keane, the first rector of the Catholic University of America and a strong Americanist, accepted an invitation to give one of the Dudley lectures in Harvard Chapel, although the series had been established in the seventeenth century to help destroy the "apostate church" of Rome); a belief in the primacy of freedom of conscience (Father Walter Elliott, a successor to Hecker as a leader of the Paulists, warned against servile faith born of fear, maintaining that bovine obedience was unfitting for Americans. Whether or not American Catholics joined secular secret societies should be a matter of conscience, the Americanists argued); a belief in the importance of education, particularly in the most modern branches of knowledge (the Americanists planned the Catholic University of America, which would foster secular as well as religious knowledge); a belief in a vigorous, active lay participation in the Church (Archbishop Ireland warned against "too much dependence upon priests"); a strong conviction that democracy was the best form of government and way of life for Catholics in America (in his book *The Faith of Our Fathers,* Gibbons actually sought analogies between Catholic doctrines and American ideals, even comparing the veneration of the Virgin to the traditional respect of Americans for womanhood and the doctrine of papal infallibility with the power of the Supreme Court); and a strong conviction that the American system of separation of church and state should be continued even if Catholics were to gain a majority in the United States in appreciation for the fair encouragement given to the Catholic religion through tax exemption of church property, the appointment of paid chaplains to the armed services, and through occasional state aid to hospitals and asylums.

These were the central views of the Americanists which, from approximately 1885 to 1893, were in ascendancy in the Church in the United States, particularly in the sees of St. Paul, Cleveland, Chicago, Peoria, Illinois, and Wheeling, West Virginia. The center of Americanist strength was in the Middle West, where for

decades there had been greater social and economic mobility for
Catholics than in the Northeast. Immigrants and second-genera-
tion Catholics played their part as pioneers in the building of
Cincinnati, Cleveland, St. Louis, Omaha, St. Paul, and other cities.
They had not been pushed into tightly packed slum ghettos in
long-established cities with rigidly defined class and religious lines.
Encounter with Protestant Americans was not something to argue
about; it was taken largely for granted. Although the nativists in
the APA were stronger in the Middle West than anywhere else,
Catholics there had developed more self-confidence in confronting
the liberal, secular culture-religion of Americanism than in the
East.

Confidence and hope were the typical psychological characteristics of the Americanists. They were not afraid to expose themselves to change because of their confidence in the truth of the
Catholic religion and of their conviction that the United States
provided fair ground rules for competition between truth and
error. That is why Ireland urged Catholics to get out of the sanctu-
ary and into the highways and the marketplaces to defend the faith
and win conversions, and why Father Walter Elliott led a series of
mission tours through Middle Western towns, in which he employed no liturgy, did not wear religious garb, and frequently
began the service with favorite Protestant hymns such as "Rock
of Ages." It is why Gibbons, Ireland, and Keane attended the
Parliament of Religions at the Chicago World's Fair in 1893,
where Keane attempted to allay Protestant apprehensions that an
authoritarian hierarchy stood between the Catholic conscience and
God, but where he also asserted his belief in the truth of Catholicism. The Americanists missed no opportunity to reach non-Catholics with the confident message that American Catholics were
happy with, and certain of, their place in the city on the hill. They
wanted Catholics to be drawn into the whirlpools of American life.
Recognizing the dangers in stepping over the boundaries of physi-
cal and psychological ghettos, still they saw the opportunities in

Catholic participation in unions, business groups, education, the professions, and social reform movements.

The leadership of men such as Ireland stirred the laity to a more active involvement in church affairs. That was particularly true in the Middle West, where clerical sympathy was highest, but the spirit of the Americanists was also reflected in newspapers edited by laymen in Boston and Brooklyn, where the episcopacy was hostile or indifferent to the Americanizers. An idea for a Catholic lay congress, originally proposed by Father Isaac Hecker in 1868, was revived by Henry F. Brownson, the son of Orestes, and because of the vigorous support of Ireland and final acquiescence of Gibbons, was held in Baltimore in November, 1889. The theme of the conference was encounter. Nearly all the major points of view embodied in the Gibbons-Ireland approach to Catholic participation in American life were underscored. Brownson urged freedom for the laity to think for themselves, and for a greater mingling of Catholics with non-Catholics. Priests and laymen alike vied with each other in proclaiming to the world that the Church in America was not "priest-ridden." Actually, the Irish pattern of priest-lay relations still prevailed in most parishes, and probably a large majority of Catholic laymen were indifferent to the battles being fought by the Americanizers who were opposed by elements of the American episcopacy and the Curia in Rome.

Leaders of the opposition, who held an essentially separatist point of view, were John Cardinal McCloskey of New York, his successor as archbishop of New York, Michael Corrigan, and Bishop Bernard McQuade of Rochester, New York. Suspicious of Catholics mixing with non-Catholics in secular activities, they watched the participation of Gibbons and Ireland in interreligious activities with jaundiced disgust. They saw in Ireland's insistence that the Church had nothing to fear from Americanism a capitulation to secular and liberal values. Their personal dislike for Ireland, especially that of McQuade, was venomous (Ireland was almost as nasty about them), but aside from personalities, they appear to have differed from the Americanizers on every important issue. In addition to the dioceses of the Northeast, they received substantial support from German-American bishops, priests, and lay journalists who were anxious not so much to promote Catholic separatism as German Catholic separatism from an Irish and increasingly Americanized episcopacy.

With the election of Pope Leo XIII following the death of Pius IX in 1878, the Americanizers believed that their point of view would prosper. Pius had reacted to the wounds of the Church with the Syllabus of Errors and the doctrine of papal infallibility. Leo was expected to be more conciliatory in his diplomatic relations with secular governments. He was known to believe in the importance of updating the teachings of the Church with respect to labor-management relations and the social welfare needs of urban populations. In these respects, he did not disappoint the Americanizers.

Between 1887 and 1893, Archbishop Ireland, usually with helpful interference from Gibbons, won a series of victories against McCloskey, Corrigan, and McQuade for control of the policies of the Church in America by appealing to Pope Leo in Rome. The first important skirmish dealt with the labor organization known as the Knights of Labor. The Knights had been previously twice condemned by Rome upon the inquiry of the Archbishop of Quebec because its members required a modified oath of secrecy. The question was whether the condemnation applied to the United States as well as Canada.

The separatists said yes, and asked the Pope for a decree condemning the organization in America. Gibbons won a vote of a majority of the hierarchy against condemnation, and when he reached Rome in February, 1887, for the ceremonies accompanying his elevation to the cardinalate, he presented a memorial that had been prepared by Ireland and Keane, who were also in the Holy City, defending the right of American workers to protect themselves through organizations such as the Knights of Labor.

The memorial argued that a harsh stand against Catholic participation in the organization would make the Church seem un-
American, and place a terrible burden of conscience on the approximately 300,000 Catholics in the 600,000-member organization. The final decision was a victory for Gibbons: toleration of
Catholic membership was granted, provided certain phrases in the
Knights' constitution which seemed to imply socialism and communism were altered.

The next skirmish won by the Americanists was over the establishment of the Catholic University of America. The separatists
were satisfied with the ecclesiastical seminaries responsible for
training priests. Bishop Spalding was not. He argued that the seminaries did not widen intellectual and cultural horizons or develop
critical faculties. The priests, he said, were getting an education
inadequate to fit them to understand the world in which the laity
lived. There was simply no genuine university education for the
clergy in America. With the establishment of the university and
the appointment of Bishop John J. Keane as first rector, the separatists were handed another defeat.

A major encyclical, *Rerum novarum,* issued by Pope Leo in
1891 encouraged the Americanizers further. While affirming the
rights of private property as stemming from natural law, Leo condemned the oppressiveness of capitalism and pointed out that
private property was not to be considered absolute. Social needs
were to be the criteria of social action. Following Leo's decision
in the Knights of Labor case, the issuance of *Rerum novarum*
made Gibbons confident that he had the Pope's support to permit
Catholics to join nonsectarian labor unions and to participate
in social action programs on a broad front.

In the same year, another vital battle between the forces of encounter and separatism issued in the conflict between the Americanizers and the Germans. The first German Catholic settlements
came in Pennsylvania in the mid-eighteenth century. From the
beginning, German Catholics tended to insist on separate treat-

ment and recognition as a minority group within Catholicism in America. For a century they battled for language rights, national parishes, and proportional representation in the hierarchy, but they were resisted by Catholic leaders from Carroll on. Between 1865 and 1900, the German Catholics were the largest Catholic immigrant group to come to America, and by 1891, German Catholics were almost as numerous as Irish Catholics. Yet American-born Catholics of Irish ancestry dominated the episcopacy, the major Catholic publications, and secular political organizations where Catholics had influence. Anxious to keep their own language and other aspects of German culture, many of the immigrants wanted priests who could hear their confessions in German and carry out traditional religious observances in the vernacular. The Germans, a large proportion of whom became farmers, spreading through the Ohio River basin to the Great Lakes and then into the prairie states beyond the Mississippi River, saw men like Ireland as interfering with the cherished customs of their fatherland. Although many of them had been farmhands in the old country, others had been small shopkeepers and landowners who had tried to escape the heavier taxes and universal military service under Bismarck, whose religious persecution, culminating in 1873 with the abolition of religious orders and the annulment of papal jurisdiction over German Catholics, drove them to seek refuge in America; and they probably felt superior in intellect and culture to American priests. By 1891, the Germans, with assistance from separatists in the East, had enough power to challenge the "interference" of the Americanists.

The struggle was crystallized when a German businessman, Peter Paul Cahensly, led European Catholic immigration societies in proposing a separate organization for German Catholics in the United States, even to the point of appointing a cardinal protector for German Catholics in America. The implication of the proposition, as Cardinal Gibbons quickly saw, might lead to separate churches for each nationality, instruction in the mother tongue, separate parochial schools, and proportional representation in the hierarchy (something which Father Hecker had proposed for the college of cardinals in order to reduce Italian influence in the universal Church, but which was impossible for the Americanists to accept within the Church in America). Gibbons, a strong American nationalist and friend of Theodore Roosevelt, William McKinley, Benjamin Harrison, and Senator Albert Beveridge of Indiana, believing this to be "his greatest battle" urgently opposed and defeated what Ireland had branded as "Cahenslyism." Final victory came when the Pope decided not to grant Cahensly's petition that national bishops be appointed. President Harrison congratulated Gibbons, who promptly reported the message to Rome.

The Americanizers were exuberant. Ireland particularly began to write and say things against the separatists at home and conservatives in Europe which he must have regretted later. The Cahensly battle was followed by another triumph. This one concerned the American economist and philosopher, Henry George, and a popular New York priest, Edward McGlynn. George's economic theories had won considerable support among Irish and German Catholic voters in New York during the hard times of 1885–86. Even in Ireland many people regarded the single tax as the solution to that country's land problem. Sufficiently encouraged by the response he received from the workers of New York, George organized the Working Men's party and ran for mayor. McGlynn, pastor of St. Stephen's parish, and one of George's strongest supporters, was extremely popular with non-Catholics, including Protestant ministers, as a sympathetic, loving champion of the poor.

McGlynn's views on most issues, proclaimed with an eloquence that was at least the match of Ireland's, were odious to Archbishop Corrigan. The priest defended the public schools, criticized government aid to religious groups, and tended to place the blame for the difficulties of the Catholic Church on Catholics themselves.

During the election campaign, he supported George by sharing the platform with Daniel DeLeon, an outspoken radical syndicalist and the Reverend Heber Newton, a liberal Protestant. Corrigan was furious and ordered him to end his political activities. Mc-Glynn refused, insisting that his rights and duties as a citizen had not been surrendered when he became a priest. When George was defeated, Corrigan issued a pastoral letter criticizing him and his theories; McGlynn answered with a defense of both. McGlynn's insubordination was intolerable to Corrigan, who suspended him from St. Stephen's and eventually had him excommunicated.

Gibbons watched the battle with dismay. He had already prevented Corrigan from having Rome place George's famous book, *Progress and Poverty,* on the Index of prohibited books. In the summer of 1892, apparently sure of his ground in Rome, he commissioned Archbishop Ireland to reopen the case by interviewing McGlynn. The outcome was hardly in doubt since Ireland sympathized with McGlynn and hoped for a chance to "break Corrigan's heart." Cleared by Ireland, McGlynn was sent by Gibbons to Rome where, in a quick interview with the Pope, His Holiness conferred a blessing on the errant priest following a declaration by McGlynn that he believed in private property. Reinstated in the priesthood, he served as pastor of a church in Newburgh, New York.

In the same year, Ireland and his friends received additional encouragement through an indirect papal decision on the vital question of the relationship of Catholics to America's public schools. Generally, separatists frowned on, and Americanists smiled on, the growing system of compulsory secular education in the United States (nearly thirty states passed compulsory education laws by 1897). Although the Third Plenary Council in 1884 had commanded Catholic parents to give their children a "truly Christian and Catholic education" and decreed that a parochial school be erected near each church, it had specifically reproved those who would withhold the sacraments from parents who failed in this obligation, and also gave bishops authority to postpone the building of parochial schools where conditions required delay.

The problem presented by the council is present today. Parochial education is encouraged but it is difficult to find the money, facilities, and teachers to do the job. Various arrangements were tried in the 1880's in an effort to resolve the dilemma. The most famous scheme was promoted by Archbishop Ireland in his own archdiocese in the towns of Faribault and Stillwater, Minnesota. The local board of education leased the parochial schools from the parish, undertaking to keep them in repair and pay the teachers while retaining the right of inspection and control. Religious instruction was given after school hours. Bishop McQuade and other separatists thought such cooperation with the secular schools was unconscionable. (Apparently most Protestants did not like it either.) He mounted an attack on Ireland's plan as inconsistent with the decrees of the Baltimore council, forcing a decision from Rome. The Vatican ruled that while the decisions of the Baltimore council with respect to parochial schools remained in full force, Archbishop Ireland's arrangements with secular authorities "may be tolerated." Gibbons was pleased, especially so since at least nine plans similar to Ireland's were in operation in his own archdiocese, and he and Ireland were especially delighted when Leo's Apostolic Delegate, Monsignor Francesco Satolli, explicitly told the archbishops assembled in New York that the Holy See did not condemn public schools. Rather, he said, the Pope, while naturally disapproving of those features of public schools which were opposed to the truths of Christianity, believed that there should be public schools in every state, "according as the circumstances of the people require." By forbidding priests to deny the sacraments to parents whose children attended public schools, Satolli stopped or slowed the building of several parochial schools. McQuade and Corrigan again were miffed. "We are all in a nice pickle," wrote the Rochester bishop in disgust.

THE DECLINE OF THE AMERICANIZERS

McQuade's view was more sour than the facts warranted. The Americanists had been winning battle after battle; but they had been making enemies too. Ireland was particularly vulnerable. He had made a thinly veiled attack on religious orders and blamed the Jesuits for the loss to Catholicism of Japan and England. He had spoken bluntly and loudly about the universal validity of separation of church and state and democracy. He seemed more ambitious with each triumph despite an implicit warning issued by Pope Leo in an encyclical in 1888, *Libertas praestantissimum,* which condemned unconditional freedom of thought, speech, and worship. Reaffirming Catholic doctrine, including important aspects of the Syllabus of Errors, Leo urged that such freedom could be allowed only in support of a just cause. He condemned various forms of liberalism which rejected the supreme authority of God in public or private affairs and the doctrine of complete separation of church and state. The Americanists virtually ignored the encyclical, Father Hecker pointing out that the Pope was writing mainly for the people of an "eastern" mentality and intended no limitation on American ideas of liberty. Gibbons went ahead with the lay congress of 1889, and after the decisions in the McGlynn affair and on public schools, he probably felt that Hecker had been correct.

If the Americanizers had been able to confine their policies and viewpoints to the United States, they might have continued to receive Leo's consistent support in their arguments with Corrigan and McQuade. But that was impossible. By definition, the Americanists believed not just in the values of personal independence and achievement, but in the mission of America to spread those values as well. They were as imbued with the spirit of America's culture-religion as any non-Catholic. Several American priests made invidious comparisons between Catholic losses in Europe and gains for the Church in America. One responded to the criti-

cism of the Cahenslyites of Catholic defections in the United States
by predicting that Americanized Catholics would one day restore
health to decadent European Catholicism. Gibbons had extolled
the ideal of church-state separation in Rome upon receiving his
cardinal's hat, probably annoying many of the French and Italian
prelates who listened to him. The cardinal's representative in
Rome, Dennis O'Connell, rector of the American College, frequently praised the American constitutional system, democratic
ideals, and the values of the New World. Ireland, the loudest
apostle of Americanism, had boasted in several lectures in Paris
that if Frenchmen would emulate American Catholics they would
achieve success over antireligious forces.

Undoubtedly Ireland's optimism seemed justified at the time,
although his indiscretion was not. Gibbons had been supported on
every major issue except one, the appointment of the Apostolic
Delegate in 1892, and even that turned out to be a blessing when
Satolli upheld the Faribault plan and praised public education.
But a series of actions and utterances emanating from the Vatican
would soon shake Ireland's self-confidence and elevate the influence of the separatists in America. From all the evidence available (and much of it is not), Leo probably wanted to support Gibbons and Ireland, for whom he had much personal affection, in
their internal battles against Corrigan and McQuade. The problem, from his point of view, was simply that the issues which had
been raised inside the United States were worldwide in implication.

The tide began to turn against Gibbons in the spring of 1893,
when he received a letter from the Pope acknowledging a com-
plaint of Corrigan and McQuade that Monsignor Satolli seemed
to have partially abrogated the intention of the council of Baltimore with respect to building parochial schools. Leo wanted it
understood that the decrees of the council were to be "steadfastly
observed." Shortly after, Gibbons met a major defeat on an issue
comparable to the Knights of Labor case. Secret nonsectarian

organizations whose members were bound by oaths were seen by some Catholic leaders as threatening the sacrament of confession, and therefore as challenging the primacy of the Church itself. The separatists wanted Catholics to have nothing to do with such organizations, and won papal condemnation of three of them, the Odd Fellows, the Knights of Pythias, and the Sons of Temperance. Later Gibbons had to be reproved for delaying the promulgation of Rome's decrees.

The condemnation of the secret societies was followed in 1895 by a decision of the Apostolic Delegate to forbid Catholic participation in interfaith congresses. This was interpreted as a direct rebuke to Gibbons, Ireland, and Keane for their involvement in the Parliament of Religions at the Chicago World's Fair. In the same year, Pope Leo issued a long-awaited encyclical to the Church in America entitled *Longinqua oceani,* which made it plain that even if many of his friends and children in America had forgotten the Syllabus of Errors, he had not. Although the Pope expressed gratification with the growth of the Church in the United States— there were now more than twelve million Catholics—he warned Americans that "it would be erroneous to draw the conclusion that in America is to be sought the type of the most desirable state of the Church," or that it would be expedient for church and state to be "dissevered and divorced in other countries as in America." Archbishop Ireland was so disappointed in the encyclical that he turned down a request of the *North American Review* to analyze it. In 1896, Bishop Keane was summarily removed as rector of the Catholic University, causing McQuade and Corrigan to rejoice. It was Ireland who was in a pickle now.

The setbacks to Gibbons and his friend, Ireland, came almost in direct proportion to the growth and popularity of Americanism in Europe. Almost all the priests or bishops urging reform on the Continent—whatever the reform—were calling themselves or were being called "Americanists." European opponents of reform felt threatened by the advancing power of the Church in America.

German prelates were still angry because of the failure of Gibbons to give special status to their countrymen and coreligionists in the United States. French monarchists hated Archbishop Ireland for his strong endorsement of the Third Republic. Bishop Keane, visiting Rome following his removal from the rectorship of the Catholic University, found growing opposition at the Vatican to Americanism in all aspects.

Leo had reason to be concerned. However his encyclical of 1888 might have been construed as not having relevance for Americans, there should have been no question concerning his encyclical of 1895, which was addressed specifically to the Church in America. Yet Ireland seemed bent on stirring up the very European Catholics who needed to be bound firmly by authority and devotion to Rome's authority. There was accuracy in the charge of the conservative *American Ecclesiastical Review* of February, 1897, that the Americanists encouraged a growing "disrespect for authority, both in matters of doctrine and discipline," at least as their views were interpreted in Europe. There was also ostensible truth in the criticism that the Americanists were constantly appealing to the judgment of the American people, whether or not their judgment was consistent with the divine plan for governing the Church.

The Pope finally felt forced to issue a definitive statement on Americanism by the publication of a French translation of a biography of Father Isaac Hecker. Written by Father Walter Elliott, the book was translated by a French liberal, Abbé Felix Klein, who, in his preface to the French edition, compared Hecker to Benjamin Franklin and Abraham Lincoln as a self-made man who had risen to success through hard work and intelligence, and, more extravagantly, also likened him to St. Augustine. Hecker was not just a good priest for America, the Frenchman maintained, but he was an ideal answer to the modern age of Protestantism and secularism. The Church had insisted on external direction and submission in order to counteract the exaggerated individualism of Protestantism in the past. Now, Klein argued, a greater emphasis must be placed on self-direction, as advocated, according to the French priest, by Father Hecker of the United States.

The main points of the biography itself emphasized Father Hecker's conviction that the modern era, characterized by widespread education and liberty, demanded a greater independence of action for individuals under the direction of the Holy Spirit. It was also necessary, according to Elliott's interpretation of Hecker, to suit the Catholic doctrine of divine grace to the modern age. The elevation of grace was to be brought about by the natural faculties of understanding and greater union with the Holy Spirit. The sacraments and prayers were helpful, but the ultimate direction of souls would come from the Holy Spirit. Hecker, it seemed from this interpretation, believed that the value of personal independence and the doctrines of Catholicism were congenial; nor did Hecker see any inconsistency between the American value of activity and Catholicism. According to Elliott, Hecker maintained that in the new age, the Church no longer needed martyrs or monasteries as much as men who would work in the toils and obligations of modern life.

The book's publication in France intensified ecclesiastical conflicts in America and Europe. Hecker was known to have been an influential adviser of Bishop Spalding and Bishop John J. Keane, and to a lesser extent of Cardinal Gibbons and also of Archbishop Ireland, who had written an introduction for the French version of Elliott's biography, praising Hecker as the quintessence of Americanism. He called attention to Hecker's belief that "the order of the day should be individual action—every man doing his full duty and waiting for no one else to prompt him." The time had passed, wrote Ireland, when the Church had to suppress individual activity. Hecker, he boasted, is largely responsible for "the flow of Catholic affairs in America."

To some of the younger French priests, Hecker became a model, even a subject for canonization. To defenders of traditional European Catholicism, he became a symbol of all that was wrong with the infection of Americanism. To his boosters, Hecker was the priest of the future, the genius of the new age. To his enemies, he was a transcendentalist Protestant devil.

In theological terms, the Americanists were accused of being Pelagianists, a fourth-century heresy which, like Arminianism, the great Calvinist heresy that had become the core of the American creed, alleged extraordinary spiritual capacities for human beings who, among other things, were not stained with original sin and had the ability to achieve grace through individual choice. Pope Leo understandably may have believed that the views attributed to Ireland, Keane, and others were raising divisive controversies which were supposed to have been resolved long ago by papal authority.

A minor American addiction to certain aspects of Pelagianism —the emphasis on the American values of independence and activity—might have been overlooked if the Americanists had not seemed to give an almost sacramental quality to the secular values and institutions of the United States. Hecker had written in a pastoral letter in 1884 that "the hierarchy of the Catholic Church in the United States shared a conviction that American political institutions are in advance of those in Europe in helping a man to save his soul, and that they promise a triumph for Catholicity more perfect than its victory in medieval times." It was time, thought Pope Leo, to set matters straight.

In a letter to Cardinal Gibbons entitled *Testem benevolentiae,* dated January 22, 1899, the Pope praised the American hierarchy and the American people, and while never implying that Gibbons or his friends held any of the positions attributed to them by their enemies, warned against a confusion of liberty with license. He then systematically condemned five errors identified with what he and everyone else was calling Americanism. First, Pope Leo warned that there was a greater need than ever for Catholics to be submissive and to be guided by the infallible authority of the Pope in order to be preserved from private error. Next, he scorned the view that men could save themselves through the Holy Ghost alone. The Holy Ghost, he stated, is no more active in the era of liberty than in times past, and external guidance was needed as much as ever before. It was also a mistake, stated Leo, to extol natural as opposed to supernatural virtues. It was definitely wrong to hold active virtues as superior to such passive qualities as humility and obedience. The fourth error imputed to the Americanists was the rejection of religious vows (Hecker believed that vows were unnecessary for the Paulists) as cramping the freedom of the individual. Finally, the Pope warned against ecumenism. If one wishes to speak with dissenters outside of the Church in friendly conference, he may do so, but only with the approval of his bishop, who should choose men for such encounters as have already given proof of their knowledge and virtue.

Despite Leo's charitable failure to mention even a single name (he even spared Elliott's book from the Roman Index), there could be no question that his strictures were intended for Americans as well as Europeans. The letter, after all, was addressed to Gibbons and not to Abbé Klein. To judge from the reactions of Gibbons, Ireland, Keane, and others, Leo XIII had condemned a fantasy. Gibbons called the condemned doctrines "extravagant and absurd," and said they had "nothing in common with the views, aspirations, doctrines, and conduct of Americans." Not a single American Catholic was obliged to leave the Church because he refused to give up the errors which the Pope had reproved. But Americanism was much more than a fantasy to the separatist Archbishop Corrigan, who had no doubt for whom the letter was intended. Bishop McQuade in Rochester was equally clear and even more specific. He gave four examples of the evils against which the Pope warned: participation by Gibbons and Ireland in the Parliament of Religions; Keane's speeches to non-Catholic universities such as his Dudley lecture at Harvard; the reluctance of Gibbons and Ireland to accept Rome's condemnation of secret societies; and their un-Catholic friendship toward the public schools.

Americanism was not a figment of anyone's imagination. It was a fundamental response to the American environment by men whose temperaments and convictions were far more congenial to the spirit and institutions of the United States than a large proportion of their parishioners and of their superiors in Rome. The Americanists not only embraced the values of personal independence and activity in the abstract, but they practiced them. Bishop Spalding had denounced self-annihilation and called for greater self-assertion among Catholics. Father Walter Elliott, Hecker's successor as leader of the Paulists, frequently warned against passivity, servility, excessive conformity, and belief in the virtue of discipline. In their private correspondence, the Americanists had resisted Pope Pius IX's emphasis on devotionals, and their enthusiasm for the cult of achievement was equal to that of Grover Cleveland or Benjamin Harrison. While they may not have meant any more than that the individual must show initiative and enterprise if he wishes to deserve grace, they were frequently understood as virtually equating independence and activity with a state of grace itself.

It was typically American of Gibbons, Ireland, and Keane that none of them were theologians. They were practical administrators and politicians who lived their democracy and Catholicism without trying to split hairs. They saw no incompability with American values and the teachings of the Church because they experienced no real tension between them in their own lives. Americans were individualistic, optimistic, and active, but so were they, and they saw in American freedom for the individual a chance to live Catholicism to the fullest.

The specific interpretations given to Hecker's views on the personal direction of the Holy Spirit, cooperation with non-Catholics, the active virtues as opposed to the passive, and opposition to religious orders may have been exaggerated by Europeans, both conservative and liberal, who overreacted in the context of their own struggle. But the basis for exaggeration could be found in the writings of Hecker and in the utterances of Gibbons, and, particularly, Ireland.

Despite Ireland's recklessness, the Pope might have continued to side with the Americanists on the issues if they had confined the polemics to within the United States. The views attributed to Hecker probably would not have been condemned had they not been taken up by Catholic liberals in Europe. When Gibbons saved the Knights of Labor from condemnation, it was on the ground that conditions in America were special. But the Americanists, particularly Ireland, often fell into the position of appearing to say that what is good for America is good for American Catholics and what is good for American Catholics is good for Catholics everywhere. It was this approach which Leo could not condone.

Several Catholic historians have attempted to minimize the effect of the Pope's condemnation of Americanism on the development of Catholicism in the United States. One has suggested that it was hardly more than hypothetical since Americanism never existed as a precisely formulated doctrine. Others have cited the comment of Archbishop Ireland in 1909 to the effect that the Pope later told him to forget the letter on Americanism since it had no practical application in the United States. Despite these demurrers, there is no question that *Testem benevolentiae* gave joy to Archbishop Corrigan and Bishop McQuade and set back the forces of encounter among American Catholics.

Pope Leo undoubtedly did not want to hurt Gibbons and Ireland, and may have intended his repudiation of Americanism primarily for European ears, but the doctrines he condemned were incontestably American in their origin, and many of Gibbons' most cherished projects were no longer feasible: Keane was out as rector of the Catholic University; participation in interfaith meetings was made much more difficult; it would be a long time before another lay congress was held comparable to the meeting of 1889. Once again, the separatists among the episcopacy could look to Rome for support against those who found the Protestant-inspired culture-religion of Americanism compatible with the aims and dogma of the Catholic Church.

To a very considerable extent, the American bishops turned their energies away from encounter with Protestant America and inward toward building Catholic schools, churches, hospitals, orphanages, and other charities. Once again, the episcopacy was confronted with huge numbers of immigrants. Now they came mainly from Italy and Poland. Hundreds of thousands of immigrants from both countries arrived in the United States toward the end of the nineteenth century and during the first two decades of the twentieth century. Most of the Italians were peasants who spread out from the port city of New York into Pennsylvania, New Jersey, Massachusetts, Connecticut, Rhode Island, Ohio, and Illinois. The Poles, also mainly peasants, settled predominantly in the region from Wisconsin east along the Great Lakes, throughout Pennsylvania, into New York State, and New England. Chicago became the largest Polish city, but Buffalo, Detroit, Milwaukee, and Cleveland each absorbed large numbers of Polish Catholics. The task of leading the newer immigrants fell to Irish priests and politicians, both of whom encouraged the growth of separatist Catholic organizations. Usually they were ethnic organizations too—Irish, Italian, Polish—but the most important organization of all was neither strictly Catholic nor ethnic. It was the local Democratic party.

ETHNIC POLITICS

Not only did the Catholic population grow more quickly than that of the country as a whole—it practically doubled between 1890 and 1928—but the relative increase of Catholic voters was even larger. In the cities of the Northeast, Irish Catholics captained the major precinct, ward, and city-wide organizations of the Democratic party. Because official government had little to do with the pressing problems of city life, poor immigrants turned to the invisible government of the party machine in dealing with oppressive landlords and employers. The machine raised its own taxes through crooked deals with businessmen, assessments from gamblers, saloons, and houses of prostitution. From these funds the party gave food and coal to the needy, helped intervene at city hall on behalf of the illiterate and frightened, procured jobs and other kinds of assistance, and paid for wonderful parades and picnics to brighten the lives of working-class families. In city after city, schoolteachers, policemen, and firemen were preponderantly Catholic. The machine not only gave jobs to the poor and the ambitious, but defended their religion in struggles which put an end to the exclusive use of the King James Bible in the schools and to the assignment of Protestant chaplains to Catholic inmates in hospitals and prisons.

Irish Catholics were at the peak of their numerical power in New York City in 1890, where they probably constituted a majority of the population. Four years before, Tammany Hall had been taken over by Richard Croker, an Irishman and a convert to Catholicism who typified the Irish view in politics. "All there is in life is loyalty to one's family and friends," maintained Croker. Here were no illusions about the Protestant world of reform and abstract justice. When Croker was asked by the chief counsel of an investigating committee in 1899 whether he was really working just to fill his own pockets, he answered, "All the time—the same as you!" Croker was succeeded in New York by Charles F. Murphy, who also knew how to take care of his own. But the Irish in New York took care of the newer immigrants too, at least as long as it was necessary to woo their votes. Bastions of Irish Catholic power were built not just in New York, but in Boston, Chicago, Kansas City, Jersey City, Hoboken, and Albany, and such colorful names as "Hinky-dink" McKenna and "Bathhouse John" Coughlin enlivened the American scene.

The "newer races," as Mayor Curley of Boston used to call them —mainly the Italians, Poles, and French Canadians—were not always satisfied with Irish leadership in the Church or politics. The Germans, anxious to maintain their old-country identity, quarreled with the Irish endlessly, but were never able to challenge Irish power in either the Church or courthouse. By 1907, a dispute between Polish Catholics and the hierarchy over control of church property and ecclesiastical jurisdiction developed into the only major and lasting schism in the history of American Catholicism with the formation of the Polish National Catholic Church of America, with over a quarter of a million communicants today living in New England, the Middle Atlantic States, Wisconsin, and Chicago, with its chief bishop located at Scranton, Pennsylvania.

The vast majority of Catholics remained faithful to their Church and their party. In Boston, where the Irish were almost a majority by the 1880's, they did not have to accommodate themselves to sizable groups of Italians, Russian Jews, Germans, Poles, or Lithuanians until after the turn of the century. With few exceptions, they had no interest in adapting themselves to the world of the Boston Yankee—Emerson, Thoreau, Hawthorne, State Street banks, the Chamber of Commerce, the Museum of Fine Arts, and Harvard University. They fought among themselves for spoils, but politics was also a way of striking back at the prestigious Yankee aristocracy who resented the advance of Irish power.

The two best-known and most influential leaders in Church and politics in Boston—William Cardinal O'Connell, archbishop of the Boston Archdiocese from 1906 and cardinal from 1911 to 1944, and James Michael Curley, elected once as governor, four times as mayor of Boston, and four times to Congress—exemplified separatist Irish Catholicism. O'Connell became the champion of Catholic morality against the corrupting influences of secularism and Protestantism. He encouraged a petty censorship of books, movies, and plays, and catered to the aggressively hostile, anti-Yankee mood of the day.

James Curley filed his nomination papers as candidate for the Boston City Council only eight months after Pope Leo's letter,

Testem benevolentiae, was received by Cardinal Gibbons. Because Curley wanted his name to head the nomination list, he and his brother John, accompanied by a score of toughs, took the nominating papers to the registrar's office on the night before filing day and blocked the entrance. Other rowdies tried to crash their line, but they held fast (although his brother received a broken jaw) and Curley's name topped the ballot. Sometime later, Curley was arrested for taking a civil service examination for letter carrier in behalf of an unqualified constituent, and served a sixty-day term in Charles Street Jail. While incarcerated, he was elected to the Board of Alderman, proving that a little rascality to help a friend in need brought no penalty at the polls. Whenever the charges concerning the incident were raised in subsequent campaigns, his supporters answered, "He did it for a friend."

Curley was no hypocrite. In a hot campaign, he lied and cheated; but he usually admitted that was part of the game. "There are times . . . when, if you want to win an election, you must do unto others as they wish to do unto you, but you've got to do it first." That was the essence of Irish politics in Boston. The tribe above all. On most issues, it was Curley and his friends against a vast array of tribal cliques. But on matters concerning the Irish as a whole there was one enemy: the Yankee Protestants who dominated business, finance, society, and the Republican party.

Curley encouraged a feeling of superiority and separateness among his constituents just as Cardinal O'Connell did. Reflecting a growing interest fostered by Irish newspapers in the re-creation of Irish history and fantasy, Curley maintained that the Irish "had letters and learning, culture and civilization when the ancestors of the Puritans were savages running half-naked through the forests of Britain. It took the Irish to make Massachusetts a fit place to live in." Curley once boasted that he destroyed a letter accepting his son for admission to Harvard and sent him to Holy Cross, a Jesuit school in nearby Worcester. It was not Curley's way, nor O'Connell's, to understand the outsiders or to have themselves understood, and Boston became the classic case of Irish Catholic separation.

Ethnic politics encourages both separatist and integrative tendencies for immigrant groups. Aside from the particular cultural background and historical situation of the group, the factors which militate for or against encounter are mainly the size of the dominant group in relationship to the others (in Boston, the Irish Catholics overwhelmed the others) and the ambitions of group leaders to go beyond local power and prestige. In New York City, Irish Catholics were forced to come to terms with other significant voting groups. Irish leaders, having successfully managed their encounter with outsiders at the local level, looked ambitiously for power at the State House in Albany and even to the White House in Washington.

In the complex politics of New York City, Tammany boss Charles Murphy and underlings such as Tim Sullivan worried about, and bargained with, the leaders of large groups of Jews and Italians. They were also forced to deal with a good number of Democrats from upper New York State (outside of Boston, the Republicans of Massachusetts maintained overwhelming power). Under the New York State Constitution, the city was largely dependent upon the actions of the state legislature. It was important to nominate assemblymen who could listen to the problems of outsiders, logroll effectively, and yet never forget their own people.

Al Smith met those requirements. Smith's record of twelve highly successful years in the State Assembly, two years as sheriff of New York County, and a term as president of the Board of Aldermen in New York City proved his extraordinary abilities even before he ran for governor. Even though he was Irish Catholic and Tammany's candidate for governor, he won handsome victories which sent him to the State House four times. Murphy saw in Smith's governorship not an opportunity to kick the other guys in the head, but "to see you make good so we can show the people that a young man who has come from the lower East Side and has been closely associated with all phases of party activity, can make good." The man who seeks high office in pluralistic America cannot afford to be parochial, and in the State House Smith abandoned Irish Catholic separatism. He surrounded himself with dedicated, competent advisers regardless of sex or religion. He did not think that a woman's place was only in the home or that Protestants and Jews ought to stay in the other party. He opposed censorship in every form and defeated a book-censorship bill which had wide Catholic backing and rejected a bill to establish a loyalty oath for teachers. He even pardoned Tim Larkin, a radical agitator who had been imprisoned under the state's criminal-anarchy law, insisting that the surest way to prove error is to give it free rein to compete with truth.

Because of his success in effecting social legislation and his extraordinary administrative efficiency, Smith rapidly won a reputation as the best governor in the country. Then came 1928. Religious hatred, ethnic slurs, and upper-class snobbery found their mark. Although millions of Protestants and secularists voted for Smith despite the Syllabus of Errors and the doctrine of papal infallibility, Smith and millions of other Catholics interpreted his defeat as a triumph of anti-Catholic bigotry. Among clerical leaders, the forces of encounter had been thwarted by Pope Leo's papal letter of 1899. Now the same tendencies among Irish Catholic political leaders had been dealt a stunning blow. It would take thirty years before another Pope and another Catholic candidate for president could reverse the separatist tide.

IV

DEEPENING TENSIONS

J OHN KENNEDY was eleven years old when Herbert Hoover was elected President of the United States. His father, having already made several million dollars, had settled the family in fashionable non-Irish, non-Catholic Bronxville, north of New York City, where they lived in spacious affluence. Young Jack, an academically average but cheerful student at nearby Riverdale School, may have taken a special interest in the election campaign which had just passed, but it is far more likely that his most serious concerns focused on the upcoming football season. Not so for millions of Catholics who attributed Al Smith's defeat to bigotry, despite the fact that more Protestants voted for him than Catholics and Jews together against a popular hero of an incumbent party in a time of prosperity. The forces of encounter had received a severe disappointment. They had worked and fought on the side of non-Catholics in labor unions, business, and on the battlefields; yet (they thought) the country was unwilling to elect a Catholic to its highest office. During the almost seventy lean Democratic years after Appomattox, the Catholics in the big cities of the North and Middle West virtually kept the party alive. But with few exceptions, Catholics had not been appointed to high positions of the government, even when the Democrats were in power. Since the founding of the Republic, only four Catholics had served in the Cabinet, and since the election of McKinley not a single Catholic had been appointed to a top judicial or executive post, with the exception of a Republican, Supreme Court Associate Justice Pierce Butler.

AMBIVALENCE TOWARD ROOSEVELT

With Franklin Roosevelt's election in 1932, Catholic expectations of recognition were palpably high, and Roosevelt did fill many key posts with Catholics. His first choice for Attorney General was the crusading senator from Montana, Thomas Walsh. For Postmaster General he chose James A. Farley, chairman of the Democratic National Committee and chief strategist in Roosevelt's brilliant preconvention campaign in 1932. At Roosevelt's side, writing presidential speeches, giving advice and cajoling congressmen was Thomas V. Corcoran, "Tommy the Cork." Others who held key posts included Frank Murphy as Attorney General (later as Associate Justice of the Supreme Court) and Joseph P. Kennedy as chairman of the Security and Exchange Commission and ambassador to Great Britain. Roosevelt's encouragement of Catholic labor leaders, his disparagement of nativism (he addressed the Daughters of the American Revolution as his "fellow immigrants"), and his program of economic relief for the unemployed helped to reinforce Democratic proclivities for a large majority of Catholics in the first few years of his administration. But hundreds of thousands of Catholics soon became dissatisfied with the New Deal and especially with Roosevelt's growing involvement in European affairs.

The vast majority of Catholics have always been bread-and-butter and status-Democrats. From 1828 on, they voted their pocketbooks and pride but not necessarily their ideology. Since Know-Nothing days they have been suspicious of the ideologies of American freedom. They voted—even the German Catholics despite common beliefs to the contrary—overwhelmingly against Lincoln, and hundreds of thousands of them turned away from Wilson after he began his crusade for the League of Nations. As long as voting for Roosevelt meant jobs and a chance to tell the upper crust to take a jump in the lake, the vast majority of Catholics remained faithfully Democratic. Soon after the 1936 election, and in some cases before, many Catholics became uneasy over what they believed to be Roosevelt's drift toward socialism and growing commitment to defending England in her quarrels with Germany. Although most Catholics did not follow Al Smith into the Liberty League in opposing Roosevelt in 1936, many other important Democrats did break with him eventually, including Farley and Kennedy, who not only felt personally slighted by F.D.R., but mirrored the sentiments of large numbers of Catholics in resenting the growing influence of liberals, internationalists, and intellectuals in the Democratic administration. The Catholic vote for Roosevelt went down sharply in 1940 and again four years later, and the disillusionment of Catholics with the President was undoubtedly stronger than the votes revealed. The opposing candidates, Republicans Willkie and Dewey, offered no real alternative to Roosevelt's pronounced internationalism and they were less sympathetic to labor than F.D.R.

By the late 1930's, many of the most strongly separatist Catholics were profoundly alienated from the policies, if not the party, of Franklin Roosevelt. Probably the most influential and famous of the Roosevelt haters was Father Charles Coughlin. Following the depression, Coughlin, who had been a radio priest in a small town in Michigan, began to issue thunderbolts against laissez-faire economics and urged a positive program to combat unemployment and poverty. The response to his self-confident baritone voice was astounding. For several years in the early 1930's Coughlin's mail averaged eighty thousand letters a week, requiring more than a hundred clerks to answer them.

The core of Coughlin's following were Catholics of the East and Middle West, particularly the Irish, but German and Polish Catholics too. From Coughlin, radio listeners received answers to troubling questions: Why was it so hard to make a living? Who manipulated the stock market and caused the depression? Who was responsible for World War I? The radio priest had the answers in bold, plain talk: international bankers, Wall Street, atheists and Communists, and, later, Jews.

As long as Roosevelt concentrated on ameliorating the depression through monetary reform, unemployment relief, and other early New Deal measures, Coughlin limited his scapegoating to international bankers and Wall Street. In the mid-1930's, as Roosevelt abandoned his early economic nationalism, Coughlin told his audience that the enemy was Jewish, communistic, and foreign. From 1936 on, Coughlin became violently nationalistic. He joined William Randolph Hearst in a successful fight against Roosevelt's proposal to have the United States enter the World Court, and organized a national political party, the Union party, personally choosing Thomas C. O'Brien of Boston to run for the vice presidency with Representative William Lemke, a maverick Republican from North Dakota.

When Coughlin's brand of separatism became increasingly anti-Semitic, George Cardinal Mundelein of Chicago made it clear that Coughlin was not speaking for the Church; but the radio priest continued to talk on the radio and encouraged the formation of paramilitary squads of storm troopers under the name of Christian Front to fight the war against the Antichrist. When the Justice Department pointed out to Archbishop Mooney in 1940 that Coughlin's broadcasts resembled Nazi propaganda, he was silenced. But he already had stirred the fears and resentment of hundreds of thousands of Catholics, encouraging defensive, parochial, xenophobic, and anti-intellectual tendencies which later would be exploited skillfully by Senator Joseph McCarthy of Wisconsin.

REVENGE THROUGH MC CARTHY

Many traditionally Democratic Catholic voters who had defected in 1940 and 1944 returned to the fold to vote for Harry Truman in 1948. Henry Wallace's Progressive party removed the stigma of ultraliberalism or socialism from the Democrats; and Truman was a plainspoken, scrappy, no-nonsense, nonideological President who knew how to work effectively with the leaders of big-city organizations. Then came a crisis of confidence in America's foreign policy. Although two terrible wars had been won, and Truman had embarked upon a program of successfully defending Western Europe against the Soviet Union, the United States appeared to be on the defensive around the world. Eastern Europe had been lost to communism. Polish Catholics were furious at what seemed to have been a sellout at Yalta. Suddenly America's giant ally in Asia, China, inexplicably had been taken by the Communists too. In June, 1950, Communists from North Korea attacked South Korea and beat back American troops in what was to become an inconclusive, incomprehensible, and enervating war.

Onto the scene came Senator Joseph McCarthy of Wisconsin. As a county judge, McCarthy had been censored by the Wisconsin Supreme Court for destroying records in an important case. As a candidate, he not only lied repeatedly about his opponents, but told blatant untruths about his war record. McCarthy was a political adventurer, a gamester who probably meant no harm, but who loved power, fame, and a good fight. By exploiting the vast disillusionment of Americans following the expansion of militant Communist power after World War II, he was able to rise from an obscure happy-go-lucky heavy-drinking United States senator to a position of terrifying power and internationally infamous notoriety in only a few years.

The Wisconsin senator was extremely popular among Protestants as well as Catholics. He received particularly strong backing from Middle Western Republican Protestants, many of whose parents and grandparents had zealously believed the Maria Monk fraud and had joined the APA and Ku Klux Klan. For them, Communists had replaced Catholics as the preeminent threat to the so-called "American way of life." It was the Communists, internal and foreign, who had ruined the promise of a new Zion. Although McCarthy's support was widespread, public opinion surveys showed consistently that he had greater strength among Catholics than Protestants. He was loved particularly in the poor Irish neighborhoods of Boston, New York, and Chicago, where anticommunism, patriotism, and Roman Catholicism became practically synonymous.

Catholics could boast that they had warned against communism for years and that they bore no responsibility for the frightening surge of Communist power. There had been few Catholics in significant policy-making positions in foreign affairs during the Roosevelt and Truman administrations—Truman's Secretary of Defense, James Forrestal, a staunch anticommunist, was an exception—although Catholic liberals in Congress such as Brien McMahon, Mike Mansfield, and Joseph O'Mahoney, whom McCarthy helped defeat in his bid for reelection in 1952, wielded considerable influence. As Thomas Murphy, prosecutor in the two Hiss trials put it at the height of McCarthy's power, "I can't even recall one Irish name among the many thousands called before the House Committee on Un-American Activities. If there was, he probably changed his name." Of course there were many Irish men and women in the American Communist party, some of them holding key positions, but they were no longer Catholics.

McCarthy hit every raw nerve of suspicion, resentment, and prejudice which American Catholics had developed in years of exclusion. Now, in one brief but rich fantasy, they could knock together the heads of Communists, internationalist Jews, and Anglophile Yankees.

Catholics, particularly Irish Catholics, behaved as if they were more American than anyone else. After all, the greatest threat to American freedom was now communism, not Catholicism. The staunchest foe of the international Communist conspiracy was the universal Holy Church. In the cold war against "godless, monolithic communism," both the international religion of Catholicism and the culture-religion of Americanism seemed threatened. One could be zealously Catholic and stridently American at the same time.

Most of the Catholic hierarchy supported or were indifferent to McCarthy, and his popularity with Holy Name societies and such organizations as the Ancient Order of Hibernians was unmatched. European Catholics were appalled. Graham Greene, the English novelist and distinguished Catholic layman, wrote that "we Catholics of Europe ... feel that a far worse enemy than communism is the kind of treacherous Catholicism which is represented by McCarthy." It was extremely difficult for a European to understand the extraordinary appeal of McCarthy's super-Americanism to those Americans who had been treated as ideological aliens.

For the first time in history, Catholic separatists could participate in the nativist vanguard. Originally, nativism was simply the antagonism of old immigrants for new. With the arrival of large-scale Catholic immigration, it became primarily anti-Catholic, not just antiforeign. Thus, it was possible for German and Swedish Protestants once recovered from the wounds inflicted by initial struggles with Yankees, to join their former foes in attacking Catholics. A third phase of American nativism came in response to the twentieth-century migrations of Italians, Jews, and East Europeans, combined with the growth of the cities. It was not just anti-Catholic, anti-Semitic, or even antiforeign; it was largely anti-urban. Irish Catholics, although by this time an older immigrant group, could not become a part of the nativist movement because they were too closely identified with newer immigrants. It was only in the fourth period of American nativism—the anti-Communist phase—that they could not only participate but also provide leadership in defending the city on the hill against an international conspiracy bent on destroying individual freedom. McCarthy's contribution was that he married strident, parochial Catholicism with opposition to America's greatest external threat.

McCarthy's message was even more appealing because it included the ironic claim that members of the Anglo-Saxon Protestant establishment—representatives of the very group that had long refused to accept the Americanism of Catholics—were the real subversives of new Jerusalem. McCarthy delighted in the prosecution of Alger Hiss and the persecution of such State Department regulars as John Carter Vincent, John Stewart Service, and John Paton Davies, all of impeccable Yankee lineage. McCarthy did not blanch in naming Dean Gooderham Acheson and George Catlett Marshall, two of the most powerful members of the establishment in the United States, as front men for traitors; and McCarthy's assistants eventually accused the Protestant clergy of constituting the most serious Communist threat to America.

Anti-Catholic nativism was largely dead. Although the election of Eisenhower returned to power precisely those elements of the population who had attacked Catholics in the past, nothing emanated from Washington which resembled anti-Catholic bigotry. Eisenhower himself had come from a Mennonite background and was now a strong if somewhat vague Presbyterian. John Foster Dulles, one of the most influential lay Protestant leaders in the United States, was an elder of the Presbyterian Church. Ezra Taft Benson, Secretary of Agriculture, was a prominent Mormon, Sherman Adams, White House Chief of Staff, was an active Episcopalian, and White House aide Gabriel Hauge was the son of a Lutheran clergyman. The Eisenhower administration was as old-stock Anglo-Saxon Protestant as that of Grant, Hayes, or Garfield; but it was not anti-Catholic in any respect.

THE RESURGENCE OF SEPARATISM

Opposition to Catholics and Catholicism as such was relegated to state and local politics, particularly in the larger cities and suburbs, where Catholics tightened their grip on the machinery of government. By 1948, nearly half the Catholic population in the United States—well over 30 percent of the entire population from 1940 on—was concentrated in cities of 100,000 or more, while three fourths of the Protestants remained in communities of 100,000 or less and on farms. In the state legislatures and city councils, liberal Protestants, often joined by secularists and Jews, fought battles with Catholics over school-bond issues, censorship, divorce laws, birth control, and child-adoption statutes. When people talked church-state issues at the local level, they were often substituting a euphemism for Catholic and non-Catholic tension reflecting basic value differences between the two groups. Because of the Catholic position on the sanctity of the family contrasted to the Protestant and Jewish emphasis on the individual, Catholics could not accept more flexible divorce laws. Because of the Catholic emphasis—compared to most Protestants and Jews—on the inability of man to choose between good and evil without a large measure of clerical assistance, a disproportionate number of Catholics supported local censorship of "evil" ideas, motion pictures, and literature. Because of the Catholic emphasis on salvation as requiring Catholic baptism, many Catholics tended to oppose the liberalization of interreligious adoption laws. Because of the increased Catholic stress on a proper religious education, Catholic pressure mounted in the 1940's and 1950's for public aid to parochial education and against the advance of secularism in the public schools.

Control over education once again became the focal point of conflict between spokesmen for American Catholicism and defenders of America's culture-religion. Because the public schools have been the primary agent of Americanization, non-Catholics usually have resisted and continue to oppose efforts to strengthen parochial schools. It is not just the principle of separation of church and state which they defend but the public school system itself. Many non-Catholics believe that the public schools are not only vital in teaching the culture-religion of Americanism, but that sectarian schools exacerbate tensions in a pluralistic society by setting some students against others. Probably there is no other sign of Catholic separatism as powerful in the minds of non-Catholics as parochial schools. The *New Republic* had warned in 1927: "The Catholic Church will remain an alien guest in the American body politic as long as it tries to form the minds of American Catholics by educational methods different from those which are used to form the minds of other American citizens." Twenty-six years later, as the controversy over aid to parochial schools mounted, James B. Conant wrote: "The greater the proportion of our youth who fail to attend our public schools and who receive their education elsewhere, the greater the threat to our democratic unity. To use taxpayers' money to assist private schools is to suggest that American society use its own hands to destroy itself."

Catholics felt caught in a double bind. Pluralism had virtually eliminated religious instruction in the schools. Archbishop Hughes himself had won the first important fight toward secularization in helping to de-Protestantize public schools. Now the Jews and others wanted to de-Christianize them in a sectarian sense. Many Jews objected to the singing of "Onward, Christian Soldiers" at commencement exercises. Some protested Christmas celebrations commemorating Christ's nativity. Jews generally accepted the view that schools, while religious in the sense of raising questions about man's existence, nature, life and death, could not give a party line, even if it was the so-called "Judaeo-Christian" line. In 1948, the Supreme Court ruled that religious instruction could not be given within the public schools, even on released time, which for Catholics meant private education became more important than ever.

The Roman Catholic bishops of the United States protested against the secularization of schools in November, 1952, insisting that man needs religion "because he is weak," and it must be fostered by the educational system. Education, they argued, was the main instrument of truth; and in an attack on secularism reminiscent of the Syllabus of Errors, the bishops maintained that "man is not free to pick and choose among the truths God has made known either through reason or revelation." In order "to save man from the eternal consequences of his fall, to pay the penalty of his sins and to restore him to his supernatural state and destiny, the Son of God became Man, suffered and died on the Cross for the salvation of all mankind." Therefore, "to attain his destiny . . . man needs not merely the truths which reason can discover; he needs also the truths which Christ has revealed; he needs the Church which Christ has established."

One could accept the bishops' insistence that humility and obedience are needed to discover God and to acknowledge and expiate guilt without agreeing with them that the public schools should share a responsibility for promoting religion. One could even accept the Catholic view of God, Christ, and the Church without feeling that public schools must promote it, as was probably the case for hundreds of thousands of Catholics. But millions of Catholic parents felt the pressure to send their children to parochial schools, and perhaps almost as many were resentful that the de-Christianization of the public schools was accompanied by a refusal on the part of most non-Catholics to provide public assistance for Catholic schools. They felt penalized because their religious convictions obliged them to support public schools which many felt they could not in conscience have their children attend. Opponents pointed out in rebuttal that Catholic children were welcome in public institutions and that it was not the state but the Church itself which imposed a double taxation on its communicants.

In the late 1940's and in the 1950's tension accelerated in many communities. Where Catholics were influential in public school systems, they pushed Bible reading, encouraged graduation exercises in churches, asked the school systems to sell property to the Church at reduced prices, and urged that children be released on school time for instruction at religious centers. While holding on to key appointive and elective jobs in the school systems of major cities and suburbs, they often tended to resent and oppose programs for upgrading the quality of and expanding public education. From their point of view, resentment was justified. They acknowledged the need for new public school facilities, but with nearly five million Catholic children in overcrowded Catholic schools, there was a pressing need for parochial facilities too. Feeling the pinch of double taxation, Catholics often opposed school-bond issues, even for higher education. In New Jersey in 1954, the voters rejected a proposal for floating a $25,000,000-bond issue to finance construction of a public medical-dental college and health center, despite support for the proposal by Governor Robert Meyner and leading physicians. The official organ of the Newark archdiocese printed a front-page editorial opposing the bond issue because Seton Hall, a Catholic institution, was also opening a medical school; and the newspaper's stand was cited by Catholic priests in several parishes at Sunday Masses. Such retaliation was bitterly resented by non-Catholics who believed that Catholics should pay for their religious convictions when they ran counter to fundamental public policy. On the other side, Catholics saw themselves as being penalized for those convictions.

By 1960, the burden on Catholics increased as parochial school populations mounted and as the stakes in federal aid to education —a new issue—suddenly became extremely high. A few constitutional issues such as approval of payment for transportation of pupils to parochial schools were settled, but a dozen more remained unresolved. Could the states provide free textbooks for parochial school students? Could building funds be provided? Lunch money? The Supreme Court had blocked any use of tax funds for the central activities of sectarian schools, but provided no firm definition of what was central. In 1960, a group of liberal non-Catholic senators attempted to extend substantial federal financial aid to Catholic institutions of higher learning but were defeated by a Senate majority, including a number of Catholics.

Censorship was another major issue which frequently divided Catholics and non-Catholics. Actually, the first recorded prosecution for obscenity in a published book took place in Massachusetts in 1821, long before Catholics were influential; and the first federal law against obscenity, the Comstock Act of 1873, was lobbied through Congress by puritanical Protestants. In the 1950's, Catholics led the crusade for censorship of immoral literature, films, and television programs. The Catholic bishops who had established a National Organization for Decent Literature in 1938, created a National Office for Decent Literature in Chicago in 1955. Composed of Roman Catholic laymen in several cities and towns, the NODL, in the words of the bishops' Episcopal Committee, was established "to organize and set in motion the moral forces of the entire country . . . against the lascivious type of literature which threatens moral, social, and national life." Again the strongest opposition to such activities came from Protestant and Jewish organizations, not without considerable Catholic help. The major constitutional issue was the legal definition of obscenity. Until a series of court cases weighed heavily against the NODL position, the battle was fought in city halls and state legislatures throughout the country.

Censorship of allegedly obscene literature was not an unpopular issue with many Protestants; but the censorious spirit of Catholics in occasionally trying to prevent discussion of controversial questions, such as birth control, was. A thorough case study of an attempt by Catholic leaders in Holyoke, Massachusetts, to prevent the appearance of Margaret Sanger in behalf of planned parenthood revealed the extent and depth of conflict—not just over the question of birth control—concerning the power of Catholics to restrict the activities and beliefs of those who opposed them, much as Protestants had done to Catholics in colonial times. The study found that a large majority of Catholics believed that they had the right to use any coercive technique necessary to protect their interests, and did not doubt their right to mold the moral consensus of the city in which they lived. It also found that there was so little communication between the Catholic majority and the Protestant minority as to make cooperative discussion virtually impossible; even more significant, there was little desire among Catholics to break down the barriers which separated them from Protestants. Catholic pressure in Holyoke actually forced the First Congregational Church to withdraw permission to an organization known as the Mothers' Health Council to use its church buildings for Mrs. Sanger's meeting. Ironically, a Catholic laywoman, the secretary of a textile workers' union, volunteered the office rooms of that organization for Mrs. Sanger's appearance despite a campaign of cajolery and threat against her and not before Mrs. Sanger's appearance had become the subject of a city-wide conflict between Catholic and Protestant leaders.

In the late 1940's and early 1950's, dozens of other issues tended to divide Catholics and non-Catholics. Should Sunday blue laws be enforced and enacted? Should the birth control statute in Massachusetts be repealed? Should interreligious adoption be permitted or encouraged? Should divorce laws be made more flexible? Should the United States send an ambassador to the Vatican?

When President Truman attempted to send General Mark W. Clark to the Vatican as a full ambassador, opposition organized by a new militant group called Protestants and Other Americans United for Separation of Church and State, blocked the appointment. After it had been made clear that Clark would be the only full ambassador at the Vatican from a non-Catholic power, Protestant churches virtually united against Truman's request. In the face of bitter controversy, Clark, presumably with the President's approval, withdrew his name.

THROUGH SECULAR LENSES

Despite the increasing wealth and status of individual Catholics, the growing power of the Catholic Church in the United States, and the continued mixing of Catholics and non-Catholics in sports, work, and war, clerical separatism appeared to be growing in the late 1940's and well into the next decade. Between 1875 and 1911, there had never been more than one Roman Catholic cardinal in America at any one time. During the next thirty-five years, many American priests were appointed to offices in the Roman congregations (governing organs of the Vatican) and to positions of Apostolic Nuncio and Apostolic Delegate to other countries, and by February, 1946, there were five American cardinals. But there was no Carroll or Gibbons among them. None of the new cardinals was as staunchly separatist as William Cardinal O'Connell of Boston had been until his death in 1944, but diocesan newspapers usually reflected a defensive, parochial point of view. Consistent support for separatism came from the *American Ecclesiastical Review* under the leadership of Father Joseph C. Fenton, a theologian from the Catholic University of America, which, originally conceived by Keane and Ireland as a force for encounter, had become a bastion of separatism. To Fenton, the Church was still in a state of siege. He and others argued that far too many American Catholics were indifferent to their religious commitment only for the sake of non-Catholics. They minimized, he insisted, their obligations out of a mistaken feeling of accommodation. When Pope Pius XII issued an encyclical, *Humani generis,* in 1950 to warn against the many errors in modern apologetics—an encyclical similar in spirit to the Syllabus of Errors and Pope Pius X's attack on modernism—Fenton believed the Pope was criticizing tendencies in the American Church.

The Catholic bishops insisted that they were devoted to the principle of separation of church and state. In January, 1948, the National Catholic Welfare Conference denied absolutely and without qualification that the Catholic bishops were seeking a union of church and state. The authors of the statement promised: "If tomorrow Catholics constituted a majority of our country, they would not seek a union of church and state. They would then, as now, uphold the Constitution and all its Amendments." But non-Catholics wondered if separation of church and state meant the same thing to the bishops that it did to them. A large number of Protestants, Jews, and agnostics committed to the secular religion of Americanism saw in Catholic actions on local school boards, the imposition of censorship restrictions, the maintenance of laws against the dissemination of birth control information, and relentless pressure for public-tax support for parochial schools, efforts to impose Catholic views on public policy. Of course, Catholics could argue back, and some did, that Catholics were no different from other groups in pressing their interests on the polity. The difference, from the point of view of non-Catholics, was that certain Catholic interests appeared antithetical to a culture-religion based on the primacy of the individual's right to make choices. Alexis de Tocqueville had warned a long time before that "the more the conditions of men are equalized and assimilated to each other, the more important it is for religion ... not heedlessly to run counter to the ideas that generally prevail." It was usually acceptable for the Amish, Jehovah's Witnesses, or even the Zen Buddhists to adopt ideas which ran against prevailing American orthodoxies; what made Catholics seem threatening was that their loyalty presumably extended, not just to another subculture within the United States, but to a foreign-based Church whose policies might be imposed on American cities and towns, and perhaps eventually on the nation. Despite the statement of the National Catholic Welfare Conference, non-Catholics frequently referred to an important book written in 1940 by two priests, John A. Ryan (known for his liberal views on social welfare) and Francis J. Boland, which asserted in an authoritative manner that if the United States ever became a Catholic country in which Protestants were numerically insignificant, the activities of non-Catholics would be restricted, and even their tax exemptions removed. Stung by such statements, a non-Catholic counteroffensive gained momentum in the Protestant and liberal secular press in the late 1940's.

One study by a Catholic sociologist of the nondenominational weekly *Christian Century* revealed a sharp rise in anti-Catholic criticism during the decade of the 1940's. In 1939, there had been only twelve editorials and no articles critical of the Roman Church; in 1944, there were eleven editorials and two articles; by 1949, twenty-six editorials and nine articles were critical of Catholics or Catholicism, or more than 8 percent of all editorials and 12 percent of the articles which appeared in the *Christian Century* that year.

Of forty-nine ministers in a Middle Western county answering a questionnaire submitted through a local council of churches, 91.9 percent believed that "if Catholics become a majority group [they] would . . . strongly influence American society toward less democratic principles and practices." Also, 68 percent believed that priests strongly influenced the vote of the Catholic laity, and 62.5 percent thought that Catholic schools tended to violate democratic traditions.

Several books appeared sounding the alarm against authoritarianism in religion and "a graduated system of power headed by a supreme and absolute commander and operating downward through successive ranks of the priesthood until it finally reaches the laity who as privates in the army have no responsibility except that of obedience" and "a church whose leaders assume the style and title of Prince." A social scientist argued: "There is an inner spiritual logic that is inescapable by which democracy and the state cannot dwell in the same house with autocracy and the church. When the Catholic Church was a small minority, the meaning of this political antipathy was insignificant; now that it has become a large minority, it constitutes a major threat to American unity and peace."

The two liberal journals, the *Nation* and the *New Republic* frequently printed articles denouncing the growth of Catholic power. The most widely noticed were authored by a Unitarian lawyer, author, and New York City official named Paul Blanshard, who wrote a series of articles in the *Nation* in 1947 attacking Catholic views on medicine, sex, and education. In the spring of the next year he advanced a series of charges that Catholic power was threatening to destroy "the American way of life"; and in 1949 he published the first of five books written over the course of eleven years, challenging Catholics to prove their loyalty to concepts of American freedom. His first book, *American Freedom and Catholic Power,* went through twenty-six printings for a total of 240,000 copies before its second edition was published in 1958 for another five printings up to the fall of 1960.

Blanshard maintained that he was writing in the spirit of Unitarians such as William Ellery Channing and Theodore Parker, who centered their attacks on the political and educational policies of the hierarchy of the Roman Catholic Church. He insisted that his only cause was that of freedom, and that his close study of Catholic canon law respecting education, medicine, marriage, divorce, annulment, and censorship persuaded him that Catholic doctrine in those matters was inimical to American liberty.

Blanshard's investigation of canon law, encyclicals, pastoral letters, and other official Catholic pronouncements was encyclopedic and heavy documentation accompanied each of his books. Catholicism, he asserted, was essentially what officials from the Pope down have proclaimed it to be. He did not make personal investigations in Catholic institutions or conduct interviews of Catholics as to the significance of canon law or papal pronouncements with respect to their attitudes, values, and behavior in everyday life.

Although Blanshard repeatedly denounced the bigotry of the Know-Nothings, APA, and such gross frauds as the Maria Monk story, he was attacked consistently by Catholic conservatives and liberals as a bigot himself. Separatist Catholics applied pressure to keep bookstores and department stores from selling his work, and succeeded in banning the *Nation* in the public school libraries of New York City because of its articles by Blanshard.

Liberal Catholics were hurt and resentful too. They acknowledged that many of the charges in Blanshard's books were true: The Church was authoritarian, the Pope did claim infallibility when speaking ex cathedra in matters of faith and morals; Catholics, even American Catholics, did kneel to gorgeously appareled cardinals with red cloaks three yards long; the Vatican was a state, and the hierarchy did wield enormous power over its flock; Catholic dogma did restrict the freedom of action—the scope of choice—of American Catholics in personal and public matters such as marriage, divorce, birth control, reading, and education; and Catholic power was growing in the United States. But Blanshard was resented by liberals because he seemed to think the Church was monolithic and because he betrayed an inadequate understanding of the organic nature of change within the Church.

He consistently played down the tendencies toward encounter among American Catholics; equally upsetting, he repeatedly took a legalistic and literalistic interpretation of change in the Church which was congenial to Catholic separatists and abhorrent to advocates of encounter.

Blanshard kept daring Catholics to deny a particular section of a papal encyclical or a specific canon law on education or marriage. The reaction of many Catholics was similar to that of Al Smith in 1928, when he was shown a published statement by an Episcopalian layman citing papal encyclicals and canon law which purported to challenge the compatibility of Smith's religion with his loyalty to the United States. As the New York governor told his close confidante, the Jewish Judge Joseph M. Proskauer, "Joe, . . . to tell the truth . . . I don't know what the words mean. I've been a Catholic all my life—a devout Catholic, I believe—and I never heard of these encyclicals and papal bulls and books that he writes about. They have nothing to do with being a Catholic, and I just don't know how to answer such a thing." Another version of the meeting had Smith throwing up his hands and asking, "Will someone tell me what the hell a papal encyclical is?"

In effect, Blanshard kept saying that canon law made it impossible for a Catholic to be a good Catholic and believe in the primacy of individual conscience. He reminded his readers that Catholic doctrine holds that whoever willfully remains outside of the Church, refusing to partake of her sacraments and obey her laws, cannot be saved. When the well-known Father Leonard Feeney of Cambridge, Massachusetts, was expelled from the Jesuit order and later excommunicated by Archbishop Richard Cushing of Boston for insisting on a literal interpretation of that doctrine, Blanshard concluded that even though Feeney was a fanatic, his view "was far more honest and accurate than the liberal make-believe adopted by Archbishop Cushing." The Vatican, Blanshard believed, stood by Cushing only for the sake of appearances in support of his "synthetic liberalism." As far as Blanshard was concerned, the Church could not really change barring a formal repudiation of Catholic doctrine by authorized spokesmen. That was a perfectly understandable picture of the history of religion from a Unitarian perspective. When William Ellery Channing and other Congregationalists no longer believed in Trinitarianism, they formally declared their disbelief and set up a new church.

In his last book, *God and Man in Washington*, published in 1960, Blanshard wondered whether presidential candidate John F. Kennedy believed in the coercive principle of canon 1374, which obliges parents to send their children to Catholic schools under pain of excommunication. He and I had disagreed in correspondence on the issue, and quoting my view that all of the rules embodied in canon law did not necessarily have operative significance in American politics, he acknowledged that the boycott of public schools was not universally enforced in the United States. Still, he asked for a specific repudiation of the coercive aspect of canon 1374. He challenged my opinion that the boycott was really irrelevant, quoting a priest to support him, and writing that "it cannot be considered irrelevant unless the Catholic Church releases Catholic candidates from an obligation to observe or promote" it.

Blanshard was begging some Catholic in high position, preferably the Pope, to come right out and say, "Can't you see. We are changing. Can't you see that this canon law or that encyclical no longer has meaning in our lives!" In rebuttal, Catholic liberals wanted to shake Blanshard into the realization that a continuing dialogue and struggle was taking place within American Catholicism to define and redefine it operationally in the context of American pluralism and personal freedom without an explicit and literal repudiation of doctrines which had been promulgated in previous times. They wanted him to understand that although the Church speaks with authority, the tactics of the local post of Catholic war veterans, or school committee members, or the utterances of a parish priest or communion breakfast speaker did not represent a studied policy of the American bishops. They could not understand why American Protestants often blamed Catholics in the United States for the policies of the Spanish government or the hierarchy in Latin America. Most of all, they could not fathom why Blanshard and critics like him gave such little weight to, or appeared to denigrate, the forces of encounter within American Catholicism itself.

THE FORCES OF ENCOUNTER PERSIST

Those tendencies, although relatively quiet among the clergy ever since *Testem benevolentiae,* and subdued among the laity following Smith's defeat and the rise of Coughlin and McCarthy, were far from dead. They showed themselves in the labor movement, intellectual activity, new publications, the struggle for racial equality, and party politics. Pope Leo XIII's encyclical on the rights and dignity of labor provided the basis of an important pastoral letter issued by the American hierarchy in September, 1919, urging support for the right of labor to a living wage through collective bargaining. The bishops signed a pamphlet written by Monsignor John A. Ryan, who in his youth had been a friend and disciple of Archbishop Ireland, and who now urged the need for minimum-wage legislation, employment, health, and old age insurance for workers, an age limit for child labor, legal enforcement of the right of labor to organize, and the need for public housing and a national employment service. The 1919 Bishops' Program of Social Reconstruction meant that members of the Catholic hierarchy were often much more sympathetic to secular social legislation than individualistic Protestant ministers. It also meant that Catholics were encouraged to take active leadership roles in the trade-union movement in America where they worked with men from different religious backgrounds.

The Catholic Worker movement, begun by Dorothy Day in the 1930's, appealed to Catholic intellectuals who were unsatisfied with such organizations as the Holy Name Society and the Knights of Columbus. The *Catholic Worker* achieved a circulation of well over a hundred thousand and within a few years thirty-three houses of hospitality were opened throughout the country to shelter the homeless and feed the hungry regardless of their religion.

In the 1920's, Catholic laymen began the publication of *Commonweal*, which ran articles critical of the failure of parochial education to produce intellectual and artistic leaders. A Jesuit theologian, John Courtney Murray, began writing a series of essays and articles in the 1940's criticizing the separatist Catholic position on church-state relationships and attempting to reconcile the standard American view with Catholic thought. In the early 1950's, Father James G. Keller developed the Christopher movement, open to all Christians with the purpose of raising contemporary education, government, labor relations, and the arts to a higher spiritual level. But it was not until the orgy of McCarthyism had passed in 1954 that Catholic efforts toward encounter and criticism of separatism became commonplace.

In May, 1955, Monsignor John Tracy Ellis, professor of Church History at the then theologically conservative Catholic University of America, read a paper entitled "American Catholics and the Intellectual Life." Ellis quoted others to the effect that the intellectual prestige of Catholicism was lower in the United States than in any other western society. "The chief blame," he said, "lies with the Catholics themselves. It lies in their frequently self-imposed ghetto mentality which prevents them from mingling as they should with their non-Catholic colleagues, and in their lack of industry and habits of work." Following the publication of Ellis' talk, a spate of self-critical articles appeared in popular and scholarly Catholic journals. Articles in *Commonweal* had been urging Catholics to abandon ghettoism for years. Now the same message was heard frequently in the influential Jesuit journal, *America,* in *Cross Currents,* a Catholic-sponsored journal dedicated to fostering Protestant-Catholic dialogue, in the Paulist *Catholic World,* in the more self-consciously scholarly and intellectual *Thought,* produced at Fordham University, and in *Theological Studies,* published at Woodstock College. Ellis had revived the debate on Catholic intellectualism begun by Brownson and continued later by Bishops Spalding and Keane. He had not said anything new, but he said it vigorously and freshly for a new generation of Catholics used to the roguism of Frank Hague, the marauding parochialism of McCarthy, and the standpat conservatism of Francis Cardinal Spellman.

For men such as Monsignor Ellis, John Cogley, William Clancy, and Father Robert Hartnett—advocates of encounter—the concept of interfaith fellowship implied a dynamic engagement with non-Catholics beyond the platitudes of the interfaith breakfast or dinner meeting. In their view, Catholic hysteria in the face of secularism, communism, or Protestantism betrayed a lack of self-confidence. The xenophobic, antiintellectual, censorious tendencies of Catholics in the 1940's and early 1950's, they argued, stemmed from fear.

Ellis' message, developed in a short book in 1956, was followed by another influential volume by Thomas F. O'Dea entitled *American Catholic Dilemma*. The dominant attitude of American Catholics, O'Dea charged, was defensive. "We must ask ourselves why some Catholics are afraid of the differences of opinion demanded by genuine pluralism." His answer was that many Catholics, despite a phony overidentification with Americanism, often were uneasy about the place of Catholics in America. Their anxiety led to retreat and a ghettolike approach to outsiders. It was difficult to break the walls of the ghetto, argued O'Dea, because mature intellectual activity among Catholics was inhibited by the basic characteristics of American Catholicism which made the ghetto in the first place: formalism, authoritarianism, clericalism, moralism, and defensiveness.

A lively debate within Catholicism began to develop on a variety of issues including censorship, birth control, and various kinds of interfaith encounters. In the spring of 1958, the literary editor of *America*, Father Harold C. Gardiner, authored a book entitled *Catholic Viewpoint on Censorship* which, while criticizing liberals for their alleged support of unbridled freedom, took Catholics, and particularly the NODL, to task for approaching art through categories of condemnation and approval, a position which Gardiner maintained was puritanical and not Catholic at all.

Despite these differences, nearly all Catholics appeared to be in agreement on the issue of aid to parochial schools. The vast majority of Catholics believed that state aid would not breach the wall between church and state. They could not see why parochial schools were any more divisive than Jewish dietary laws. Nor could they understand why non-Catholics refused a solution comparable to that reached in 1918 in heavily Protestant Scotland, in which Catholic schools were transferred to local school boards and became part of a general state system, freeing Scottish Catholics from the double financial burden which they had previously borne. In Scotland, the local public authority, assuming financial responsibility for the schools, was given power to appoint teachers in Catholic schools after the Church had passed on their religious qualifications. A comparable system appeared to work satisfactorily in the Netherlands too. Why not in the United States?

But many non-Catholics were not persuaded that Jewish dietary laws were in the same category as parochial schools. Education, not diet, was the bulwark of American freedom. Nor did they find the analogy between the United States and Scotland compelling. In America, the question was not just how to provide for the religious education of Presbyterians and Catholics as in Scotland, or members of the Dutch Reformed Church and Catholics as in the Netherlands. In this country, there were millions of Jews, Mormons, Jehovah's Witnesses, and others who came under the protection of the First Amendment. More important, here—unlike Scotland and the Netherlands—there was a culture-religion of freedom to be taught to all which had its own rituals, symbols, heroes, and dogma.

The tension over education seemed as sharp as it had ever been, but Catholics and Protestants were beginning to talk to each other about it in a serious and respectful way. Fewer voices were heard repeating the 1947 charge of Cardinal Spellman that Protestant criticism of parochial schools amounted to "bigotry" and "a crusade . . . against the Catholic Church in the United States." In the spring of 1958, the Ford Foundation's Fund for the Republic sponsored a week-long seminar on Religion in a Free Society, bringing together Catholics, Protestants, Jews, and secular humanists including Paul Blanshard. The topics for discussion were precisely those which had absorbed the attention of Ireland, Keane, and Gibbons sixty years before: Religious Pluralism and Civic Unity; the Meaning of Separation of Church and State; Religion and Education; Religion and Secular Culture; and Religion and the Free Society.

The meeting was an eye-opener even for the managing editor of *Commonweal,* long experienced in discussions with non-Catholics. He concluded that sincere men were still genuinely concerned that should Catholics become a majority, they would throw out the Constitution to give their own religion a preferred position. "If one judges from this seminar, what do many non-Catholics see?" queried editor James O. Garrick. "They see not the Church of Christ that Catholics behold but a huge monolithic structure, a kind of vast pressure group, intent on restricting here, banning there, and picketing everywhere. Catholics are not, of course, completely to blame for this distortion of the Church that takes place in the public eye. We suffer from a heritage of centuries of mistrust and enmity. But Catholics often help to perpetuate this distorted image."

Laymen who were anxious to reshape the Catholic image with respect to church-state questions, segregation, and interreligious encounter began to find leadership in three Jesuits, John Courtney Murray, Gustave Weigel, and Robert F. Drinan, who brilliantly advocated acceptance of religious pluralism in America. In September, 1947, Archbishop Joseph E. Ritter of St. Louis ended segregation in the schools of his archdiocese. In Washington, the integration of parochial schools was begun by Archbishop Patrick O'Boyle in the fall of 1948. In 1954, Archbishop Joseph F. Rummel of New Orleans denounced three bills in the Louisiana legislature which were intended to frustrate the antisegregation decision of the United States Supreme Court. In the same year, the University of Notre Dame received an award from a Negro newspaper, the *Chicago Defender,* for breaking off athletic relationships with Southern schools which practiced Jim Crow on the playing field. In March, the director of the National Association for the Advancement of Colored People praised Bishop Vincent S. Waters of Raleigh, North Carolina, for abolishing segregation in his diocese; and in April of that year, Archbishop Robert E. Lucey of San Antonio, Texas, decreed that no child would be refused admittance to a Catholic school in his archdiocese because of color, race, or poverty.

Aside from these efforts toward encounter with Negroes and others concerned with segregation, there were few voices heard in the episcopacy against Catholic separatism. Bishop Bernard J. Sheil of Chicago, known mainly for his work in cooperation with public agencies in relationship to underprivileged youth, was practically alone in opposing Senator McCarthy. Archbishop Richard Cushing of Boston, whose sister had married a Jew, freely participated in interfaith activities, and in February, 1956, was honored by a Lowell, Massachusetts, lodge of B'nai B'rith for serving the cause of human brotherhood. But most of the hierarchy were usually suspicious of liberals, secularists, and Protestants who criticized the Church. In the summer of 1954, Samuel Cardinal Stritch of Chicago banned Catholic participation in the World Council of Churches meeting at Evanston, Illinois. Shortly after, a public opinion survey revealed that 22 percent of the dioceses in the United States forbade Catholic participation in the National Conference of Christians and Jews, although about 75 percent actually did participate. Laymen anxious to widen opportunities for encounter with non-Catholics received little encouragement from most of the highest leaders of the Church.

ENCOUNTER IN POLITICS

Politics was another matter. As Catholic voters became proportionately more numerous, many Catholic politicians moved from their local base of power to assume wider responsibilities. In 1958 and 1959, Catholic governors were elected in the predominantly non-Catholic states of Pennsylvania, Ohio, California, and Hawaii. Catholics were sent to the United States Senate from Connecticut, Massachusetts, Michigan, Minnesota, and Maine in 1958. In Min-

nesota, an Irish Catholic candidate for the Senate, Eugene Mc-
Carthy, not only defeated a Protestant Scandinavian in the Democratic primary but won over a Protestant Scandinavian Republican
in the general election; and in Maine, the Polish Catholic Democrat, Edmund Muskie, carried all but two of sixteen counties over
his Protestant Republican opponent. In Ohio, gubernatorial candidate Michael DiSalle beat the Protestant Republican incumbent
by nearly half a million votes. California's Edmund G. Brown
walloped a veteran Republican opponent by one million votes. In
Protestant Montana, Senator Mike Mansfield received 76 percent
of the votes, and in Alaska, Senator E. L. Bartlett won 85 percent.
Each of these men represented resurgent liberalism in the Democratic party, but they also symbolized the growing efforts of Catholic laymen to reach beyond their own community for direct contact
with non-Catholics in politics. To win in a large state meant
knowing and being liked by non-Catholics as well as coreligionists.
Pluralist politics required encounter.

On the eve of the 1960 election, Jesuit Father Walter J. Ong
wrote a book with the prophetic title *American Catholic Crossroads*. In his essay on "Father Hecker and the American Situation," Father Ong, like Hecker, saw "the Catholic vision [as] a
vision which opens lines of communication between men, not one
which closes them." Speaking for the nascent but emergent forces
of encounter, the author saw the desire "to keep to ourselves, to
keep pure of any defilement by avoiding contact with those different from us" as a kind of parochial isolationism which had long
handicapped Catholics in America. Father Ong asked for an end
to "fencing in" and urged an outgoing, positive Catholicism as
Father Hecker had done in the nineteenth century.

A great deal of encouragement came from Rome as the new
Pope named John, who was not expected to be much more than
a caretaker leader, surprised the world with ecumenical intent
and action. He quickly established a Commission for the Promotion of Christian Unity, and arranged for meetings with the Arch-

bishop of Canterbury, the Patriarch of the Eastern Orthodox Church, and with Jewish lay leaders. A call went out for the convening of the first Vatican Council since 1870 from the old peasant Pope who was preparing in thought, action, and written word to reevaluate papal doctrines promulgated only a half century before. And in America, the political stage was set for the entrance of another Catholic named John.

V

NOT THE CATHOLIC CANDIDATE

WHEN Al Smith ran for President in 1928, approximately twenty million American Catholics constituted 16 percent of the population. By 1956, there were more than thirty-five million Catholics (at least 20 percent of the population) in the United States, and their strategic location in the big cities made their votes especially important under the American electoral college method of choosing Presidents. In that system the winner in one big state such as New York takes all of that state's electoral votes (based on the number of seats in the national House of Representatives plus two), more than compensating for the possibly larger numerical losses in a half-dozen small states. More than 80 percent of the Catholic voters lived in fewer than a dozen key industrial states including those with the largest electoral college vote.

By the spring of 1956, Democratic politicians talked of the possibility of a Catholic vice presidential candidate. Careful studies had shown that whenever a Catholic ran in a congressional contest, whether as a Republican or Democrat, he usually picked up 10 percent more of the Catholic vote. Such information was significant in light of the sharp decline in the Catholic vote for Democratic presidential candidate Adlai Stevenson in the 1952 election.

THE VISIBILITY OF KENNEDY

The Catholic most often mentioned as a vice presidential possibility was John Fitzgerald Kennedy, the youthful senator from Massachusetts. Kennedy's closest staff aide, Theodore Sorensen, prepared a memorandum to be distributed by John Bailey, chairman of the Democratic party in Connecticut and an early Kennedy booster, which purported to show that a Catholic would be an important asset on the ticket with Stevenson in 1956. Not everyone agreed. Catholic Mayor David Lawrence of Pittsburgh, one of Stevenson's closest advisers and an astute politician, told the former Illinois governor that a Catholic on the ticket would mean certain defeat. The Speaker of the House of Representatives, the politically wise Sam Rayburn from Texas, agreed.

At the convention, Stevenson surprised everyone by throwing the vice presidential nomination open for decision by the delegates. Abraham Ribicoff, a Jew who had been elected governor in heavily Catholic Connecticut, John Bailey, and Kennedy's brother Robert hastily organized a campaign on the convention floor for Senator Kennedy against Estes Kefauver and Hubert Humphrey. Kennedy lost the nomination to Kefauver but won the attention and acclaim of important Democrats because of his attractive personality and proved vote-getting appeal. He became a national figure; and suddenly his name was frequently mentioned as a candidate for the presidency in 1960.

Kennedy was unquestionably available, but there were several obstacles to his nomination: youth; a relatively undistinguished record in the Senate; Massachusetts was not a large pivotal state; the opposition of Lyndon Baines Johnson and Hubert Humphrey; the neutrality of Adlai Stevenson; the availability of Stuart Symington of Missouri, who was supported by Harry S. Truman; and, most important of all, Jack Kennedy was a Catholic.

The argument that a Catholic vice presidential candidate would strengthen the national ticket was not transferable when that same Catholic became a candidate for the presidency. When the Gallup poll asked voters in October, 1948, "If your party nominated a generally well-qualified person for President and he happened to be a Catholic would you vote for him?" 34 percent of the Protestant and 6 percent of the Jewish respondents said no. There was always the possibility that in the secrecy of the voting booth, others also would say no. Protestants might elect a Catholic to the Senate or as governor, but would they elect one to the highest office of the land? For many Americans, the Al Smith defeat in 1928 provided a resounding negative answer. The statehouse yes; but the presidency no!

It was not a question of numbers. Unitarians had always constituted a small denomination; but they had had four Presidents. Three Presidents, Jefferson, Hayes, and Lincoln, officially belonged to no church, but that had not been an obstacle to their nomination and election. As seen by millions of Americans, the issue was simply a question of the suitability of a Roman Catholic in the presidency. The first Catholic candidate for President, Charles O'Conor, a prominent New York lawyer, had been selected in 1872 by a splinter group of Democrats in opposition to the nomination of Horace Greeley at the regular Democratic convention to run against President Grant. O'Conor's vote total was negligible, a mere 29,000 as opposed to 2,800,000 for Greeley and 3,600,000 for Grant. Because the contest was really between Greeley and Grant, O'Conor's candidacy did not produce a flood of vitriolic anti-Catholic literature comparable to that thrown against Smith in 1928. Following Smith's defeat, when Hoover carried the normally Democratic states of Texas, Virginia, North Carolina, Florida, and Tennessee, and when Smith had even lost his own state of New York, it was assumed generally that while an able Catholic might be elected chief executive of the largest state in the Union, no Catholic would be sent to the White House.

PRESIDENTIAL AVAILABILITY

To be available for the presidency in America has usually meant not being identified with a pronounced religious, sectional, economic, or ideological point of view. Because democracy depends not on counting noses but on unity, and because America is a medley of many ethnic, religious, sectional, geographic, and occupational interests, the nominating process tends to select men who can promote consensus or unity and to screen out those who are strongly identified with a particular point of view even when they are of high ability.

Ever since the second Jackson election of 1832, when presidential nominations were taken out of the hands of a congressional elite and made the responsibility of state and courthouse politicians who represented a widening democracy, it has been especially important to nominate someone who would not run the risk of offending sizable blocks of voters. The very diversity of American life encouraged a search for men who represented the common denominator of Americanism. When candidates were identified with a sectional, economic, or religious point of view, as with Henry Clay, William Jennings Bryan, Al Smith, or Wendell Willkie, they usually lost. Dozens of outstanding public servants have been passed over exactly because they embittered large numbers of voters in the course of their careers. United States senators were thought to be bad risks, no matter how high their ability, because their views on all the important issues of the day were on record. Such men as Daniel Webster, John C. Calhoun, Thomas H. Benton, Rufus Choate, Charles Sumner, Henry Cabot Lodge, William Pitt Fessenden, Hamilton Fish, and Lucius Q. C. Lamar had extraordinary talent and conviction, but they held widely known controversial views in the United States Senate.

It is the business of the nominating convention to coalesce the various centrifugal factions which constitute an American political party and not to divide them. Just as the parties cannot afford to be ideological, they dare not nominate, except at great risk, and under conditions of extraordinary social change, a candidate who threatens a significant element of the party's coalition. Since elections are close, and since both parties comprise overlapping and competing interests, the tendency is to seek a man who will offend no one.

State governors have often been nominated because they have not been involved in national issues. The better known and more pronounced their records (New York's brilliant reform governor Samuel J. Tilden, Al Smith, and Adlai Stevenson) the less likely their success. Grover Cleveland and Franklin Roosevelt, both of whom proved to be superior Presidents, received the nomination not because of their outstanding achievements, but because they were "available." Woodrow Wilson had much more of a record than either Roosevelt or Cleveland, but he won the presidency only because the Republican party was badly split. When the position of a governor on vital national issues was known, as in the case of William H. Seward, who was an active crusader for the rights of Negroes, he was counted out in favor of a barely known Illinois lawyer, Abraham Lincoln, despite the fact that Seward may have been the most effective man in government in the United States at the time.

Ever since Washington, military heroes have been the single most important source of presidential nominees. As heroes in defense of all Americans, military men are vital assets in politics to a highly dispersive, pluralistic society beset by centrifugal forces of interest and background and unified mainly by a culture-religion. They are particularly welcome in a political party whose fortunes are low because of internal schisms. Hence, the Whig nominations of William Henry Harrison and Zachary Taylor and the Republican choice of Dwight Eisenhower in moments of ebbing prestige and power. Only Jackson, Harrison, Taylor, Grant, and Eisenhower were major military heroes; but the minor military records of Generals Rutherford B. Hayes, James A. Garfield, Benjamin Harrison, and William McKinley were exploited to the fullest. From Grant to Cleveland, a military record was almost a prerequisite for nomination.

Military men are not chosen because Americans revere the martial spirit. The most martial of our heroes interested in presidential politics usually do not receive the nomination or, when they do, lose the election. Generals Winfield Scott and Winfield S. Hancock were beaten in the nineteenth century. In more recent times, General Leonard Wood lost the nomination to Harding and Admiral George Dewey and Generals John Pershing, George S. Patton, and Douglas MacArthur, despite their brilliant military exploits and willingness to accept the nomination, were never seriously considered in convention. President-makers and Americans generally have preferred citizen-soldiers who not only win glory in the field but who—with the exception of Washington— look and talk like ordinary folk, and with the inclusion of Washington seem to be indifferent to, if not above, politics and other sectional, party, or religious ties.

In their time, there were no Americans more popular than George Washington, William Henry Harrison, Zachary Taylor, Ulysses S. Grant, and Dwight Eisenhower. In battle they had led men of all classes, races, religions, and ethnic groups. They symbolized united effort against a foreign or subversive enemy who threatened the culture-religion of Americanism. These sterling, valiant defenders of Zion were admirably available: safely Protestant, largely indifferent to religion and politics, and promoters of consensus.

Washington was an obvious choice to unify the country after a period of war against Britain and sectional strife. Taylor, "Old Rough and Ready," the most popular man in the United States since Washington, never voted for President until he himself ran. Grant and Eisenhower had managed to vote only once, Ike for

Republican Dewey in 1948, and Grant for Democrat Buchanan in 1856. The military heroes all advocated morality and frugality and denounced corruption. They insisted that they did not talk politics but had, in Taylor's phrase, "cardinal principles," or in Eisenhower's words, "beliefs" which transcended political strife. Their appeal was national and the Democrats as well as the Whigs, who finally nominated them, wanted Harrison and Taylor as candidates. President Andrew Johnson urged Grant to run as a Democrat and Truman attempted to persuade Eisenhower to succeed him.

One did not have to be a governor from a large state or a military hero to receive the nomination. Warren Harding was elected directly from the Senate (the only man since Garfield), but he was little known. A Horatio Alger hero such as Herbert Hoover was acceptable and electable even though he wore a business suit. Hoover, born in modest circumstances in West Branch, Iowa, was another nonpartisan symbol of American unity. Orphaned as a child, he worked his way through Stanford University and then around the world as a mining engineer. At the age of twenty-five he became chief engineer of the Chinese Bureau of Mines at a salary of twenty thousand dollars annually. By 1908 he had laid the basis for a personal fortune and had become a prominent figure in a dozen important international ventures.

After he administered Belgian relief following World War I, he seemed to Associate Justice Brandeis "the biggest figure injected into Washington life by the war." Here was a hero for America: independent, a doer, and a man of large charity. His politics remained obscure, and a number of young Democrats thought him a likely candidate for the presidency. One of them was Franklin D. Roosevelt, who, after talking with Hoover late in 1919, said: "He is certainly a wonder and I wish we could make him President of the United States. There could not be a better one."

KENNEDY AND PERSONALITY POLITICS

By the traditional rules of the game, many factors militated against Kennedy's candidacy. He was not a governor from a large state but had served in the Congress for fourteen years where his votes were on the record. More important, he was a Catholic, which in the minds of many made him unavailable by definition. A Catholic was overly identified and committed; a Catholic was too divisive. Al Smith had been nominated only because the convention, having rejected him in 1924, could not refuse him four years later without seriously damaging the party itself. To win the nomination Kennedy would not only have to demonstrate repeatedly that he was free from ecclesiastical pressures of any kind but that he had the kind of personality that could win in 1960.

Personality politics was never more important than when John Kennedy projected his candidacy for the presidency in 1956. Ideology and party have always counted less in America than in Europe. Now, the sweeping social changes of the mid-twentieth century reduced their significance in presidential contests even more. The old bases for such party alignments as did exist were crumbling. The sectional divisions which formed the basis of the two-party struggle from the Civil War until 1928 had been replaced in the 1930's and 1940's by competition between a Republican combination of voters from the upper middle classes, small towns and farms, older ethnic groups and Protestants versus a Democratic coalition of urban industrial workers, Catholics, and newer ethnics. By 1956, even those coalitions were being shattered by the impact of social and technological change.

Americans were on the move more than ever before. In any single year as many as 15 to 20 percent changed their residence. Farmers were still leaving for the city in droves and city dwellers were spreading to the suburbs in even larger numbers. In the year that Kennedy decided to run for the presidency, more than 30 million persons lived under urban conditions in a continuous area stretching more than 600 miles from Boston to Virginia. Altogether, well over 100 million Americans lived in what the Census Bureau defined as metropolitan areas. In the urban suburbs, Republicans and Democrats alike were forced to grapple with the problems of traffic and schools. The most marked government employment and payroll increases were in cities with populations from 10,000 to 25,000. No less than the cities, the urban suburbs found it difficult to meet the mounting cost of highways, modern schools, and urban renewal without federal help. American politics could no longer be based primarily on sectional agricultural divisions or even urban-rural conflict. The problems of social life were increasingly national and there was not only a growing recognition and acceptance of the roles of federal government in dealing with those problems, but there was also grudging acquiescence in the need for experts.

The spread of affluence in an expanding middle class also tended to blur old party distinctions. As measured by 1947–49 dollars, the gross national product—even without counting defense spending—increased by more than one third between 1948 and 1956; and during the same period per capita real disposable income—the dollar constant again—increased 18 percent. Because of labor success at the bargaining table and progressive taxes on corporate and individual incomes begun during the New Deal, American workers steadily improved their relative economic standing during the 1930's, 1940's, and 1950's. Even after adjustments for price increases, the weekly wages of factory earners rose from slightly more than sixty dollars in 1948 to almost eighty dollars by 1956. By the mid-1950's, more than 30 percent of all families had incomes of more than five thousand dollars, compared to only 20 percent in 1948. The redistribution of real income revolutionized consumption habits, putting tail fins on Fords as well as Lincolns and a copy of the latest Paris design within the reach of office girls. By 1956, Americans owned 51 million telephones, 50 million cars, and 40 million television sets. Each year they bought more than

4 million new washing machines and 12 million new radios. Popular culture also helped to level differences between economic strata.

Despite the record outpouring of goods following World War II, employment growth was much greater in the service than in the production industries. The fastest growing occupation in the 1950's was selling; next, the clerical occupations; third, the professions. In 1920 there were almost twice as many Americans engaged in the production of goods as in the performance of services. By 1956, the year Kennedy came on the national scene, there were more people in white-collar jobs than factory workers and farmers combined.

Foreign policy issues in the mid-1950's also tended to disrupt the old bases of party preference. The new problems of defense and diplomacy—frighteningly complex and technical—were not put easily in terms of class, status, or even ethnic interest. Voters do not divide along economic lines on such issues as the recognition of Communist China, the cessation of hydrogen bomb tests, or the guided missile program. To the extent that they perceive such issues to be significant they give their votes—not so much on the basis of economic or even old-country interests—to the candidate who seems best able to deal with them. An important study of the 1952 election showed that Eisenhower's appeal to many Americans was precisely that they presumed he was best able to handle the Korean War.

The migration of Negroes to the North and the developing struggle of American Negroes everywhere for votes, decent homes, and jobs was also helping to change the character of American politics. The number of Negroes registering to vote in seventeen border states more than tripled between 1940 and 1956. Between 1944 and 1956, the number of Negroes legally able to vote in a Democratic primary election in Florida rose from zero to more than 128,000. It was in the North that Negro political gains were largest. Until 1910, some 90 percent of all American Negroes had lived in the South. By the mid-1950's, 35 percent of the nation's almost 18 million Negroes lived in the North and West, and each year the proportion was increasing. The rate of Negro population growth in the big-city states of New York, California, Pennsylvania, Illinois, and Michigan, casting a total of 156 electoral votes in 1956, was spectacular.

The weakening of traditional party loyalties was abetted by the rising level of education in America and extensive use of television by candidates for national and congressional offices. More than 75 percent of the nation's sixteen- and seventeen-year-olds were in school compared to 43 percent in 1920. Just a few generations before, only two out of every ten Americans finished high school. In the 1950's, a high school diploma was just a beginning. Candidates were forced to present themselves over and over again on television in the living rooms of an increasingly educated electorate.

These dynamic social changes resulted in a crazy-quilt pattern of political results. Democratic candidates were making inroads in the Middle Western farm areas and in the suburbs. Republicans were making gains in traditionally Democratic city strongholds and in the South. There was probably more split-ticket voting in 1956 than ever before. President Eisenhower carried 329 of the nation's 425 congressional districts while G.O.P. candidates for Congress won only 201 seats; in 41 states carried by Eisenhower, Republicans lost 11 Senate battles while winning only 18. Most voters still called themselves Democrats or Republicans, but a growing number were ready to split their tickets. A study by the Survey Research Center at Ann Arbor, Michigan, revealed that in the 1952 election only four out of every ten Americans agreed that "a voter should vote for the same party for President and Congress." As many as one third of the voters classified as strong Democrats and one half of the strong Republicans reported they would be willing to split tickets and vote for the man rather than the party.

Personality politics also meant that old-style political organizations were diminished in importance. The traditional political organization, which in the cities had depended on graft, patronage, low business ethics, poverty, immigration, and the absence of state action in the welfare field was being replaced by a new system of political leadership. Political victory usually meant (and still does to a large extent on the local and county level) jobs, favors, and opportunities to make what George Washington Plunkett used to call "honest graft." Party workers did not play at politics for fun or foreign policy. In the mid-1950's, the workers who stuffed the envelopes, manned the polls, rounded up voters on election day, organized street corner rallies, and rang doorbells came increasingly from pressure groups (in Michigan, the United Automobile Workers constituted the single most important element in the Democratic party), the civic-minded (an example would be the California Democratic Clubs, a powerful organization in the Golden State made up primarily of well-educated, reform-minded young voters), and unaffiliated volunteers who enthusiastically clustered around the candidate whose personality and programs seemed appealing. Volunteers formed national organizations to back presidential candidates out of a feeling of deep personal loyalty and commitment to the man.

This was the background of change in American politics in 1956 when John F. Kennedy, who narrowly missed being nominated for Vice President on the Democratic ticket, decided he would run for the office of President four years later. The increasingly independent voting habits of Americans provided Kennedy with his greatest danger and opportunity. Anti-Catholic Protestants and Jews who normally voted Democratic might switch in even greater numbers than they had in 1928; but if voters thought less in stereotypes than in 1928, Kennedy might be able to reach them as a personality regardless of his religion. If, in addition to ability, he could communicate a forceful independence as a politician and as a Catholic, the presidency might be his.

Fortunately, such independence was the central feature of Kennedy's own personality and background. Kennedy, whose Pulitzer Prize-winning book, *Profiles in Courage,* stressed the theme of independence in politicians under pressure, could claim an unusual degree of self-sufficiency: the son of a strong father, he almost wholly disagreed with him on political issues; the product of city politics, he was not tied to any machine; the possessor of a liberal record in Congress, he refused to be labeled as a liberal; elected to the Senate on a platform of doing more for Massachusetts, he supported the St. Lawrence Seaway bill, supposedly against the interests of his own state; a prolabor congressman in the House of Representatives, he helped to lead an investigation of labor abuses as a senator; a lifelong Democrat, he admitted voting for Republican Senator Leverett Saltonstall when he ran for reelection from Massachusetts in 1954; a decorated war veteran, he stated on the floor of the House of Representatives in 1949 that "the leadership of the American Legion has not had a constructive thought for the benefit of the country since 1918"; a senator from Massachusetts, the locus of strongest support for McCarthyism, he enraged the most partisan McCarthyite paper, the *Boston Post,* by refusing to support McCarthy in his censure fight in 1954 and by consistently voting against important McCarthy nominees to high posts; an Irishman, for whom loyalty to the tribe is supposed to be the first allegiance, he was the only Democratic representative from Massachusetts to refuse to sign a petition requesting President Truman to pardon James Michael Curley in prison for mail fraud; and a Roman Catholic, he, as Richard Cardinal Cushing of Boston was to say later, wore his religion "lightly."

As Kennedy crisscrossed the nation in an effort to build grass-roots support for his candidacy in 1957 and 1958, voters wanted to know whether he was truly independent of his Church. Kennedy's family was known to be devout and close to the Catholic hierarchy, and his father had been a heavy contributor to Catholic churches and charities. During his first years in Congress, Kennedy supported federal aid to education programs in which private and parochial school students would share funds for bus transportation, nonreligious textbooks, and health services. In 1947, he had declined to attend the dedication of the memorial chapel in a Protestant church on the advice of Cardinal Dougherty of Philadelphia. As he explained in 1960, Kennedy based his refusal on the fact that he had no credentials to attend as a representative of the Catholic Church, but he would have been delighted to join in the memorial had he been invited as a public official. In 1954, he indicated that since Presidents Roosevelt and Truman had favored representation at the Vatican, he would vote for an ambassador to the Papal See if a nomination were submitted to the Senate, a position he reversed two years later. These facts—his family's devotionalism, his 1947 failure to attend an interfaith service, and his early support for peripheral public aid to religious schools— would constitute the sum of evidence advanced to support the charge that Kennedy would favor his religion in the White House.

HE WORE HIS RELIGION LIGHTLY

Actually, Kennedy had never shown any special interest in Catholicism. He had spent only one year in a Catholic school, and that taught by laymen. The rest of his education was in private and public schools, including the strongly Protestant-influenced Choate and Harvard. He displayed a remarkably candid irreverence toward ecclesiastical authorities, especially in private. In public, he made it clear that he believed America's politics to be beyond the reach of papal influence. During a congressional hearing on federal aid to parochial schools in 1947, he challenged a witness: "Now, you don't mean the Catholics in America are legal subjects of the Pope? I am not a legal subject of the Pope." When the witness continued to assert that all Catholics had a dual allegiance which compromised their Americanism, Kennedy blurted, "There is an old saying in Boston that we get our religion from

Rome and our politics at home, and that is the way most Catholics feel about it."

By 1958, Kennedy knew that many Americans were still afraid of the alleged power of an authoritarian, hierarchical Roman Church to discipline the faithful, including American officeholders. He realized that he would have to make his views on church-state questions unequivocally explicit. He did not regard every voter who doubted the desirability of a Catholic in the White House as a bigot. As he told Unitarian Ted Sorensen, he would have to answer all reasonable as well as unreasonable questions. He could not afford to be defensive or silent to questions which seemed unfair or even insulting. This approach was far different from that of Al Smith, who could not understand anti-Catholic attacks as having any reasonable basis at all. Kennedy understood their historical roots. Once convinced that the religious issue could not be buried, he was determined to bring it out into the open as much as possible on a basis of reason. He felt it unjust that other presidential contenders were not questioned on the relationship of their religious beliefs to their fitness for the presidency; but he recognized that Catholics, because of the nature of their universal authoritarian Church, were under special suspicion.

Late in 1958, Kennedy gave off-the-cuff answers to a reporter from *Look* magazine doing a story on possible Catholic candidates in 1960. The article, which came out in March, 1959, quoted Kennedy as saying: "Whatever one's religion in private life may be, for the office-holder nothing takes precedence over his oath to uphold the Constitution and all its parts—including the First Amendment and the strict separation of church and state. Without reference to the presidency, I believe as a Senator that the separation of church and state is fundamental to our American concept and heritage and should remain so."

Kennedy stated his unequivocal opposition to the appointment of an ambassador to the Vatican—a position he had taken since 1956—stating: "Whatever advantages it might have in Rome—and

I'm not convinced of these—they would be more than offset by the divisive effects at home." The senator strongly praised the First Amendment to the Constitution, insisting: "There can be no question of federal funds being used for support of parochial or private schools. It's unconstitutional under the First Amendment as interpreted by the Supreme Court." He made a distinction between extending support "to sustain any church or its schools," and "fringe matters [such as] buses, lunches, and other services," which he saw as primarily social and economic.

The editors of the Jesuit weekly, *America,* were "taken aback ... by the unvarnished statement that whatever one's religion in his private life ... nothing takes precedence over his oath." The Paulist *Catholic World* complained that "Kennedy's views were out of line with the majority of Catholics" and that "the most regrettable statement by Kennedy was his opposition to federal aid to parochial schools." The *Catholic Review* in Baltimore accused him of going overboard to placate the bigots. Even *Commonweal,* the liberal lay Catholic journal, took issue with Kennedy on the constitutionality of federal aid to parochial schools, although it otherwise commended him on his straightforward answers to extremely difficult questions.

Despite considerable critical mail from Catholic constituents, Kennedy refused to qualify his *Look* interview. He denied that he was appeasing bigotry, badly interpreting the Constitution, or violating Catholic views on church and state. He backed his opinions by introducing a federal aid to education bill limited to public schools. Later, he was alone among presidential aspirants in opposing as unconstitutional a Senate amendment authorizing funds for nonpublic schools. Other actions appeared at variance with the opinions of a majority of Catholic clerics. He supported economic aid to Communist Yugoslavia and Poland, and in November, 1959, he said it would be wrong to refuse or reduce foreign aid to any country that used funds for birth control programs, although he opposed making such programs a condition of assistance.

Only a few days before Kennedy stated his views on foreign aid and birth control, the Catholic bishops of the United States criticized "population alarmists" (a position for which Kennedy might have qualified) and urged opposition to national or international programs which permitted birth control methods to be employed in contravention of the Catholic version of moral law. Kennedy mused aloud to Sorensen that the bishops' declaration was an indication that the hierarchy did not want him to be a candidate. He complained that they issued their statement deliberately at a critical time or else were thoughtless in not realizing how much harm it might do.

Many Protestant leaders were impressed by Kennedy's forthrightness. The associate director of Protestants and Other Americans United for Separation of Church and State (POAU) called Kennedy's *Look* interview "a courageous stand." Kennedy was a little annoyed at the sense of wonderment expressed by Protestants at his independence. As he told Williams College Professor James MacGregor Burns: "My faith is a personal matter and it doesn't seem to me conceivable, in fact it is impossible, that my obligation as one sworn to uphold and defend the Constitution could be changed in any manner by anything the Pope could say or do." Sorensen has written: "His own attitude has always been one of respectful independence, far less impressed by the political power of the Church than any of his Protestant critics." In the spring of 1959, he had written a Colorado woman:

> As a public official, sworn to uphold the Constitution, I have no obligation to any private institution, religious or otherwise. My obligation is to the good of all. . . . We live in a liberal, democratic society which embraces wide varieties of belief and disbelief. There is no doubt in my mind that the pluralism which has developed under our Constitution, providing as it does a framework in which diverse opinions can

exist side by side and by their interaction enrich the whole, is the most ideal system yet devised by man. . . . I cannot conceive of a set of circumstances which would lead me to a different conclusion.

Privately, Kennedy was angered by reports of local clerics who were alleged to oppose interfaith activities or public school bond issues; and he criticized and poked fun at prelates whom he thought to be hypocritical or overly conservative.

While most Jews and many Protestants were delighted by Kennedy's explicit position on church-state matters, some friendly Protestant leaders wondered if the candidate had not gone too far in the direction of secularism. "Strangely enough," wrote the Right Reverend James A. Pike, Bishop of the Episcopal diocese of California: "Senator Kennedy's statement [in *Look*], far from posing the threat of ecclesiastical tyranny, would seem rather to represent the point of view of a thoroughgoing secularist, who really believes that a man's religion and his decision-making can be kept in two watertight compartments." Robert McAfee Brown, a friendly critic of Catholicism, wrote in *Christianity in Crisis* that Kennedy had demonstrated "that he is a rather irregular Christian." The associate editor of the *Christian Century*, Martin Marty, saw Kennedy as "spiritually rootless and politically almost disturbingly secular."

OLD FEARS AND HATES

While some Protestant leaders showed concern over Kennedy's secularism and others welcomed it, a third group simply did not believe him. A large number of fundamentalist Protestants disregarded his record and statements and, like an organization of Alabama Methodists, attributed his candidacy "to the political machinations of a determined, power-hungry Roman hierarchy." The theme of such opposition was familiar. Roman Catholics by definition were obliged to submit to an authoritarian Church directed from Rome. An unsigned editorial in *Christianity Today*, an influential Protestant journal which included the Reverend Billy Graham as one of its contributing editors, stated: "Informed Protestants believe not at all irrationally that the interests of the nation are safer in the hands of one who does not confess to a foreign, earthly power." The president of the nine-million-member Southern Baptist Convention declared that he would not "stand by and keep my mouth shut when a man under control of the Roman Catholic Church runs for the presidency."

In the spring of 1959, a Gallup poll found that 57 percent of those asked preferred Kennedy to Nixon for the presidency; but fewer than half had expressed any awareness of Kennedy's religion. A year later, with the number of persons aware of his religion substantially increased, an equal number of respondents chose Nixon as preferred Kennedy. The Massachusetts senator realized that the only way he could prove his availability despite his Catholicism was to win votes in primary elections. Only if he swept the primaries could he scatter the favorite-son candidates, win a substantial block of delegates, beat key competitors, and show that Protestants would send a Catholic to the White House.

When Kennedy arrived in Indianapolis to file a petition to enter the Indiana primary in March, 1960, he was met by a group calling themselves the Indiana Bible Baptist Fellowship. Coming directly from an all-night prayer meeting at their church, they challenged the candidate to a debate: *Resolved,* That a Roman Catholic President cannot impartially defend the Constitution and advance the true welfare of the United States while remaining true to his religion. Later, Kennedy said at a press conference that the demonstrators were entitled to their views but that "I also believe in the First Amendment which provides for the separation of church and state," and "I also believe in Article Six which says that there shall be no religious test or religious qualification for public office."

In the early months of 1960, a soul-searching debate over Kennedy's candidacy took place within Protantism itself. A Lutheran convention stated that it would be unfair to oppose a candidate on the basis of his religion, and the Council for Social Action of the United Church of Christ said that a denial of Kennedy on religious grounds would be a rejection of basic American values. An article in the *Christian Leader* in January maintained, "It is difficult to believe that informed Americans can really think that the election of a Roman Catholic will give over the reins of power to Vatican control." But the problem of conflicting loyalties troubled many Protestant writers. Extreme views appeared in the *Christian Heritage* (Disciples of Christ). "America today stands at the crossroads of destiny," maintained one article. "On the one hand, communism, on the other, Romanism. We have come on a straight course thus far. Are we going to stay on that course, or are we going to barter our democratic principles for a totalitarian system, to be either enslaved or liquidated at the hands of despotic tyrants?" Other publications, such as the nondenominational *Christian Century,* were less vociferously opposed to a Catholic in the presidency but were still negative. Even friendly periodicals like the *Lutheran* worried about the question of ecclesiastical pressure.

The first major primary test came in Wisconsin, where 32 percent of the population was Catholic. Religion was the dominant issue. On the Sunday before the election, the *Milwaukee Journal* listed the voting strength of three types of voters in each county: Republicans, Democrats, and Catholics. Voters leaving political gatherings were questioned as to their religious affiliation, and a major advertisement appeared in the newspapers questioning whether Kennedy could possibly be truly independent in view of the allegiance he must owe to the Pope as Christ's vicar on earth.

Although Kennedy won in Wisconsin against Minnesota's Hubert Humphrey with more votes than any candidate in the history of that state's primary, and ran surprisingly well in certain farm areas, his victory was attributed by many to the votes of Catholic Republicans who took advantage of the state's open primary system. Since Kennedy made his best showing in the three most heavily Catholic districts, while Humphrey led in the two most strongly Protestant districts, many Catholics undoubtedly did vote for the Massachusetts Irishman out of pride, as many Protestants voted against him out of fear. That Kennedy could not have won without substantial Protestant approval seemed obscured in much postelection talk.

The contentiousness of some of the campaign literature in Wisconsin brought into the open the fears of many Catholics that Kennedy's candidacy would be harmful to the unity of America and the social and economic aspirations of Catholics. Such views were held by several members of the hierarchy and political leaders such as Pennsylvania's governor David Lawrence, whose fears seemed justified only a short time after the Wisconsin victory when one thousand delegates to the annual meeting of the Missouri Baptist Women's Missionary Union gave a singing assent to a prayer asking "the Lord's blessing and assistance" in electing a Protestant President of the United States.

CONVINCING PROTESTANTS

More than ever, Kennedy had to prove that his election to the presidency did not depend on Catholic votes. He would have to win a victory in an overwhelmingly Protestant state. There were many reasons why he should not have entered the West Virginia primary against Hubert Humphrey. Humphrey was an authentic child of the New Deal. Personally having known poverty, and long identified with welfare programs and labor unions, Humphrey had a special appeal for the dispossessed coal miners of West Virginia. Kennedy, with his clipped Harvard accent, urbane manner, and smartly tailored two-hundred-dollar suits would be seeing real poverty for the first time in his life. More important, West Virginia had only a 3 percent Catholic population. But that was precisely the reason Kennedy had to make West Virginia a crucial test of his ability to get votes.

He decided on a strategy for meeting the religious issue in West Virginia and the nation. He would reassert his independence of ecclesiastical pressure as often as was necessary and attempt to stigmatize as bigots those who remained opposed to him on religious grounds only. His first task would be to make clear his independence; his second, to put the haters on the defensive. He tried the approach with any group of voters who would listen at outdoor meetings or in local high school gymnasiums in West Virginia; and he decided to try it in a major national speech before the American Society of Newspaper Editors too.

In that speech, he reviewed his stands on education, birth control, and the appointment of an ambassador to the Vatican, arguing that "there is only one legitimate question . . . would you, as President, be responsive in any way to ecclesiastical pressures or obligations of any kind that might in any fashion influence or interfere with your conduct of that office in the national interest? My answer was—and is—no. I am not a Catholic candidate for President." Kennedy reiterated that he completely believed in the separation of church and state (he thought that federal assistance to parochial schools was unconstitutional, although many Protestants believed otherwise; he believed it would be wrong to appoint an ambassador to the Vatican, although it was last proposed by Baptist Harry Truman). As President, he asserted that he would be guided by his conscience, and be completely independent of direction from the Pope or any other Church official.

Having defended his independence, Kennedy attacked those who opposed him despite his views and his voting record. His private religious views were personal, he said, and he should not be singled out to explain their relationship to his constitutional responsibilities. Those who made a special test for him because he was a Catholic and who persisted in ignoring his record and refusing to believe his answers were plainly unfair. "Are we to admit to the world—worse still, are to admit to ourselves—that one third of our population is forever barred from the White House?" Kennedy asked. The candidate concluded his plea for fair play by asserting: "If there is bigotry in the country so great as to prevent fair consideration of a Catholic who has made clear his complete independence . . . then we ought to know it. But I do not believe this is the case. I believe the American people are much more concerned with a man's views and abilities than with the Church to which he belongs."

Influential Protestant leaders were favorably impressed. Sorensen worked behind the scenes with the Very Reverend Francis B. Sayre, Jr., dean of the Washington Episcopal Cathedral and grandson of Woodrow Wilson, and Methodist Bishop G. Bromley Oxnam—long known as an opponent of the Catholic hierarchy on church-state questions and currently a leader of POAU—in enlisting other ministers to sign an open letter to their "fellow pastors in Christ" urging consideration of all candidates on the basis of ability alone without respect to their religious affiliation. The letter, issued from Dean Sayre's office, was signed by thirteen nationally known Protestant leaders who said: "We are convinced that each of the candidates has presented himself before the American people with honesty and independence, and we would think it unjust to discount any one of them because of his chosen faith." But the opinions of Dean Sayre and Bishop Oxnam were not necessarily shared by Episcopalians, Methodists, and members of Pentecostal groups in West Virginia, where the Episcopal bishop announced his opposition to a Catholic candidate and a Baptist minister distributed copies of a fabricated Knights of Columbus oath purporting to show that Catholics in power would destroy Protestants.

In rebuttal, Kennedy again asserted his independence and asked for fairness. He told the students at Bethany College that if he received a political directive from his archbishop, "I simply would not obey it." No priest or Pope could influence his decisions, he asserted, and he hoped that anti-Catholic prejudice would not determine theirs. He was a free man; were West Virginia voters fair men and women?

In a televised question-answer program with Franklin D. Roosevelt, Jr., that closed the primary campaign, he repeated again that he "would not take orders from any Pope, cardinal, bishop or priest, nor would they try to give me orders. . . . If any Pope attempted to influence me as President, I would have to tell him that it was completely improper." He pointed out that Catholic Boston had given a huge plurality to Baptist Harry Truman in 1948 "because of the man he is." Kennedy concluded, "I would like the same fairness Harry Truman was shown."

The voters of West Virginia were more than fair. The Massachusetts senator won an incredible 61 percent of their votes and carried all but seven of West Virginia's fifty-five counties. The fair-play strategy had paid off brilliantly. The candidate joyfully but mistakenly concluded that the religious issue had been "buried here in the state of West Virginia."

Within a few days Kennedy admitted that the issue was still very much alive. In an apparent contradiction of the open letter he published one week earlier, Bishop G. Bromley Oxnam joined Eugene Carson Blake of the United Presbyterian Church in an article in *Look* magazine to state his uneasiness about the possible election of a Roman Catholic to the presidency. While Oxnam and Blake agreed that it would be utterly wrong to stir up prejudice and bigotry, they believed it was perfectly fair to "worry about how the religious affiliation of a candidate may affect the fulfillment of his official duties." They worried about "how a Catholic President could square his political duties with the 'official' position of the Church to which he owes allegiance on questions that range from the use of public funds for parochial schools . . . to the conduct of foreign affairs." They praised Kennedy's frank answers to difficult questions but noted with concern that "Senator Kennedy was vigorously attacked by many important Catholic journals in the United States" for his views on separation of church and state.

Kennedy felt caught in a double bind. If a member of the hierarchy approved of his candidacy, as did his own archbishop of Boston, Richard Cardinal Cushing, Kennedy was in trouble with Protestants who saw evidence of a Catholic plot. When members of the hierarchy criticized him, the inference was drawn that Catholics really did not approve of separation of church and state and that Kennedy was some kind of an oddball Romanist.

When the Vatican newspaper *L'Osservatore Romano* editorialized that the Church "has the duty and the right" to tell Catholics how to vote, Kennedy was forced again to issue a statement that his support of church-state separation "is not subject to change under any conditions." When Vatican sources were reported as saying that the editorial applied to Americans as well as others, although it had earlier been believed to be aimed at Communist candidates in Italy, Kennedy remarked privately, "Now I understand why Henry VIII set up his own church." He wondered again if there was some plan to hinder his candidacy among the more conservative prelates in Rome and the American hierarchy.

West Virginia had at least proved that under some circumstances a majority of Protestant Democrats would vote to *nominate* a Catholic for President. The question remained: Would enough Protestants, Democrats and independents, vote for Kennedy to elect him President? On May 21, Kennedy won his eighth primary, defeating Wayne Morse, a proponent of federal aid to parochial schools, in his home state of Oregon. When the Democrats convened to nominate a candidate for President, it was certain that Kennedy would have more first-ballot strength than anyone else. The Massachusetts senator was fortunate in that his opposition, with the exception of Senator Stuart Symington of Missouri, also failed to fulfill the traditional requirements of availability. Lyndon Johnson was labeled as the southern candidate and was strongly opposed by labor, liberals, and Negro groups. Hubert

Humphrey had been blasted out of contention by Kennedy's primary victories, and Adlai Stevenson was marked as a two-time loser. When the opposition was unable to agree on a single stop-Kennedy candidate, the convention delegates awarded Kennedy a first-ballot triumph.

In his speech accepting the nomination, Kennedy once again stated his views on church and state before a nationwide television audience. He acknowledged that by nominating a Catholic the Democratic party had taken on what many regarded as a risk. He repeated the themes of his West Virginia victory, asserting that he was an independent man who happened to be a Catholic. He would uphold the Constitution and "reject any kind of religious pressure or obligation that might directly or indirectly interfere with my conduct of the presidency in the national interest." The American people, he hoped, would "render a free and fair judgment" and no American "considering the really critical issues facing the country, will waste his franchise and throw away his vote by voting either for or against me solely on account of my religious affiliation. It is not relevant. I am telling you now what you are entitled to know: that my decisions on every public policy will be my own—as an American, a Democrat, and a free man."

CLARIFYING THE ISSUES AGAIN AND AGAIN

Kennedy's nomination was the signal for intensified anti-Catholic agitation despite his acceptance speech. In the last week of August, a Minnesota Baptist convention declared that Roman Catholicism posed "as serious a threat to America as atheistic communism." A few days later, the general presbytery of the Assemblies of God, claiming to speak for over half a million members, and disclaiming any religious bias, charged that the Roman Catholic Church was guilty of bigotry "as reflected in its position of infallibility of its leadership." Also in the first week of September, the Baptist state convention in Arkansas gave approval to a letter sent to the state's eight Democratic presidential electors signed by the vice-president of the convention which said, "We cannot turn our government over to a Catholic President who would be influenced by the Pope and by the power of the Catholic hierarchy." Kennedy's brother Robert admitted that religion was the biggest political issue in the country, and the executive director of the Fair Campaign Practices Committee, which had been established in 1954 as a response to the McCarthyite excesses of the 1950 and 1952 campaigns, expressed alarm at the growing circulation of rabidly anti-Catholic material.

Kennedy knew the religious issue would be raised repeatedly, and he was prepared to be patient. He told a Portland, Maine, audience on September 2: "There are a good many Americans who are concerned about the question of religious freedom. The power of the President is great. There are a good many Americans of goodwill who want to hear my views on the question of religious liberty, constitutional separation of church and state and so on. I have given these views on every occasion that I am asked and I am glad to give it [sic] again." To help answer reasonable questions and neutralize religious hostility, he appointed a former staff member of the National Council of Churches who had worked on the Sayre-Oxnam open letter with Sorensen to head a "community relations" division which was kept busy in the campaign answering from six hundred to one thousand letters every week and distributing information to local Democratic leaders on how to deal with the religious issue through panel discussions, interfaith appeals, and statewide committees.

The most formidable attack on Kennedy as a Catholic candidate for the presidency came on September 7 with the foundation of an organization of prominent clergymen called the National Council of Citizens for Religious Freedom. One hundred and fifty ministers and laymen, including the famous Norman Vincent Peale (author of *The Power of Positive Thinking*), Daniel A. Poling, editor of the *Christian Herald*, L. Nelson Bell, editor of *Christian-*

ity Today (and the father-in-law of Billy Graham), and Harold
J. Ockenga, a former president of the National Association of
Evangelicals, representing thirty-seven Protestant denominations,
signed a statement insisting that Kennedy was unacceptable for the
presidency because no Catholic could be free of his hierarchy's
"determined efforts . . . to breach the wall of separation of church
and state." Peale was reported as saying: "It's a good thing to have
this crisis forced upon us; it will bring us together . . . our American culture is at stake." In elaboration of the signed statement,
Peale and Ockenga told a press conference that it was inconceiv-
able to them "that a Roman Catholic President would not be
under extreme pressure by the hierarchy to accede to its policies
with respect to foreign relations . . . including representation to
the Vatican." Later, in the face of criticism of Protestants, and
perhaps from the newspaper readers of his syndicated column,
Peale withdrew from the group, saying that he had attended only
one meeting. But Kennedy was once again put on the defensive.

On the same day, the POAU also issued a statement denouncing
bigoted literature as "trash" and praising Kennedy to the extent
that he repudiated the policies of the Catholic Church with respect to birth control, public school attendance, and other church-
state issues. But it added: "When a candidate belongs to an organization which champions such a policy [partial union of church
and state], it is not bigotry or prejudice to examine his credentials
with utmost care and frankness and to ask how far his commitment
goes."

Many leading Protestants came to Kennedy's defense. The
Methodist Church Board of Missions journal *World Outlook,* the
American Jewish Congress, and individual Protestants and Jews
pointed out that it was unfair to refuse to accept Kennedy's statements and voting record at face value. The views of the candidate,
and not the views of Catholic Popes, should be the basis for judging him. The influential Reinhold Niebuhr and John C. Bennett,
of Union Theological Seminary, both of whom were vice-chairmen

of the Liberal party in New York, accused the Peale g
"blind prejudice." Not so, responded George M. Doherty,
ber of the group, who insisted that criticism of the Roman
Church was based on a "deep-seated concern for the mair
of those human freedoms . . . which are basic to the American way
of life."

At a press conference, Kennedy stated that he believed in the
separation of church and state "just as strongly as Doctor Peale or
anyone else." While Kennedy was disappointed in having to constantly defend himself on the religious question, a secret report,
prepared by Simulatics Corporation, showed that by mid-Septem-
ber Kennedy had probably lost all of the votes he would lose as a
result of anti-Catholicism and that continued forthright discussion
of the issue might actually gain some votes. He prepared to give
still another definitive statement on church and state, and accepted
an invitation to speak before the (Ministerial Association of Greater
Houston) an audience of several hundred ministers and about an
equal number of laymen.

Probably no President has ever made as important a speech on
church-state matters as Kennedy did in Houston. The young senator joined the issues forcefully and clearly. "I believe in an
America," he said, "where the separation of church and state is
absolute—where no Catholic prelate would tell the President
(should he be a Catholic) how to act and no Protestant minister
would tell his parishioners for whom to vote—where no church
or church school is granted any public funds or political preference—and where no man is denied public office merely because his
religion differs from the President who might appoint him or the
people who might elect him."

Kennedy told the ministers that he wanted a chief executive
"who can attend any ceremony, service, or dinner his office may
appropriately require him to fulfill." He asked not to be judged
on the basis of selected quotations from the statements of Catholic
Church leaders, usually from foreign countries. "I do not consider

these other quotations binding upon my public acts; why should you? . . . I am wholly opposed to the state being used by any religious group, Catholic or Protestant, to compel, prohibit, or persecute the free exercise of any other religion. And that goes for any persecution at any time, by anyone, in any country."

Kennedy pledged that "whatever issue may come before me as President, if I should be elected—on birth control, divorce, censorship, gambling, or any other subject—I will make my decision in accordance . . . with what my conscience tells me to be in the national interest, and without regard to outside religious pressure or dictates. And no power or threat of punishment could cause me to do otherwise."

Before his speech, Kennedy had been reassured by his friend Bishop John Wright of Pittsburgh that, contrary to public belief, no public act of a President could possibly lead to his excommunication and that he, as a Catholic, had not sworn allegiance to the Pope. The speech had been reviewed by Father John Courtney Murray and John Cogley as well as members of the candidate's personal staff, and Kennedy's confidence with respect to Catholic doctrine and public policy pervaded every line of the talk. Once again Kennedy forcefully insisted: "I am not the Catholic candidate for President, I am the Democratic party's candidate for President who happens also to be a Catholic. I do not speak for my Church on public matters, and the Church does not speak for me."

Following the applause which came at the close of his speech, Kennedy directly answered pointed questions. When asked by a Baptist minister to appeal to Richard Cardinal Cushing to present Kennedy's views on church and state to the Vatican, so that they might become the authorized views of all Roman Catholics in the United States, Kennedy retorted: "As I do not accept the right of, as I said, any ecclesiastical official to tell me what I should do in the sphere of my public responsibility as an elected official, I do not propose also to ask Cardinal Cushing to ask the Vatican to take some action." Applause burst from the audience; a minister rose to state his admiration for Kennedy's courage, but doubted that the senator's views represented the position of the Catholic Church. Kennedy shot back: "I believe that I am stating the viewpoint that Catholics in this country hold toward that happy relationship which exists between church and state." The minister responded, "Let me ask you, sir, do you state it with the approval of the Vatican?" Kennedy replied, "I don't have to have approval in that sense."

One minister put Kennedy on the defensive with a question concerning the Syllabus of Errors. The candidate acknowledged it was still part of church doctrine, but pointed out (inaccurately) that it was from several centuries in the past. When a minister quoted a series of statements from the *Catholic Encyclopedia* on the right and duty of the Roman Catholic hierarchy to instruct its flock in politics, Kennedy said simply that although he had not read the *Catholic Encyclopedia,* he found "no difficulty" in disagreeing with the statement quoted.

As time ran out, the candidate expressed his conviction that such questions were reasonable. He understood the historical basis of Protestant fear. "I don't want anyone to think that because they interrogate me on this very important question [the Syllabus of Errors] that I regard that as unfair . . . or unreasonable, or that . . . somebody who is concerned about the matter is prejudiced or bigoted. I think this fight for religious freedom is basic in the establishment of the American system and therefore any candidate for the office, I think, should submit himself to the questions of any reasonable man.

"My only objection would be"—here Kennedy was interrupted by strong applause and he had the opportunity to point out the unfairness not of those who ask questions, but of those who refuse to listen to answers. "My only objection would be if somebody said, 'Regardless of how much evidence he's given, . . . I still wouldn't vote for him because he's a member of that Church.'"

In typical understatement, Kennedy concluded, "I would consider that unreasonable."

THE TRIUMPH OF REASON

The Houston speech was a turning point for many Protestant leaders. On the day of his talk, a "Statement on religious liberty in relation to the 1960 campaign" was published by one hundred distinguished Americans of all major religious backgrounds, including the dean of the Yale Divinity School and the Presiding Bishop of the Episcopal Church, which revealed a keen understanding of the diversity within Roman Catholicism. The authors of the statement proposed a series of ten guidelines in the 1960 election, including the principle that no member of any faith be excluded from public office on the basis of his religious affiliation.

Following the Houston speech, the *Christian Century* switched from opposing Kennedy to neutrality. The nondenominational *Christianity in Crisis,* a liberal, sophisticated journal concerned with modern theology and world affairs, became even more sympathetic. Several Protestant periodicals which had opposed Al Smith, including the *Unitarian Register and The Universalist Leader* and the *Lutheran,* announced their support for Kennedy. But these were exceptions. Most Protestant periodicals were either skeptical or hostile. Two Presbyterian publications, *Presbyterian Life* and *Christianity Today,* argued that it was not enough for Kennedy to have made his position clear on church-state relations. The Church itself would have to announce acceptance of his views. The *Christian Heritage* kept up its opposition, even resuscitating such wild accusations as the charge that Rome plotted the assassination of Lincoln.

Despite the widespread opposition of Protestant periodicals, a study of letters written to the editors of eighteen such journals compared with the letters written during the Smith campaign in 1928 showed that while two thirds of the letters to the editors in the earlier contest opposed the election of Smith, only about half were opposed to Kennedy. One new theme pointed out by many letter writers in 1960 was that Kennedy might be more resistant to Catholic pressures than a Protestant President, an appraisal probably shared by several members of the Roman Catholic hierarchy.

No matter what Kennedy could say or do, a hard core of anti-Catholic opposition remained, particularly in the South and Southwest. Among the religious bodies which took a public stand against the election of a Catholic in 1960 were the Southern Baptist Convention with 9,000,000 members; the Assemblies of God Church, Springfield, Missouri, with 556,000 members; the American Baptist Association with 600,000 members; the Augustana Lutheran Church with 582,000 members; the Conservative Baptist Association of America, with 275,000 members; and the General Association of Regular Baptist Churches with 126,000 members. The National Association of Evangelicals urged a massive anti-Catholic action program for Reformation Sunday, pointing out that the election of Kennedy would mean the end of the United States as a Protestant nation. Plans were laid for prayer meetings, special services, and other offerings by Protestant groups for the last two Sundays in October. Buttons were to be worn on the street and at the job carrying the words "Stand Up and Be Counted" with the numerals "1517" to remind Protestants to follow Martin Luther's courageous action in nailing his ninety-five theses to the door of Wittenberg Castle Church in 1517.

Despite or because of some of these attacks, surveys showed major Kennedy gains among Jewish voters and more modest advances among liberal Protestants. To these groups, Kennedy's views on church-state relations and other issues were clearly persuasive. Among the Jews particularly, skepticism gave way to massive support, which was astounding to some because Kennedy's father was frequently alleged to have been anti-Semitic and indifferent to the plight of Jews under Hitler.

More than opposition from fundamentalist Protestants, Kennedy worried about a pastoral letter issued by the Roman Catholic bishops of Puerto Rico. In Puerto Rico, at the height of Kennedy's own election campaign, the Catholic bishops advised the faithful not to vote for the party of Governor Muñoz Marín because of his positions on sterilization, birth control, and the teaching of religion in the Puerto Rican schools. The governor, a divorced Catholic, had not recommended the granting of time off from public schools for religious instruction to the dismay of the bishops, one of whom, Bishop James E. McManus, said that to vote for Marín would be a "sin of disobedience."

There was immediate speculation in the Kennedy camp that certain members of the hierarchy looked unhappily on the prospect of his election. Protestant newspapers were alarmed, and the liberal Catholic magazine, *Commonweal,* strongly supporting Kennedy, pointed out the irony in Protestants believing there was a hierarchical plot to help Kennedy's election: "The pastoral letter by the bishops of Puerto Rico . . . should demolish these doubts once and for all," it remarked ruefully. In Boston, Richard Cardinal Cushing, aware of the danger to his good friend John Kennedy, issued a statement of his own, pointing out that while the discussion of the relationship of moral issues to politics may take different forms that "whatever may be the custom elsewhere, the American tradition, of which Catholics form so loyal a part, is satisfied simply to call to public attention moral questions with their implications and leave to the conscience of the people the specific political decision which comes in the act of voting." Perhaps at the prodding of someone friendly to Kennedy, the Apostolic Delegate to the United States said that he was "confident the Roman Catholic hierarchy in the United States would never take political action similar to that of the Puerto Rican bishops." To this assertion, Cushing added his amen, declaring that "for ecclesiastical authority here to dictate the political voting of citizens . . . has never been a part of our history and I pray God that it never will be." The trouble with the statement of the Apostolic Delegate, as Senator Kennedy well knew, was that Puerto Rico is American soil and its bishops were American bishops. Kennedy told Sorensen that if the voters realized that, the election would be lost.

The voters did not realize it, and Kennedy wisely decided against devoting an entire speech to discuss the pastoral letter issued in Puerto Rico. It was more effective, he thought, just to repeat his own views in response to questions. An opportunity came on the television program "Face the Nation," on Reformation Sunday, when he restated his belief in a neutral, secular state in which all religions were permitted but none favored. He repeated that the Constitution and his conscience happened to be in close harmony and said:

> I want the people free to practice all their various religions. We are quite unique in this regard. I mean, many of the countries in Europe have a close union between church and state. We don't . . . all of us happen to believe that we don't want an official state church. If ninety-nine percent of the population were Catholics, I would still be opposed to it. I do not want civil power combined with religious power. Now that's my view. . . . I want to make it clear that I am committed as a matter of personal deep conviction, to this separation. Now, what is there left to say?

Reformation Sunday, October 30, 1960, came eight days before election. Hopes for a nationwide campaign against Catholicism were smothered by effective opposition within the Protestant churches. For the first time in many years, no mass Reformation Day rallies were held in St. Louis, Missouri; and ministers in other cities attacked Protestant bigotry rather than the thirteenth-century Catholic Church. The Anti-Defamation League of B'nai B'rith, the American Jewish Congress, the National Conference of Christians and Jews, the General Board of the National Council of the Churches of Christ in the U.S.A., the Fair Campaign Practices Committee, and the genial fairness of President Eisenhower and Republican candidate Nixon had succeeded along with Kennedy's forthright utterances in promoting a general climate of fair play.

In that climate of fairness, Kennedy narrowly defeated Richard Nixon for the presidency of the United States. Did he win in spite of, or because of, his religion? There is no doubt that Kennedy's religion helped reinforce the Democratic proclivities of most Catholics, about 80 percent of whom chose Kennedy. How many would have voted for Nixon against Stevenson, Humphrey, Johnson, or Symington is impossible to say. Surveys revealed that more than three out of five Catholics who voted for Eisenhower in 1956 switched to Kennedy, but it cannot be determined how many would have voted Republican if Kennedy had been a Protestant. The Catholic vote for Kennedy was 3 to 6 percentage points higher than for Truman in 1948, but it is almost as misleading to compare Democratic votes between 1948 and 1960 as if they were constant in a qualitative sense as it would be to compare dollars. The 1948 GOP candidate was the singularly unattractive Thomas E. Dewey, and while Nixon could not have had the appeal of an Eisenhower for Catholic voters, even against Adlai Stevenson, he did represent a post-McCarthy militant anticommunism which had been proved attractive to Catholics. Also, by 1960, large numbers of Catholics had moved to the suburbs, away from their lower-class and lower-middle-class origins and presumably were more vulnerable to Republican appeals on domestic issues.

The Survey Research Center of the University of Michigan, whose conclusions and data are highly respected by political scientists, reported that Kennedy lost more votes than he gained because of his religion. The center's study showed that Kennedy's overall loss from Protestant Democrats was at least 4,500,000 votes, considerably more than the number of Catholic Republicans and independents who chose Kennedy. Since the majority of Catholics who switched from Eisenhower to Kennedy probably would have voted for a Democratic candidate anyway, it seems likely that Kennedy's religion hurt his candidacy. It was certainly no surprise to most political analysts that Kennedy was hurt numerically; nor was it a surprise that his religion helped where it counted most, in the big-city states with large blocks of electoral votes. Being a Catholic may have cost him a victory in Florida, Kentucky, Virginia, Tennessee, and Oklahoma, but it may have elected him in Illinois and Michigan.

It was not surprising that a majority of Protestants had opposed Kennedy. They had opposed every Democratic presidential candidate since the Roosevelt election in 1936. Nor was it news that a substantial number of Catholics voted for the Democratic nominee as they had done for every Democratic presidential candidate in forty years with the single exception of the Eisenhower victory in 1956. What was most significant in the Kennedy victory was that the Massachusetts Catholic received a higher percentage vote from Negroes and Jews than Catholics, and more Protestants voted for him than all his Catholic and Jewish supporters combined. Since Protestant-Catholic tensions in America had actually become more complex and deep in many respects in the 1940's and 1950's than they had been in the 1920's, Kennedy's victory was a triumph of reasonableness and fair play.

The Protestant-Catholic division in America was still meaningful at the polls, but it was not decisive. Nixon won a huge plurality in the states of Iowa, Kansas, Nebraska, North and South Dakota, where the culture of rural Protestant America prevailed. He won a majority of voters in the border states, traditionally Democratic, yet Protestant with heavy pentecostal and pietistic influence, where fears of Roman Catholicism were widespread. Kennedy did best in the six states of New England, the most heavily Catholic section of the country, winning 56 percent of the votes cast, almost as much as Nixon had won in the five farm states of the Middle West. As Theodore H. White put it in his magnificent report, *The Making of the President, 1960:* "There is no doubt that millions of Americans, Protestants and Catholics, voted in 1960 primordially out of instinct, kinship, and past." White reported on four predominantly Baptist precincts in Milton County, Kentucky, which gave Kennedy only 35 percent of the vote, and of five predominantly Catholic precincts in the same county which awarded him 88 percent, a pattern which was repeated across the country.

Yet the results also showed unmistakably that approximately 40 percent of the Protestants of America voted for the Catholic candidate. Kennedy had taken his religion and his politics into a forceful, direct dialogue on the most persistent fear in American history, subversion of Americanism by the Roman Catholic Church, and he had won many converts to his view that Catholics could believe in, give expression to, and direct the future of the American Zion conceived and nurtured by Protestants more than two hundred years before.

VI

PROMISES TO KEEP

JOHN F. KENNEDY served only slightly more than a thousand days as President; but he was well on his way toward becoming an American hero even before his assassination. Kennedy's appeal, as evidenced by the outpouring of grief in Latin America, Africa, Asia, and even in the Soviet Union and Yugoslavia, went far beyond the United States. Like Franklin Roosevelt and Gandhi, he was able to communicate to millions outside of his own country. Like them, he seemed to bring hope to the nearly hopeless. Probably his widespread appeal derived from a combination of a profound sense of tragedy and an equally strong sense of confidence that man could live with and transcend tragedy. So often he seemed to be saying: The condition of man is universally troubled; the blame cannot be easily placed; there are no simple formulas to rectify it; but, leaving behind slogans and self-righteousness, answers can be found day by day.

Kennedy was a hero to millions in the world, but he was a special hero in his own culture because he eloquently articulated and dramatically exemplified its dominant values: personal independence and achievement; American mission; and a belief in a benevolent God who looks favorably on the new Zion of the United States of America.

Culture-heroes reflect the dominant values of a culture. They

189

may be saints (Mary) or gods (Zeus). They may be religious leaders (Mohammed or Moses). In some societies they are philosophers and teachers (Confucius, Maimonides, or Lao-tse). Elsewhere they may be conquerors (Alexander the Great or Napoleon). Or they may be queens and kings (Elizabeth I or Victoria and certain emperors of Japan). In European nations, poets, artists, and musicians such as Shakespeare, Hugo, Goethe, and Beethoven have been honored as heroes.

HEROES IN AMERICA

In the United States, heroes have not been noted for ideological, aesthetic, or religious qualities. Whether they are folk heroes or historical figures, they have been preeminently independent men of action. We have worshiped the great achievers, especially if they rise by one suspender and show unusual independence on the way. The frontier hero from Daniel Boone to John C. Frémont who conquers the wilderness and his enemies on his own has meant a great deal to Americans. After the election of Andrew Jackson until the twentieth century, almost every presidential candidate attempted to associate himself with the frontier. Some campaigns, such as that of William Henry Harrison, were virtually manufactured out of whole cloth in order to fit the design.

Another hero type has been the swashbuckling lumberjack, the most famous being the legendary Paul Bunyan, who was popular in the late 1800's and the early 1900's. Another is the lonely cowboy, usually self-sufficient, always on the move and fast on the draw, who remains a hero to the present day. The Horatio Alger hero who rises from rags to riches—see *Luck and Pluck, Sink or Swim, Ragged Dick,* or *Tattered Tom*—was a special favorite of Americans in the late nineteenth century. The great athlete in fact (Jim Thorpe or Babe Ruth) or fiction (Frank Merriwell or Jack Armstrong) have been worshiped as heroes in America.

Most important of all American heroes is the presidential hero who not only expresses the values of the culture in word and action but who unifies the pluralistic and divisive forces in American life as a national symbol. One may quarrel with the judgment of historian Allan Nevins that "no President was more universally esteemed and beloved during his first years in office than John F. Kennedy had been," but there is no question that the nation's youngest President was already an exciting popular hero to millions. He was quick-witted, handsome, athletic, and forceful. His wife was stunning, sensitive, and gracious. The children were bright and full of promise. Kennedy was a special hero to Catholics because of his singular accomplishment as the first Catholic President and to Negroes because of his late but wholehearted commitment to civil rights. He was admired by artists and intellectuals because of his encouragement to them. He was a favorite of youth, partly because he was young, and partly because he reached young people imbued with the traditional ideals of the culture—independence, achievement, and mission—through such ventures as the Peace Corps, but also because he seemed to understand a growing chorus of young Americans caught in the breakdown of traditional values who sensed the absurdity and tragedy of the twentieth century and who usually identified with something called the existential point of view. Despite his commitment to politics, Kennedy seemed to be unusually free from cant and cliché. He seemed to be saying that the old answers are no longer adequate.

Kennedy was not repudiating the old values of the culture. Like Jefferson, he believed in change. He agreed that each generation had to discover the meaning of life for itself, but also like Jefferson, he believed in personal independence, achievement, the mission of America, and in God; and like other presidential heroes, he spoke and wrote eloquently of his beliefs.

Neither Kennedy's general popularity nor his special appeal to such groups as Catholics, Negroes, Jews, artists and intellectuals, and young people would have been enough to assure him a place in the pantheon of presidential heroes which has included Washington, Jefferson, Jackson, Lincoln, Wilson, and the two Roosevelts. No Presidents had higher transient popularity than Grant or Coolidge. Nor would martyrdom alone have been enough to have established Kennedy as an authentic culture hero. Both Garfield and McKinley were shot down by assassins' bullets. The Kennedy legend grew after his death—countless schools and streets were named for him and more than ninety books were written about him within two years—because he fulfilled the requirements which Americans have always set for presidential heroes.

Just as transient popularity is no guarantee of lasting recognition, a record of political accomplishment does not necessarily elevate a President to the status of culture hero. James K. Polk achieved all of his major objectives; Woodrow Wilson failed in several of his. Performance without the eloquent articulation and personification of fundamental American values is not enough. Kennedy would be the first to admit that his legislative accomplishments were not extensive, but neither were Jefferson's nor Theodore Roosevelt's.

THE PRESIDENCY AND AMERICAN VALUES

To understand how Kennedy could become a presidential hero in less than three years it is necessary to look at the nature of the presidency in relation to American values and character. At the time of its creation, the presidency was a unique institution. Elected by a national vote rather than by the legislature, the office combined the ceremonial and religious significance usually invested in kings and the political power later given to prime ministers. Because the President speaks to the nation and for the nation with a single voice, he is in an extraordinary position to command the loyalty and the affection of the American people.

Originally, the presidency was intended to be a limited office. Its powers were to be curtailed precisely because Americans opposed any authority that would interfere with the personal independence of small farmers and merchants. While Americans nearly always have been anxious to constrain the powers of the presidency, they have supported independence and activity in Presidents. They have tended to insist on limiting the institution, but they have made culture-heroes out of those men who were most talented in acquiring and using power within the framework of those limitations. The outstanding example is Franklin D. Roosevelt. Elected to unprecedented third and fourth terms, Roosevelt had become a presidential hero even before his death. By November, 1945, just a few months after he died, polls showed approximately 60 percent of the American people favoring a constitutional amendment to limit future presidents to two full terms, and by the spring of 1951 the requisite number of state legislatures had ratified a constitutional amendment to prevent Americans from ever again indulging themselves in a third-term President.

The fear of a strong executive goes back to the sixteenth- and seventeenth-century struggles by middle-class Whig Protestants to extend their freedom by expanding the powers of Parliament against the king. The men who wrote the American Constitution were Whigs and Protestants who knew that the tyrannical Stuart kings and George III were checked by the growing independence and power of Parliament. They knew that the Petition of Rights had been forced on unwilling monarchs by the legislature. They realized that the English Bill of Rights was the result of the Glorious Revolution by English Protestants against James II. The arrogance of King George was fresh in their minds, and they identified popularly elected colonial legislatures with expanding personal freedom and overbearing governors appointed by the Crown with English attempts to limit independence. The problem of the writers of the Constitution was to create an executive strong enough to exercise what amounted to imperial rule over a vast domain but weak enough to stop even the slightest suspicion of potential tyranny. Public opinion, to the extent it existed, centered to a large degree on opposition to a strong executive. In *The Federalist* papers, Hamilton spent a good deal of time attempting to quiet the fears of many of his constituents that the President conceived in the new Constitution was an embryonic English king. Enemies of the Constitution attempted to picture the new executive as a king or Pope with the power to destroy individual liberty, and Hamilton attacked critics who saw the new President as "superior in dignity and splendor to those of the King of Great Britain ... seated on a throne surrounded with minions and mistresses, giving audience to the envoys of foreign potentates in all supercilious pomp of majesty."

In another *Federalist* paper, Hamilton disclaimed any alleged similarity between the presidency and the monarchy in England. Point by point, he compared the Crown to the American Chief Executive contemplated by Article II of the Constitution. Executive authority was to be vested in a single man but, argued Hamilton, that ended the resemblance to the king of Great Britain. The king, he pointed out, was a hereditary monarch; the President was to be elected for four years. The American President could be impeached; the king could be deposed only by assassination. The President would have only a qualified veto over legislation; the Crown then possessed an absolute negative. The President could not dissolve the legislature, which would be independent of him; the British monarch might prorogue Parliament at any time. The President would share his appointment power with the Senate; the king could create offices on his own.

The presidency was intended to be limited through the separation of legislative, judicial, and executive powers and through an ingenious system of checks and balances. "Let us separate," the founding fathers said, "the executive from the legislative power, but let us not separate them altogether." The President was given what were then thought to be minor legislative duties: he was obliged to report to Congress and he was given a qualified veto over legislation. The Congress, especially the Senate, was given extensive executive powers, including participation in the ratification of appointments and treaties. The Congress was to set up executive departments, define their authority, and appropriate money to staff them.

It was the power to appropriate—what the English used to call the power to vote supplies—which most Americans believed would assure congressional supremacy in the new federal system. That is why Madison could write that "in a Republic the Legislature in the last analysis necessarily predominates." It was no accident that the Executive was excluded from the amendment-making process. In *Federalist 53* either Hamilton or Madison wrote: "Wherever the supreme power of legislation has resided or has been supposed to reside, also has the full power to change the form of the government." This function was to be shared by Congress with the states, but not with the President. The legislature was also given full impeachment power, and the authority to create federal courts in addition to the Supreme Court and to define their jurisdiction. In the minds of most constitutional authors, the legislature was intended to be the final arbiter of disputes between branches of the federal government.

Large accretions of power to the presidency under Jackson, Lincoln, Wilson, and the two Roosevelts have made the office we know today, but one has only to read Woodrow Wilson's famous treatise on congressional government, written in 1885, to realize that even a hundred years after the Constitution was written, the presidency remained subordinate to Congress. Wilson wrote: "There is always a center of power: where in this system is that center? In whose hands is self-sufficiency lodged, and through what agency does that authority speak and act? ... Unquestionably the predominating and controlling force, the center and source of all motive and all regulative power is Congress."

PRESIDENTIAL HEROES

While nineteenth-century Americans viewed a strong presidency with suspicion, they repeatedly applauded energy and achievement in Presidents. From Washington on, they were wary of the institution but made heroes of the men who gave it life. Desiring personal independence for themselves, Americans feared power in the Executive; but they enthusiastically endorsed the very Presidents who displayed the same qualities of personal independence. The hagiolatry of the American culture-religion rests almost entirely upon the worship of Presidents who, when they are strong, provide considerable psychic income for Americans with few other unifying national symbols. When James Parton consulted a map of the United States in 1859 to discover which famous persons had given their names most frequently to American places, he found the name of Washington 198 times, Jackson 191, Franklin 136, and Jefferson 110.

Neither Jefferson, Jackson, Lincoln, Wilson, nor the two Roosevelts had the usual backgrounds of heroes in other cultures. They were not primarily soldiers, lawgivers, chieftains, or prophets. Their personalities varied widely: T.R. blustered and Jackson was earthy; Jefferson was cultured, Franklin Roosevelt urbane and Wilson imperious. Lincoln resembled none of them in background, looks, or demeanor. What they had in common was a capacity to articulate and personify the values of the culture. Because each of them eloquently interpreted and advanced the tenets of the culture-religion and personified them in action, they became heroes to generations after.

Although they were spokesmen for the culture-religion, they were not ideologues because Americans are essentially anti-ideological. They were primarily men of action who were anxious and willing to stretch the power of the presidency to the limit. They became heroes, not just because of their advocacy of personal freedom for others, but because they insisted on independence for themselves in relationship to the courts and Congress. They saw in the presidency (in Teddy Roosevelt's words) a "bully pulpit" from which to preach and act, and in being President (in Wilson's language) an opportunity "to be as big a man" as one could.

Madison and Jefferson were as one in their devotion to the values of personal independence and achievement and American mission, but they differed considerably in their ability to articulate and to exemplify those values in the presidency. Madison had been instrumental in the creation of an independent executive at the constitutional convention, and in Congress he played a key role in giving the President the power to remove the heads of executive departments. Once in office, he acquiesced in the prevailing republican view of legislative preeminence. He was a model of self-restraint, even deferring to a clique in the Senate in the selection of his own Cabinet. Finally, Madison was pushed by Congress into the War of 1812. Jefferson, by contrast, did not hesitate to use personal and institutional power to make the Louisiana Purchase, which he thought to be of dubious constitutionality but in the best interest of the nation. Jefferson, like Washington, probably would have been a culture-hero to succeeding generations even if he had not been President. The fact that both of them defended the independency of the presidency with considerable force against the legislature—as in Washington's neutrality proclamation and Jefferson's purchase of Louisiana—enhanced their status as heroes.

Action in the presidency is not enough to make a hero, but it is indispensable. Presidents who preside but do not lead may enjoy wide popularity but they can never become culture-heroes in the long run. The Presidents who became heroes were not synthesizers or harmonizers; they attempted to impose their view of the national interest on Congress. Because they created issues, Washington, Jefferson, Jackson, Lincoln, Wilson, and the two Roosevelts were deeply hated as well as loved in their time.

Jackson radically transformed the power base of the presidency. Both Hamilton (for Washington) and Jefferson had established their power in Congress almost as a prime minister does in England. Each built his party in the legislature through skillful behind-the-scenes maneuvering, but Jackson was the first President to back his institutional power with mass support. In his attacks on the Bank of the United States and the sectionalism of the South, Jackson spoke boldly and acted decisively. To all future Presidents he left a legacy of presidential power which consisted of four parts: first, a theory that the President, as much as Congress, is a direct representative of the people; second, belief that the veto power should be exercised when the President disagrees with Congress on policy as well as on constitutional grounds; third, a conviction that the President possesses complete power to remove subordinate executive officers; and finally, the knowledge that presidential leadership requires the support of a political party based upon mass participation and organized for national action.

James Madison, Franklin Pierce, and James Buchanan proved that national crisis is not enough to make a President into a culture-hero. Abraham Lincoln demonstrated that the American people need and want decisive, independent action in the presidency in order to advance freedom. Probably no President has done more to promote freedom in America; yet Lincoln, more than any other Chief Executive, assumed dictatorial and unconstitutional powers. No President before or since has been deified as Lincoln, and no other Chief Executive so clearly violated the American conception of limited power in the presidency. In personal matters, Lincoln was often indecisive, slow, and even weak; in political matters, he had the ability to knife through a mass of issues and to act decisively. Of equal importance, he had the gift of words to give expression to the most fundamental ideals of the culture.

Lincoln came closer than any other President to being a dictator. He clamped a blockade on the ports of seceded states, a measure which had heretofore been regarded as contrary to the Constitution except when the government was engaged in a foreign war. He directed the Secretary of the Treasury to advance two million dollars of unappropriated funds to three private citizens of New York who were unauthorized to use it. He directed that the post office be closed to treasonable correspondence and authorized the arrest by civil and military agencies of persons alleged to be disloyal. He told the commanding general of the Army to suspend the writ of habeas corpus between Washington and Philadelphia and later in a small area between Washington and New York, despite the almost unanimous opinion that the constitutional clauses regulating the suspension of the writ was directed to Congress alone. Lincoln solved that particular problem, as Franklin Roosevelt was to meet a similar situation later, by having his attorney general write an opinion justifying his action (this one stipulated that the President had the power and duty to suspend the writ in times of crisis). When Chief Justice Taney disagreed in the Merryman case, Lincoln followed Jackson's precedent in the Cherokee Indians case, when a decision by Chief Justice Marshall went against the President. Then Jackson had said, "John Marshall has made his decision, let him enforce it." Lincoln, less truculent than Old Hickory, ignored Taney's decision.

Because Lincoln combined poetry with power as no other President, he is first among American culture-heroes. His qualities of patience, tolerance, humor, sympathy, empathy, and kindliness are rare in anyone, let alone a politician. But those qualities of character would not be enough to make Lincoln a culture-hero. His decency was matched by a personal independence and pragmatic activism in the presidency.

William Howard Taft and Theodore Roosevelt provide a contrast which explains a great deal about American values and character. Taft, when thought of favorably at all, is regarded as a jolly and decent fat man who served as President and Chief Justice (a view which underestimates his really important contributions). T.R. has become a genuine hero to many. The major difference

between them was not in matters of policy. It was in the super-
abundance of energy and decisiveness which Roosevelt brought to
his job and the eloquence with which he interpreted American
values. After both men left the presidency they wrote books in
which they described their theories of presidential power. Roosevelt's doctrine has come down as the theory of stewardship. He
wrote in his autobiography that the most important factor in his
administration, apart from certain personal qualities he demanded
in subordinates, was "the theory that the executive power was
limited only by specific restrictions and prohibitions appearing in
the Constitution or imposed by Congress under its constitutional
powers." Roosevelt criticized Taft for welcoming congressional
investigations of executive offices which he, Roosevelt, would not
tolerate. T.R. boasted that he appointed unpaid presidential com-
missions to report to him without the sanction of Congress, but
that Taft, the weakling, discontinued them under pressure from
the legislature.

Taft claimed that "the President can exercise no power which
cannot be fairly and reasonably traced to some specific grant of
power or justly implied ... and necessary to its exercise." In retrospect, it seems clear that Roosevelt's and Taft's theories were
rationalizations of personal temperament. Taft preferred to wait
and mediate. T.R. wanted to act and control. For all his adolescent
blustering, Roosevelt—there were even teddy bears—became one
of the most popular heroes in American history. For T.R., every
battle was a charge up San Juan Hill, himself at the head of the
forces of righteousness, rallying his army, relishing the fight. For
generations afterward, Americans applauded.

To the extent that Woodrow Wilson achieved the status of culture-hero, it has been mainly because of his eloquence in expound-
ing American ideals and his assertion of presidential power. "The
President is at liberty, both in law and conscience, to be as big a
man as he can," wrote Wilson. During his first administration, he
displayed incredible initiative and energy in accomplishing legis-

lative reforms which have stood the test of time. His strong sense
of mission—"making the world safe for democracy"—was ethnocentric, and, in retrospect, showed a deficiency in his understanding
of human nature and history, but it touched the messianic quality
of American personality in a powerful way. Probably the reason
Wilson has not meant more to Americans is that, unlike Jackson
and Roosevelt who showed their greatest strength under incessant
attack, the former Princeton professor was badly rattled after he
lost control of Congress in 1918.

By contrast, Franklin Roosevelt was effective even under strong
attack. He eloquently spoke and wrote about the ideals of the
culture-religion but was also an unusually skillful and crafty politician. As was true of other Presidents who became culture-heroes,
Roosevelt was a dynamic, active Chief Executive who fought with
Congress and the courts to maintain his independence, impose his
will, and implement his view of American ideals and interests.
Americans still cite the whirlwind of Roosevelt's first hundred
days in office with approving admiration and remember his four
freedoms as an expression of America's messianic belief in liberty.

In his short time in the presidency, Kennedy fulfilled the requirements of an American culture-hero. The trauma of his murder and
the dignity and grandeur of the national weeks of mourning which
followed probably will help to enlarge the Kennedy legend for
generations to come.

Kennedy in the presidency epitomized the values of the culture-
religion of Americanism. From early childhood he had been trained
in the importance of personal independence and achievement.
Except for instilling a staunch loyalty to the immediate family
and convictions about independence and achievement, Kennedy's
father did not try to force a particular line of thinking or career
on Jack. Joe once boasted to a friend that he had set up trust
funds for each of his children so that they would be completely
independent financially and "could look me in the eye and tell
me to go to hell." He encouraged John and his older brother Joe,

junior, to study with the socialist theoretician, Harold J. Laski, at
the London School of Economics, even though the father thought
Laski was "a nut and a crank." The elder Kennedy relished a good
verbal battle at the dinner table, especially if the two boys fought
on the same side against him.

The mother, Rose, attended Mass early each morning and assumed the task of hearing the children in their nightly prayers and
their catechism lessons every Friday afternoon. The father made
certain that the boys would achieve a degree of independence even
from their religious background by sending them to Dexter Acad-
emy in Brookline, where they may have been the only Catholics
in attendance, and to Choate and Harvard, where they rubbed
shoulders with the sons of upper-class Yankees. Joe Kennedy was
determined that his sons would be able to stand on their own two
feet, encounter the Protestant world and succeed within it. His
own father, Patrick, was a saloonkeeper and a political boss in the
tough North End of Boston, who had virtually no social contact
with the highborn, well-to-do people of Beacon Hill. Joe had
amassed great wealth in banking, real estate, movies, and the liquor
industry, but he was blackballed when he sought membership in
the Anglo-Saxon Cohasset Country Club. Determined that his
sons would not be treated as outsiders, Joe Kennedy assumed responsibility for training them in self-reliance and the will to win.

The children were pushed into individual sports to develop
initiative and competitive feelings. "Daddy was always entering us
in public swimming races, in the different age categories so we
didn't have to swim against each other. And he did the same thing
with us in sailing races," said President Kennedy's sister Eunice.
"The thing he always kept telling us was that coming in second
was just no good. The important thing was to win—don't come
in second or third—that doesn't count—but win, win, win." The
father would not permit failure. When the boys raced on Nantucket Sound, he followed them in his boat and berated them in
the evening for the mistakes he noted. The boy who sloughed off

in a sailing race was sent to eat in the kitchen in disgrace. The elder Kennedy wrote Jack at Choate that while he did not expect his second son to be a genius, he wanted him to get all there was out of what God had given him.

Joe Kennedy once remarked that no interest of his was as great as his interest in his children. He told a reporter that when Jack and Joe, junior, even as small children, were scheduled to play in a baseball or football game, he would try to attend the game, no matter how busy he was or even if he was as far away as the west coast. "That way," he said, "they know you are interested, really interested, and when you tell them something it means something."

At his father's table, John Kennedy learned to fight; in the touch football games at Hyannis and on Nantucket Sound, he learned the rewards of victory; but he also knew defeat. He frequently lost fights with his older brother. (When the two boys raced around the block on bicycles in opposite directions and collided, Joe, junior, picked himself up without a scratch, but Jack had to have 28 stitches.) Jack was not only younger than Joe, junior; he was less robust and frequently ill. He could not possibly match his brother's athletic prowess at Choate or Harvard, particularly in the sport that meant the most, football. He played hard and wanted to win desperately at anything he tried; his stamina was good and his will unquenchable; but his physique was not always adequate.

Winning games at Choate and Harvard was important, but young Kennedy did not seem to have any particular vocational goal in mind. He toyed with the idea of law school following graduation but discarded that plan in favor of graduate courses in business administration at Stanford University. He left Stanford after only a semester in February, 1941, and took an aimless tour of Latin America. In the summer, he decided to enlist in the Army, but was disqualified because of a back injury he had suffered in a college football scrimmage three years before. When he was rejected by the Navy too, he worked for five months to strengthen his back through exercises, and in September, only a few months before Pearl Harbor, he passed the Navy fitness test.

His older brother, Joe, junior, talked of running for President even as an adolescent. There was no question as to what Joe wanted; it was the presidency, nothing less. By July, 1944, he had completed two years of duty as a bomber pilot in the European theater and had received orders to return home. Instead, he volunteered to fly a Liberator bomber with 22,000 pounds of high explosives over heavily fortified Nazi submarine pens on the Belgian coast. The plane exploded over the English Channel and Joe Kennedy, Jr., was dead.

Jack Kennedy said later that he might never have run for office if his brother had lived. He might have become a journalist, an officer in the foreign service, or a professor of political science. He might eventually have gone into politics himself; but it was Joe's death that opened up the possibility of running for Congress which led him to the highest office in the land.

KENNEDY AS A CATHOLIC

In the course of his childhood, adolescence, and young manhood, Jack Kennedy developed extraordinary self-confidence to match his belief in the importance of self-sufficiency and personal achievement. Nowhere could this be seen more clearly than in his feelings and attitudes about his religion. From the evidence available, Kennedy did not feel either inferior or superior because of his Catholicism. To feel so would be, in some measure, to be dependent on it. Even with respect to the religion of his birth, Kennedy had a sense of detachment.

It was after spending one year (his thirteenth) at a Catholic prep school, Canterbury, that Jack Kennedy was sent to the select Episcopal Choate. There and at Harvard he periodically went to church and received Communion, neither hiding his Catholicism nor boasting about it. At Harvard, he belonged to the St. Paul's

Catholic Club, but he also mixed with non-Catholics on the Harvard *Crimson,* the Spee and Hasty Pudding clubs, and in classes.

As a youth, he appears not to have been particularly interested in devotionals. Nor did he reveal any special interest in the often praised Catholic virtues of obedience and piety. He was attracted rather to assertive and individualistic virtues extolled in one of his favorite poems, William Ernest Henley's "Invictus." Henley thanked

> . . . whatever gods may be,
> For my unconquerable soul.

and concluded:

> It matters not how strait the gate,
>   How charged with punishments the scroll,
> I am the master of my fate;
>   I am the captain of my soul.

To assert that one is the captain of one's soul is to state the essence of the Arminian faith of Americanism and come close to an important aspect of the Catholic heresy of Pelagianism. It was a faith which Kennedy would carry into the presidency and defend in speech and action. Kennedy made it clear repeatedly that his most powerful belief was in the capacity of man to master his fate, overcome circumstances, and mold his environment. His speeches in the presidency drew heavily for inspiration from others who shared that belief. He probably quoted Jefferson more than anyone else but other favorites included William Ellery Channing (the Unitarian), Patrick Henry (a Deist), and the anticlerical Giuseppe Mazzini. It probably did not occur to Kennedy that he frequently quoted from men who had expressed hostility to Catholicism, including Carl Schurz, William Jennings Bryan, and George Bernard Shaw. Although Kennedy would never have endorsed their anti-Catholic views, he was perfectly aware that he was somewhat detached from his own religion. He once wrote to John Cogley of *Commonweal:* "It is hard for a Harvard man to answer questions in theology. I imagine my answers will cause heartburn at Fordham and B.C. [Boston College]." Another time, when Arthur Schlesinger, Jr., handed him a speech draft in the 1960 campaign with the observation that it was possibly too Catholic, Kennedy replied with a smile, "You Unitarians [meaning Schlesinger and Sorensen] keep writing Catholic speeches. I guess I'm the only Protestant around here." Kennedy was also aware that his strong views on the separation of church and state might lead some Catholics to suspect his commitment to the Church. He reminded a 1961 gridiron dinner audience of a popular anti-Catholic story following Al Smith's defeat in 1928. As told by gleeful non-Catholics, Governor Smith, immediately on learning of his loss to Hoover, sent a one-word telegram to the Pope: "Unpack!" Tongue in cheek, John Kennedy said that after his stand against federal aid to parochial schools, the Pope sent him a one-word wire. This one said: "Pack"

Unlike Al Smith, John Kennedy lived almost entirely apart from the world of Holy Name societies, Knights of Columbus, and Communion breakfasts. Rather than the typical deference of politicians toward men who wear the collar, Kennedy enjoyed quips at their expense. Once speaking at a dinner with an overweight monsignor, Kennedy called it an "inspiration ... to be here with ... one of those lean ascetic clerics who show the effect of constant fast and prayer, and bring the message to us in the flesh." Once Kennedy even took off on his favorite passage from Ecclesiastes ("A time to weep, and a time to laugh; a time to mourn, and a time to dance") with a political quip "A time to fish, and a time to cut bait."

Kennedy's irreverence did not constitute a rejection of Catholicism. Religion was something one accepted as decided by birth, like blue eyes or the fact that one's right leg was shorter than one's left. It should not be necessary to defend one's blue eyes; nor was it particularly important that other people had brown or hazel eyes. Kennedy accepted the Catholicism he had inherited without apology. He does not appear to have gone through the agonizing doubts felt by so many liberal, intellectual Catholics. While he resented politicians who paraded their religion for political purposes, he was proud of the set of military identification dog tags which were inscribed: "Kennedy, John F . . . Commander-in-Chief-O [blood type]—Roman Catholic."

Cardinal Cushing has written that he does not think that Kennedy would want to be called "a very religious man" in the usual sense. Although he regularly attended Mass each Sunday, he did not, according to Sorensen, care "a whit for theology." But there is no doubt that Jack Kennedy believed in a supernatural force usually called God, and there is no reason to believe that he did not accept Catholic dogma on matters of faith and morals, although he kept his opinions on such matters to himself. Sorensen has said that in all their eleven years of close association, Kennedy never discussed his personal views on man's relation to God. But Kennedy's speeches, particularly after he was elected, frequently included references from the Protestant version of the Bible and often asked for divine guidance; and Cardinal Cushing has said that Kennedy as President became a more prayerful man than he was before.

To Kennedy, being a good Catholic did not mean either that he had to be surrounded by Catholics or that he could not sharply disagree with clerical authorities on questions of public policy. Kennedy brought several Irish Catholics with him to the White House from Massachusetts in the same manner that President Johnson has staffed his office with long-time political associates from Texas, but he was disinterested in the religious backgrounds of men he considered for high positions. His personal secretary in the White House was a Methodist, and his closest staff associate a Unitarian (Sorensen's three assistants were all Jews). With the appointments of Arthur Goldberg as Secretary of Labor and Abraham Ribicoff as Secretary of Health, Education, and Welfare, there were two Jews in the Cabinet for the first time in history.

Kennedy would not accept the view that priests had any special competence in public matters. A cleric who was angered by his answer at a Catholic girls' school that "recognition of Red China was not a moral issue," queried: "Senator Kennedy, do you not believe that all law comes from God?" The senator answered heatedly, "I'm a Catholic so of course I believe it—but that has nothing to do with international law."

ON CHURCH AND STATE

On church-state issues, Kennedy in the presidency maintained his position that a strict separation was the best possible arrangement in a pluralistic, democratic society, despite mounting pressure from members of the Catholic hierarchy. The President's hopes for a rapid passage of a bill giving federal financial assistance to public schools were smashed when Cardinal Spellman denounced Kennedy's task force report on education as "unthinkable" for not giving parochial schools equal consideration. The President complained privately that the cardinal had never said a word about Eisenhower's bills for aid to public schools only, and prepared for a long, divisive and unsuccessful fight to push through legislation limited to assisting public schools according to his view of the Constitution. When the National Catholic Welfare Conference, speaking for the hierarchy in the United States, demanded the defeat of Kennedy's bill unless loans to nonpublic schools were added, the President wondered aloud at a press conference if some clergymen had changed their views "merely because of the religion of the occupant of the White House."

Kennedy realized that many Catholic parents resented the burden of what they thought to be double taxation. But he saw no other alternative. Public funds made it possible for everyone to go to school. If Catholic, Lutheran, or Jewish parents wanted to send their children to special schools, they should pay the costs. The President had no objection to amending the National Defense Education Act, first passed in 1958, to increase loan funds for private school education in areas necessary for national defense, but he was strongly opposed to any breach in what he thought to be the constitutional wall of separation of church and state.

A few Catholic publications, many laymen, and Cardinal Cushing supported the President's general position, although not in every detail; but Kennedy was correct in believing that a majority of the hierarchy were opposed to both him and his bill. Spellman declared that passage of the school-aid bill would mean the end of Roman Catholic parochial schools in the United States. Tension in the country and in the House of Representatives mounted. One group of legislators was opposed to aiding religious schools in any respect; another vowed to stop any bill that did not include such aid. Finally, a combination of conservative Democrats and nearly all Republicans killed the measure. Until his death, Kennedy believed that the kind of aid which Spellman advocated was not only unconstitutional but harmful for the country; but he was constantly on the lookout for permissible ways to help Catholic children as well as non-Catholics further their education.

Kennedy also disagreed with a majority of the hierarchy on the question of religion in the public schools. Since he believed religion to be a personal matter, he defended the Supreme Court's 1963 decision banning the recitation of formal prayers and Bible reading in the public schools. There was an immediate call from Catholic leaders and Protestant churchmen, supported by many powerful governors and members of Congress, for a constitutional amendment to permit religious activity in the schools.

Evangelist Billy Graham called the Supreme Court ruling "another step toward secularism." Cardinal Spellman warned that it was another example of the aim of secularists "to strip America of all her religious tradition." Opinion polls showed a majority of voters to be unsympathetic to the Court's decision. Yet when the President was asked about the furore at his press conference, he urged "that we support the Supreme Court's decisions even where we may not agree with them. . . . We have in this case a very easy remedy and that is to pray ourselves. And I would think that it would be a welcome reminder to every American family that we can pray a good deal more at home, we can attend our churches with a good deal more fidelity, and we can make the true meaning of prayer much more important in the lives of all our children."

IRISH OR HARVARD?

The President also opposed a majority of the hierarchy on other issues. He maintained a strong position in opposition to appointing an ambassador to the Vatican, remarking to a press conference that he saw no need for more direct communication with the Holy See than was provided by the embassy in Rome. Kennedy supported efforts of the federal government in the area of population control by increasing research grants and supporting the United Nations efforts to make birth control information available to other countries requesting it; and he vetoed a bill providing for the censorship of obscene publications in the District of Columbia on the ground that it had serious constitutional defects.

Kennedy's favorite poet, Robert Frost, advised the President-elect to be more Irish than Harvard. Probably Frost meant that Kennedy should be tough, loyal, and courageous, qualities the Irish had shown through the centuries. Perhaps Frost also meant that the young Chief Executive should be guided by his heart and his feelings even more than by his head. Whatever he meant, it would have been impossible for Kennedy to be more Irish than Harvard and become a culture-hero. He enjoyed his Irish friends from Boston and he loved his sentimental journey to Ireland in 1963, but he symbolized exactly the opposite of many of those characteristics which were considered to be stereotypically Irish in American politics. To outsiders, the Irish were often seen as tribalistically defensive in their Catholicism, fatalistic and submissive, anti-intellectual and suspicious of liberalism, and unalterably opposed to coexistence with the Communist nations. As seen, Kennedy was not a defensive Catholic. Far from fatalistic, he told one audience in rejecting the inevitability of war that "our problems are man-made; therefore they can be solved by man. And man can be as big as he wants." In his second State of the Union Message he said that his program was designed to overcome "arbitrary or irrational" restraints on human activity and "to make society the servant of the individual and the individual the source of progress." In a speech to the Liberal party of New York in 1960, he said that he believed "in human dignity as the source of national purpose, in human liberty as the source of national action . . . and in the human mind as the source of our invention and our ideas." He concluded: "Liberalism . . . faith in man's ability . . . reason and judgment . . . is our best and only hope in the world today."

Liberalism had been a bad word in many Irish-American homes for generations. Kennedy's thirst for ideas, his joy in the company of intellectuals, and his support of artistic activity made him seem quite different from other Irish Catholics who had served in high administrative posts before. Except for Thomas Corcoran, the Irishmen around F. D. Roosevelt, such as Farley and Kennedy's own father, were distrustful of theoreticians and intellectuals. High-placed Irish Catholics in the Truman administration, such as Maurice Tobin, Secretary of Labor, Matthew Connelly, Truman's appointments secretary, and Attorneys General J. Howard Mc-Grath and James McGranery, were competent in their fields but not known for intellectual curiosity. (James Forrestal, who was suspicious of liberals, was an exception.) Kennedy was not the only intellectual Irish Catholic in politics. Senator Brien McMahon of Connecticut, author of the law establishing civilian control of atomic energy, had a brilliant and liberal record before his death in 1952. Eugene McCarthy of Wisconsin, a self-styled liberal intellectual Catholic (he is supposed to have said that he was more intellectual than Stevenson, more liberal than Humphrey, and more Catholic than Kennedy), resembled a college professor even more than the junior senator from Massachusetts. But neither had a national following and neither was a particular darling of the Irish, such as Curley or Joseph McCarthy.

Kennedy went to the universities for some of his closest advisers. He probably appointed a higher proportion of academicians—there were fifteen Rhodes scholars—to important posts than any of his predecessors, including Franklin Roosevelt. He invited artists and intellectuals to the White House regardless of their political predilections in order to give recognition to excellence of spirit and mind. He entertained Nobel prize-winning scientist Linus Pauling at a party on the evening of the same day that Pauling had picketed the White House in protest against Kennedy's policies in Vietnam. He honored cellist Pablo Casals with a Presidential Freedom Award, although Casals' deep and long hostility against the Catholic-supported Franco regime in Spain was well known.

Kennedy's liberalism on welfare state issues was consistent with the Irish Catholic tradition in politics, but his profound commitment to the cause of Negro rights was not. Ever since the days when abolitionist societies were often led by anti-Catholic ideologues, most Irishmen appear to have been suspicious of civil rights advocates. Kennedy himself was aware that his decision to make the cause of Negro rights a moral as well as a political and constitutional issue would bring disapproval in the Polish and Irish Catholic communities of the North where Negro pressure was mounting for integrated schools and Negro assertiveness was associated in the minds of many Catholics with crime in the streets. Although Kennedy's decision to give leadership to the cause of civil rights had been preceded by a period of hesitancy, his strong advocacy of freedom of the mind specifically and civil liberties generally went back to his service in the Senate, where he was on record against loyalty oaths and unrestricted wire tapping.

Although Kennedy eventually was accepted by most liberals as their leader, he was suspect for a long time for having failed to attack Senator Joseph McCarthy when they both served in the upper chamber. The President had never been a McCarthy supporter, but a critical illness kept him from delivering the prepared speech in support of the censure motion against McCarthy in 1954, and he had never spoken against McCarthy in public, perhaps out of respect to his father, who warmly endorsed the Wisconsin senator, or his brother Robert, who at one time was employed on the staff of McCarthy's committee, or in deference to the vast majority of his Irish Catholic constituents who were wildly enthusiastic about McCarthy. Or possibly Kennedy believed that the best way to deal with the issues raised by McCarthy was not to denounce the man but to be counted when the votes were taken on those issues. In addition to his record on civil liberties, he voted against the confirmation of Robert Lee, a McCarthy protégé, as a member of the Federal Communications Commission, and of Scott McLeod, the McCarthyite security chief of the State Department, as ambassador to Ireland. Although some never forgave Kennedy's failure to denounce McCarthy publicly (he was caustic in private), most liberals eventually agreed that Kennedy's commitment to liberalism, rationality, and basic decency in politics made him the very antithesis of McCarthy.

On cold war issues, Kennedy completely abandoned the rhetoric of liberation which had been promoted by John Foster Dulles and was so popular among Polish and Irish Catholics. There was no talk from Kennedy about rolling back Communists in Eastern Europe. He consistently promoted a policy of peaceful coexistence with the Soviet Union, and appointed to key positions the very people who had been favorite targets of the right-wing crusade against coexistence (Chester Bowles, Adlai Stevenson, Arthur Schlesinger, Jr., George Kennan, Charles Bohlen, Paul Nitze, and others). Kennedy neutralized Laos, reduced the American commitment in the Congo, and sought unsuccessfully to limit American military involvement in Vietnam. In September, 1961, he called for a "peace race" in a speech before the United Nations General Assembly. Later, he achieved what he called his greatest triumph, the ban on nuclear tests in the atmosphere. At American University in 1963, he praised the Russian people for their many achievements, saying that "no government or social system is so evil that its people must be considered as lacking in virtue." To thaw the cold war—not win it—was Kennedy's strongest ambition in the presidency.

Not only did Kennedy make it abundantly clear that he was independent of ecclesiastical pressures and of Irish Catholic stereotypes, but he asserted his independence in relationship to Congress too, and dominated his own administration in the tradition of presidential culture-heroes. After Eisenhower's deference to Congress, and John Foster Dulles and George Humphrey, Kennedy seemed especially to epitomize presidential self-reliance. No President is self-reliant in the sense that he can make decisions without the help of others; but Kennedy communicated an enthusiasm for the responsibility and authority that was his. Following his Cuban confrontation with Khrushchev, he told the American people: "I bear the responsibility of the presidency of the United States and it is my duty to make decisions that no adviser and no ally can make for me." Even after the debacle at the Bay of Pigs, Kennedy acknowledged sole responsibility for the disastrous, abortive invasion of Castro's Cuba. Probably nothing contributed more to Kennedy's image of personal independence besides his stand on church-state issues than his successful fight against the representatives of the steel industry to prevent a substantial rise in steel prices in 1962. In that confrontation Kennedy appeared in the tradition of Jackson fighting the Bank or Franklin Roosevelt denouncing the money changers and telling businessmen that they were not going to fool the President of the United States and defy the national interest. The immediate reaction in the country was ambivalent. Many thought that Presidents ought not to employ such massive power against businessmen as Kennedy did in using the F.B.I., stimulating congressional investigations, and threatening antitrust suits; not long after the President's victory, negative reactions faded. What mattered later was that Kennedy had defended the presidency and the public interest as he saw it.

KENNEDY AS CULTURE-HERO

Kennedy was as devoted to the cult of personal achievement as Benjamin Franklin had been. His favorite poetry, according to his wife, praised the natural and active virtues in man's nature. He liked Tennyson's line: "How dull it is to pause, to make an end,/To rust unburnished, not to shine in use!" And he quoted approvingly Tennyson's old Ulysses who, though "made weak by time and fate," remained "strong in will/To strive, to seek, to find, and not to yield." Longfellow's "Psalm of Life," he took as his own credo, believing that neither enjoyment nor sorrow "Is our destined end or way;/But to act, that each to-morrow/Find us farther than to-day." No President ever took more to heart or was more systematically trained to live by Longfellow's advice to ". . . be up and doing,/With a heart for any fate;/Still achieving, still pursuing. . . ." He knew by heart a favorite passage from Shakespeare's *King Henry V* in which the sovereign, preparing for battle on St. Crispin's day, disparages the "gentlemen in England, now a-bed" who "Shall think themselves accurs'd they were not here,/And hold their manhoods cheap whiles any speaks/That fought with us upon Saint Crispin's day." Returning from his wedding trip in October, 1953, Kennedy had his wife read his favorite poem, "I Have a Rendezvous with Death" by Alan Seeger, revealing his own desire to confront dramatic challenges and accept heavy burdens. Mrs. Kennedy later learned by heart the words he liked so much:

> But I've a rendezvous with death
> At midnight in some flaming town,
> When spring trips north again this year,

And I to my pledged word am true,
I shall not fail that rendezvous.

Kennedy's favorite poet was Robert Frost, and the President never tired of quoting Frost's "But I have promises to keep,/And miles to go before I sleep,/And miles to go before I sleep." He was, as Mrs. Kennedy has written, always "looking for new margins," because "life piled on life was all too little for him." The books he read and liked best were almost entirely biography and history, and he especially loved political biography. The point of view or the position of a hero did not matter. (That also was true of the men he described in *Profiles in Courage*.) Sam Houston, Lincoln, Calhoun, Talleyrand, and John Quincy Adams all fascinated him.

Kennedy believed in his own ability to influence events and in the capacity of Americans to protect and extend freedom. Presidential heroes have always set their sights high and communicated a sense of confidence and hope not only to their own generation but to others that followed. Kennedy was fond of urging the American people to leave "fear astern," in Jefferson's phrase, and of reminding them, in the words of Franklin Roosevelt: "The only thing we have to fear is fear itself." In his third State of the Union Message he welcomed the winds of change and boasted that they were turning in America's favor. To the National Democratic Convention which nominated him he said: "My call is to the young in heart, regardless of age; to the stout in spirit, regardless of party; to all who respond to the scriptural call: 'Be strong and of good courage: be not afraid, neither be dismayed!' " And then: "Recall with me the words of Isaiah: 'They that wait upon the Lord ... shall mount up with wings as eagles; they shall run, and not be weary. ...' " Kennedy concluded, "Then we shall prevail."

America's presidential heroes have always asked for energy, action, and achievement over obstacles. From the time of his campaign, the theme of which was to get America moving again, Kennedy complained about the missile gap (which later proved to have been exaggerated), stagnation in the economy, and a sense of purposelessness in American life in the 1950's. He thrust his finger forward, shook it at audiences from Burbank to the Bronx, and told America it must get moving again. Whether he was talking about space, a race to the moon, or economic growth, Kennedy insisted that the United States must be first, not second or third, but first.

He told a New Jersey audience in September, 1960: "It is tempting to try to hide in the storm shelter—or the bomb shelter —tempting to try to escape the winds of change. But it cannot be done. We have to act—and to act along new lines." Two days later he told a Raleigh, North Carolina, audience that the journey ahead would require "effort and sacrifice. But I believe that this people of this state—and the people of all America—can again begin its forward march." Shortly before the election he reminded an audience in Warm Springs, Georgia, of the problems facing the United States, and asked them to remember the speech which Franklin Roosevelt had written for delivery after his death, which closed: "The only limit to our realization of tomorrow will be our doubts of today. Let us move forward with strong and active faith." To the United Nations in September, 1963, Kennedy urged a continuation of the struggle for human progress and referred to Luke: "No man who puts his hand to the plow and looks back is fit for the kingdom of God." Another favorite quotation came from Phillips Brooks, who advised Americans: "Do not pray for tasks equal to your powers. Pray for powers equal to your tasks." Kennedy liked to quote Archimedes, "Give me a place where I can stand—and I shall move the world." He quoted from William Bradford to an Inter-American Economic and Social Council meeting: "All great and honorable actions are accompanied with great difficulties and must be both enterprised and overcome with answerable courage." He reminded a New York audience that it was Theodore Roosevelt who said: "The credit belongs to the man who is actually in the arena—whose face is marred by dust and sweat

and blood—who knows the great enthusiasms, the great devotions
—and spends himself in a worthy cause—who at best if he wins
knows the thrill of high achievement—and if he fails, at least fails
while daring greatly."

Kennedy not only called for action; he epitomized it. His whirlwind of activity—executive orders, legislative proposals, and trips
to Vienna and Berlin—put him constantly on the front pages and
left an indelible impression of energy and achievement, even when
achievement was more apparent than real. He was aware that a
President who takes strong action disturbs the tranquility of the
people and divides the nation. As the first President in history
to put the full weight of his office behind the Negro struggle for
justice, he faced opposition from key congressional leaders and the
indifference and hostility of most white Americans. On the morning of his murder in Dallas, Texas, the *Dallas Morning News* published an advertisement which contained a number of questions
virtually accusing the President of cooperating with the American
Communist party. Even after the assassination, a fourth-grade class
in Dallas was reported as clapping and cheering at the news. Kennedy suffered in temporary popularity because he took strong
stands on several issues, but without such action he could not
possibly have become a legend in his own time.

Like other presidential heroes, Kennedy preached and exemplified personal independence and achievement; like them, he also
communicated a strong belief in America's mission to promote
freedom and prosperity. The slogan, "The New Frontier," was intended to stimulate the same messianic impulses which had responded to Wilson's New Freedom and Franklin Roosevelt's New
Deal. From his inaugural address, when he urged Americans not
to ask what their country could do for them but to ask what they
could do for their country, Kennedy's speeches repeatedly called
for action to fulfill America's destiny. If each individual had a
mission to live up to his potentialities, it was the national mission
to promote freedom everywhere. To a Miami, Florida, audience in

October, 1960, he exclaimed: "If we move forward, freedom moves forward. . . . I sound the alarm not with the idea that if this country is doomed, but with the idea that if this country moves again, nothing can stop it." And then from First Corinthians, he asked: " 'Who will prepare for the battle if the trumpet sounds an uncertain note?' " He told a San Francisco audience that he believed that the nation had reached a turning point in its life when "we can make this a time of greatness—a time of which history will truly say, when reciting our perils, that we lived by the scriptural injunction: 'Everyone shall help his neighbor, and shall say to his brother: be of good courage.' " In North Carolina, Thomas Wolfe's native state, he reminded his Raleigh audience of Wolfe's belief that " 'the true fulfillment of our spirit, of our people, of our might, and immortal land is yet to come.' " To a Waterbury, Connecticut, audience two days before the election, Kennedy spoke again of the American mission of freedom. He recalled to his listeners that at the time of the American Revolution, Thomas Paine had said that the cause of America was the cause of all mankind. "Now, in 1960," the candidate exhorted, "the cause of all mankind is the cause of America." Kennedy prophesied: "If you fail here, if we drift, if we lie at anchor, if we don't provide an example of what freedom can do in the 1960's, then we have betrayed not only ourselves and our destiny, but all those who desire to be free and are not free."

In his second State of the Union Message, Kennedy saw America as "commissioned by history . . . to fulfill the world's hopes by fulfilling our own faith." He welcomed the national role as "a great defender of freedom in its hour of maximum danger." Kennedy felt it was his good fortune to be President at such a time. It was his fate and that of all Americans "to live with the struggle we did not start, in a world we did not make . . . while no nation has ever faced such a challenge, no nation has ever been so ready to seize the burden and the glory of freedom." It was America's mission, Kennedy reminded a Philadelphia audience in 1962, quoting Abraham Lincoln, to extend liberty not only "to the people of this country, but hope to the world—'that in due time the weight shall be lifted from the shoulders of all men, and that *all* should have an equal chance.' " On his trip to Ireland in 1963, he reminded the Irish Parliament of William Jennings Bryan's insistence that "the humblest nation of all the world, when clad in the armor of a righteous cause, is stronger than all the hosts of Error." Only a few days before his death, Kennedy told a New York audience to heed the words of the Apostle Paul to the Galatians: " 'Let us not be weary in well doing: for in due season we shall reap, if we faint not.' " The President went on in a manner familiar to those who remembered his inaugural address: "And let the word go forth—to all who are concerned about the future of the human family—that we will not be weary of well doing and we will faint not; and we shall in due season, reap a harvest of peace and security for all members of the family of man." In the speech he was to have delivered to a Dallas audience on the day of his death, he said: "We in this country, in this generation, are by destiny rather than choice, the watchmen on the walls of freedom."

Like other great presidential heroes, Kennedy apparently believed that America's mission to promote human freedom had been commissioned by divine Providence. Kennedy did not believe that Americans were more capable of freedom than others. Nor did he believe that the defense of freedom excused xenophobic hatred toward those who did not share America's view of freedom or its historic mission. But Kennedy did believe that God intended human beings to be free from natural and man-made oppressions, and the United States of America had the responsibility and the power to promote that cause. In his eloquent inaugural address—perhaps one of the best half-dozen expressions of American values —the young President rephrased the American mission of the apocalypse by pointing out that the inauguration symbolized

> ... an end as well as a beginning, signifying renewal as well as change, for I have sworn before you and Almighty God the

same solemn oath our forebears prescribed nearly a century and three quarters ago.

The world is very different now. For man now holds in his mortal hands the power to abolish all forms of human poverty and all forms of human life. And yet the same revolutionary beliefs for which our forebears fought are still at issue around the globe—the belief that the rights of man come not from the generosity of the state, but from the hand of God.

We dare not forget that we are the heirs of that first revolution. Let the word go forth from this time and this place, to friend and foe alike, that the torch of liberty has been passed to a new generation of Americans—born in this century, tempered by war, disciplined by a hard and bitter peace, proud of our ancient heritage, and unwilling to witness or permit the slow undoing of those human rights to which this nation has always been committed and to which we are committed today at home and around the world.

Kennedy apparently believed there was nothing incompatible between belief in a benign supernatural God and a culture-religion which makes man "the captain of my soul." Kennedy exclaimed: "Let us go forth to lead the land we love, asking his blessing and his help, but knowing that here on earth God's work must truly be our own."

Although Kennedy forcefully argued that the impulse toward religion should never be used as an element in the cold war or in partisan strife of any kind, he frequently associated God with the mission of the United States to spread liberty. At Independence Hall in 1962, Kennedy said: "But it was in this hall that the theory [of independence] became a practice; and that the word went out to all, in Thomas Jefferson's phrase, that 'the God who gave us life, gave us liberty at the same time.' " In his second State of the Union Message, after calling on Americans to fulfill their mission to defend freedom, he concluded, "And in this high endeavor, may God watch over the United States of America." In his third State of the Union Message, Kennedy told the nation: "We steer our ship with hope" and "with thanks to Almighty God for seeing us through a perilous passage, we ask his help anew in guiding the good ship 'Union.' "

To expect the help of God in fulfilling their mission, Americans had to trust him. In his speeches, Kennedy revealed a simple trust in a benign God whose hand moves in a shadowy but benevolent way in the affairs of men. It was a trust which gave Abraham Lincoln (according to his own words) and Franklin Roosevelt (according to Mrs. Roosevelt's testimony) the conviction that they were doing God's work on earth. Kennedy evidently felt the same way. He told an audience in February, 1961: "No man who enters upon the office to which I have succeeded can fail to recognize how every President of the United States has placed special reliance upon his faith in God. Every President has taken comfort and courage when told, as we are told today, that the Lord 'will be with thee. He will not fail thee nor forsake thee. Fear not— neither be thou dismayed.' "

In October, 1960, at the Springfield Armory, Kennedy quoted from Lincoln's farewell speech to his friends in Springfield: "My friends, I now leave with a task before me greater than any which has rested upon any President since the time of Washington. Without the assistance of that Divine Being who attended him, I cannot succeed. With that assistance, I cannot fail."

Only forty-eight hours before his election, Kennedy reminded a New England audience of a letter which Lincoln wrote a hundred years before. The great emancipator told a friend, "I know there is a God, and I know he hates injustice. I see the storm coming and I know his hand is in it. But if he has a place and a part for me, I believe that I am ready." Kennedy's listeners heard him paraphrase Lincoln, "We know there is a God and we know he hates injustice. We see the storm coming, and we know his Hand is in it. But if he has a place and a part for us, I believe that we are ready." One and a half years later, at the tenth annual Presidential Prayer breakfast, he repeated Lincoln's words and his own. At the dedication breakfast of the International Christian Leadership

Movement in February, 1961, he asked his audience to join him in a prayer given by General George Washington in 1783: "That God would have you in his holy protection, that he would incline the hearts of the citizens . . . to entertain a brotherly love and affection one for another and finally that he would most graciously be pleased to dispose us all to do justice, to love mercy, and to demean ourselves with . . . the characteristics of the divine Author of our blessed religion, without an humble imitation of whose example we could never hope to be a happy nation." The new President went on, "The guiding principle and prayer of this nation has been, is now, and shall ever be, 'In God We Trust.' "

Trust in a God who helps those who help themselves has been an essential attribute of the American culture-religion. That such trust puts God in the role of helper to man has never seemed to bother most Americans. One trusts God because he has blessed Americans with the opportunity for freedom and prosperity. Kennedy, in his annual message to Congress in 1961, said: "In the words of a great President [F. D. Roosevelt], whose birthday we honor today, closing his final State of the Union Message sixteen years ago, 'We pray that we may be worthy of the unlimited opportunities that God has given us.' " One trusts God in America, then, not so much for solace or salvation but for putting the good life within the grasp of energetic, independent men.

In his advocacy of America's culture-religion, Kennedy was as much an Arminian or Pelagian as Washington (Church of England), Jefferson (Deist-Church of England), Jackson (Presbyterian), Lincoln (Deist-nonaffiliated), and Franklin Roosevelt (Episcopalian). He told the Zionists of America convention in August, 1960, that he shared with the Jews "the belief that each person is responsible for every person, and, as children of God, we each have infinite potentialities for moral growth." The Pelagians believed that everything created by God is good, including human nature. They also believed in free will, making sin a matter of human choice. Adam had been created with free will but his sin and guilt were not transmitted to the generations which followed. God's grace facilitated goodness, but it was up to man to choose his path. With the other presidential heroes, Kennedy believed that given social arrangements which provide for equality of opportunity, each man faces the burden of choice between good and evil and between inaction and achievement. With them, he believed that other doctrinal and theological differences were not important. What mattered, Kennedy asserted, was that "there is generally consensus on those questions . . . the basic presumption of moral law, the existence of God, man's relation to him." Americans, he told an interfaith meeting at Kings Point, New York, shared a "sense of brotherhood with the infinite" regardless of their sectarian affiliation.

John F. Kennedy was a mid-twentieth-century representative of the self-confident Catholic response of encounter with the American environment. He symbolized those forces which John Ireland and Al Smith represented at earlier times in different contexts. He believed with other presidential heroes that religious faith is a personal affair, that ecclesiastical authorities had no special claim over public officials, and that God had placed man on earth to exercise freedom and excellence in achievement, and that it was up to individual men and women and the United States of America to fulfill God's purpose. To Kennedy, there was nothing in these beliefs which was incompatible with the sectarian religion of his birth, including its theology and authoritarian form of church government.

Because he was a Catholic, representing the one sectarian religion thought to be at odds with the culture-religion of Americanism, Kennedy, as a culture-hero, helped to broaden the basis of consensus in American life by encouraging the forces of encounter within American Catholicism, and by opening the minds of non-Catholics to new opportunities for human communication, learning and growth in dialogue with Catholics.

VII

THE VALUE OF OUR TIME

T HE CULTURE-RELIGION of Americans is more than its Protestant inheritance but it cannot be understood apart from it. American Protestants have revealed a pronounced and distinctive unity (when compared to other world religions) in the belief that God must be experienced immediately and directly and that conceptualization of that experience is a task for the believer alone, checked only against the biblical text. This has been the central belief of most American Protestants regardless of whether they belong to the Lutheran, Reform, or other churches of the sixteenth-century Reformation, the churches of the seventeenth-century Puritan Revolution, such as Congregationalist and Quaker, the churches of the eighteenth-century Awakening, such as Methodist, Baptist, or Unitarian, or the churches of the nineteenth-century revivals, such as Disciples of Christ and Seventh-day Adventists. It has been a belief which, when mixed with other elements of the American environment, has affected the values, behavior, and psychological style of all Americans in contrast to Europeans and Asians; but it is originally and remains essentially a Protestant belief.

CLASH OF STYLES

The psychological style of a people (psycho-cultural might be the best word) describes their *ways* of perceiving, understanding, believing, feeling, and communicating. Americans, and especially Protestant Americans, have a distinctive psychological style as foreign observers from the eighteenth century to the present have observed consistently. It is a style which rests to a considerable degree on the Protestant principle of an empirical God-encounter (as seen most dramatically at revival meetings), whether it is called conversion, faith, or a decision for Christ. The Protestant emphasis on the individual's unassisted encounter with God in the American environment has promoted an empirical, intuitive, subjective (as opposed to theoretical, deductive, and authoritative) psychological style which not only divides Americans from other cultures but which, to a lesser extent, has separated Protestants from Catholics in America. The archetypal Protestant, in insisting that the individual stands alone in relationship to God and opposing metaphysical intellectualism, tradition, and authority, has recoiled from Catholic indulgences, confession, dependency on priests, the distinction between mortal and venial sins, and the Catholic emphasis on mercy and forgiveness.

Against this style is the Catholic style, which rests on the belief that man must be incorporated into God's visible society called the Church to share the life of Christ who is God as well as man. Except for the mystics, Christians do not experience God immediately in the simple direct way described by Protestants. The truth of his revelations is in the possession of the Church, and its divinely empowered organs will express it. Religion may be personal, but it is complicated and mysterious and not something that can be intuited by the individual. That is why Latin has been important to the liturgy and why Communion is a vital sacrament. It is why the religious wear special clothes, and why important distinctions are made between the sacred and profane, as in the creation of religious orders with special vows. Moral questions are seen as complicated, requiring authoritative interpretation and guidance. The Bible says that thou shalt not kill, but how does that answer the questions of war, abortion, or euthanasia? Salvation requires the avoidance of sin, but who decides which sins are mortal and which are not? Out of such beliefs has emerged a psychological style emphasizing mystery, tradition, obedience, devotion, and the need for coherence and order. To Catholics, it sometimes seems that the Protestant view of man veers crazily from one extreme to the other. Fundamentalists and Puritans emphasize man's utter sinfulness; liberal Protestants talk of man as no less perfect (or at least perfectible) than God himself. Thus, while some Protestants, obsessed by man's depravity, lurch off on crusades against drinking, gambling, and sex, others, imbued with hope for man's perfection on earth, attempt to engineer utopian communities such as Oneida, Brook Farm, and New Harmony.

While the Protestant style, and the beliefs and values from which it sprang, has dominated in America, important value differences remained between Catholics and non-Catholics, at least through the 1950's. One study in 1958 revealed that a significantly higher proportion of Jews and Protestants than Catholics valued intellectual autonomy above obedience in the raising of children. There were differences between Protestants and Catholics in each socioeconomic class, the largest at the highest level. A 1953 survey showed that Protestant and Jewish children were expected by their parents to display more independence and assume greater responsibility at an earlier age than Catholic children. A 1958 study revealed that a much higher proportion of Protestant clergymen and laymen than Catholics in the same categories believed they had a right to question what their churches teach.

The culture-religions of Americansm has gone beyond Protestantism in emphasizing personal independence and achievement, and American Catholics from John Carroll on have had to confront a transmogrified Protestantism in America which European Catholics traditionally have seen as a liberal secular anathema to the Church. But Carroll and large numbers of American Catholics, particularly those from the middle and upper classes, and most especially those from English backgrounds, have always disagreed with the European continental view. They have promoted encounter with, and adaptation to, the American environment without fearing the loss of their Catholicism. They have become thoroughly Americanized with respect to ideology and psychological style while maintaining their own identity as communicants of the Roman Catholic Church.

Probably the most important leader the forces of encounter have ever had was John F. Kennedy. He came on the national political scene at a time when the spirit of encounter among American Catholics was relatively subdued and Catholic spokesmen of parochial defensiveness seemed to many Protestants and Jews to be unusually active. There were exceptions, in the editorials and articles of *Commonweal* and *Cross Currents* (a Catholic-sponsored journal dedicated to fostering a Protestant-Catholic dialogue), the serious intellectual scholarship of *Thought* (Fordham University) and *Theological Studies* (Woodstock College), in the theology of John Courtney Murray, in the writings of Father Ong, Monsignor Ellis, and Father Weigel, in the liberal statements of Cardinal Cushing, Bishops Sheil and John J. Wright, and in the ecumenical action of leading Catholic governors and United States senators. The forces of encounter also could assert that most American Catholic leaders did not accept the dominant European Catholic view of church-state relations, as promulgated most recently and systematically by Pope Leo XIII. Regardless of these signs of encounter in the Church in America, most Jews and Protestants writing on Catholicism in the United States stressed their fear that Catholics, whatever their country, were bound to believe in one true Church and would impose their view of faith and morals on others wherever they had power. They pointed to a statement in the Jesuit journal, *La Civiltà Cattolica,* which appeared in 1948 and which argued that the Roman Catholic Church, being the only true Church, could adopt toleration of other forms of worship only as a matter of necessity. Everyone should understand, the article maintained, "that the Catholic Church would betray her trust if she were to proclaim, theoretically and practically, that error can have the same rights as truth." Non-Catholics decried Catholic persecution in Spain and in certain Latin-American countries, and more important, they complained of the imposition of Catholic truth in matters of faith and morals on local communities through pressure tactics, as in the Margaret Sanger case in Holyoke, and with respect to legislation affecting education, censorship, divorce, and sterilization in several states.

WINDS OF CHANGE

Within a few years after the election of Kennedy, Catholicism in America was to erupt with new vigor and diversity and the forces of encounter would become dominant. Before half of the decade of the 1960's was over, it became clear that the culture-religion of Americanism had profoundly affected American Catholics, even as it had influenced Jews, Buddhists, and Protestants themselves. To a considerable extent, John Kennedy was a symbol of the dynamic impact of the American environment on Catholicism. Like many Catholics of his generation, he esteemed not the virtues of humility, mortification, penance, chastity, poverty, and abnegation, but those values of independence and achievement which Americans have cherished since the eighteenth century. If the real difference between the Catholic and Protestant communities lay in their distinctive conceptions of virtue, as some Catholic writers maintained, Kennedy made clear that the American experience had blurred the difference. Between the supernatural and the natural, the theoretical and the empirical, the traditional and the new, the authoritative and the subjective, there was no doubt as to where Kennedy fit. He was the antithesis of the stereotyped separatist, parochial, anti-intellectual, superstitious, tribalistic, and fatalistic Catholic of Protestant literature and conversation. But the stereotype, while based on a core of reality, never suited hundreds of thousands of Catholics from Carroll to Spalding to Kennedy.

The 1960's saw an outbreak of Catholic activity and self-criticism which would have been unthinkable ten years before. A vast range of questions were suddenly wide open for debate: the relationship of the laity within the Church; the problem of self-determination or conscience for the individual Catholic; and the relationship of Catholic dogma to democratic values. No subject was immune from scrutiny, including birth control, divorce, parochial schools, and even the papacy itself. In addition to *Commonweal* and *Cross Currents,* articles challenging basic assumptions appeared in *America, The Sign, Ave Maria, Jubilee, Perspectives,* and a new weekly newspaper, the *National Catholic Reporter.* (Most avant-garde and irreverent of the publications was *Ramparts,* edited by Catholic laymen.)

The *National Catholic Reporter* was typical of the winds of change (a favorite Kennedy phrase) blowing through the Church in America. Its editors gave writers freedom to question every conceivable issue, including the celibacy of priests and nuns, the validity of the ban on mixed marriages, and the value of private confession. Its weekly circulation during the first year of publication (October, 1964–October, 1965) jumped from eleven thousand to more than fifty thousand. A survey of its readers revealed that the new Catholic emphasis on self-criticism appealed especially to upper-class and upper-middle-class parishioners in the Middle West and Middle Atlantic states. Only 6 percent of its readers came from New England, America's most solidly Catholic region. Its lay audience—30 percent of its readers were individual clergymen or sisters—was highly educated and well to do, 71 percent of all readers being college graduates and 34 percent having master's degrees. Nearly all heads of households were business or professional men with an average income of nearly fourteen thousand dollars.

Separatism was far from dead. Only in the Middle West could it be said that vigorous lay activity was an important feature of life in the Church. Elsewhere, particularly in Kennedy's New England, laymen were more passive. On some issues, such as racial segregation in the schools, the clerics of New England, led by Richard Cardinal Cushing, were much more willing to risk encounter than a majority of their parishioners. Many priests and nuns complained that there were far too many laymen suspicious of change in the status quo in America and within the Church. Other key members of the hierarchy were less open to encounter than Cushing. Los Angeles' James Francis Cardinal McIntyre and, to a lesser extent, New York's Francis Cardinal Spellman looked suspiciously at the new ferment within the Church.

THE NEW BREED

Much of the ferment in Catholicism was created by young men and women in their twenties and thirties labeled by sociologist Father Andrew Greeley as the "new breed." The new breed was characterized more by skepticism than anything else. They wanted to know the why of things. They were individualistic and assertive. They admired pragmatism, efficiency, and competence. They began to show up in classrooms in Catholic colleges and universities, on picket lines, in the Peace Corps, and in the book review sections of newspapers and magazines.*

In 1962, Donald J. Thorman wrote a stirring plea for lay activity in a book entitled *The Emerging Layman*. The following year, an associate editor of *Commonweal*, Daniel Callahan, already a

---

* The Peace Corps, with its secular missionary emphasis, was expected to draw heavily from Protestants. Young men and women from relatively lower socioeconomic backgrounds were not expected to be able to afford two years of volunteer service; but many Catholics from just such backgrounds joined the Peace Corps, indicating their preference to work in a secular movement backed by the American government rather than turn their idealism toward more clearly defined sectarian activities. Although the Peace Corps keeps no statistics on religious affiliation, it seemed to me during my tenure as Director of the Peace Corps in the Philippines (1961–63), that approximately 40 percent of the six hundred volunteers who served with me were Catholic, and I was especially surprised at the number who were ex-seminarians.

prolific writer and then a teaching fellow in Roman Catholic Studies at Harvard Divinity School, won the national Catholic Book Award for his tightly packed volume entitled *The Mind of the Catholic Layman.* In 1964, Michael Novak, almost as productive and even more controversial than Callahan, wrote *A New Generation: American and Catholic* and the *Open Church: Vatican II, Act 2,* both stressing ecumenical themes. In 1965, Callahan published two more books, *Honesty in the Church,* a personal critique of the Church, and edited *Generation of the Third Eye: Young Catholic Leaders View Their Church,* a compilation of twenty-two essays by third-eye ones (a name invented by Father Murray for the new breed).

Other books were even more aggressively self-critical, such as *Objections to Roman Catholicism,* edited by Michael de la Bedoyere (editor of the Catholic journal *Search*), which contained seven trenchant critiques of what heretofore had been usually considered fundamental Catholic points of view. Some new-breed books concentrated on a specific issue, such as Mary Perkins Ryan's *Are Parochial Schools the Answer?* The author thought not, and so did a surprising number of her reviewers. A half-dozen books appeared on the subject of marriage and birth control in the early 1960's, including Novak's *Experience of Marriage,* a collection of thirteen soul-searching testimonies by Catholic couples concerning the searing emotional problems imposed by the Catholic position on birth control.

The generation of the third eye wrote on the themes of dignity and conscience, self-direction and autonomy, openness and awareness, commitment and relevance, and encounter and action. Of the self-styled third-eye ones, Callahan wrote that they are a generation

> . . . cut loose from many of its roots, from the nurture of old traditions, [which] looks constantly into itself . . . nothing, or almost nothing, is safe from scrutiny. I do not hesitate for a

moment (well, yes I do sometimes) to cast a probing eye on the most sacred and revered things. I have no special compunction about evaluating the word of a Pope as stringently as that of my local mayor. I do not hesitate to pass sharp judgment on the piety or effectiveness of priests or laymen of evident good will. I don't blanch from speculating about the possibility that Christianity may be false.

John Leo, a regular commentator in the *National Catholic Reporter,* wrote that the new stance means that Catholics are becoming irreverent like other Americans. The Church, once on the defensive, is no longer under siege; Catholics can afford to be self-critical, too. To Novak, the ideal Catholic meets the risks and choices of reality head on. Before an audience of students from twenty-two colleges, Novak asserted his agreement with Protestant theologian Paul Tillich's concept of doubt. Unbelief is the basis of the kind of honest and personal commitment welcomed by God, he maintained.

Nearly all who wrote *Generation of the Third Eye* agreed that American Catholicism was intellectually too narrow. They attacked reflex or rote Catholicism and what some of them called "the Index mentality." They were antagonized by the symbols of separatism and complained about the lack of inner commitment among contemporary Catholics. They generally agreed, as one priest put it, that there was too much emphasis on the role of the priest in the Church.

These were the things they were against. What were they for? A typical answer would be the assertion of Father Laurence Brett that the first and most important task of every Catholic was as a human being; his first obligation was the development of as many human potentialities as possible. They stressed, in the words of another priest, that "our strictest obligation is to discover and maintain the intensity of that selfhood which is our innermost reality." Agreeing with Albert Camus that the aim of man's life is to increase the sum of freedom and responsibility in his being,

Father Bernard Murchland maintained that such a goal cannot be fulfilled in any automatic way simply by going to a Catholic school or by regularly attending church. "I really can represent no one but myself," wrote Rosemary Ruether in admitting that she considered Luther's understanding of grace to be more profound than that of the Council of Trent. Inadequate as it might be, she was convinced that her own "poor reason" was the best guide she had to understanding the nature of grace.

What Father Murray called the "will to self-direction" was the basic theme of Callahan's *Honesty in the Church*. Callahan saw life in pluralistic America—where the individual Catholic is exposed from every side to philosophies and ways of life which challenge his childhood teaching—as a spur to honesty. American Catholicism itself inhibited personal honesty through "an educational system which stresses humility and submissiveness, which leads the individual always to assume he must be in the wrong if he questions authority, and which impresses upon him day in and day out the superiority of its wisdom to his." Callahan maintained that the Church was meant to be a source of freedom and self-liberation, but it too often threatened individual integrity through the introduction of fear of authority. The child is taught that he dare not raise questions. When in doubt, Callahan wrote, he is often advised to turn from difficult subjects altogether or to pray. Rather than be searchingly honest, he is told to trust the authority of the Church or even the consensus of the community.

The Church can tell the individual who he is and what he is and what he should do in a general way, agreed Callahan, but "it cannot climb into our minds and emotions and actively shape the person we should become ... in the end we are on our own ... to let others, whatever their stature or office, form our inner life is to abdicate our human freedom." Integrity, Callahan maintained, goes far beyond formal honesty; it means being real in relationships, even with priests and bishops, and above all, with oneself.

KENNEDY AS SYMBOL AND CATALYST OF CHANGE

What, if anything, did the resurgence of the forces of encounter and the new existential ferment in American Catholicism have to do with John F. Kennedy? Even if Kennedy had been a school-teacher or a journalist, the new breed of American Catholics probably would have appeared in the 1960's. Many factors were at work to break down the walls of Catholic separatism in the United States and elsewhere. The most important was the election of Pope John XXIII and his two extremely influential encyclicals, *Mater et magistra* and *Pacem in terris* and the convocation of the Vatican Council. Also important was the profoundly penetrating self-criticism and ecumenism of several important European theologians such as Henri de Lubbec and Yves Congar and the extremely significant work of the French Jesuit philosopher and paleontologist, Teilhard de Chardin. The very social changes in America which produced a Kennedy—social class mobility for Catholics, the growing influence of secular education, the spreading encounter of Catholics with non-Catholics in war and work—were also factors in the growing strength of advocates of self-criticism encounter.

Kennedy was mainly a symbol of change among Catholics in America, but he was also a catalyst. Although he represented an old and significant response of American Catholics to the environment of the New World and the challenge of new Jerusalem, Kennedy, by becoming the most influential lay Catholic in American history, made the path of the new breed and the generation of the third eye much easier. Because no one in American history had ever become so completely identified with inter-religious encounter as Kennedy, his election gave hope to the forces of encounter. As a culture-hero, Kennedy could not help but inspire other lay Catholics to identify with him, and he undoubtedly gave many of the laity the courage to voice their doubts. Here was a layman who was not only occasionally flip and irreverent toward the clergy, but he seemed certain of his own positions in opposition to members of the hierarchy, and was admired all over the world as the most representative American of his time.

Without Kennedy, the forces of American pluralism, the rapidly developing thought of Catholic theologians, and the influence of Pope John would have stimulated the American laity to new introspection anyway. With Kennedy, questions and doubts were brought more rapidly and forcefully into the open. Kennedy was a sign but he was also a stimulus who made it easier for Catholics to peel away their defenses both in and outside the Church. Young men and women who had never heard of de Lubbec or Congar or who had not even read *Mater et magistra* could see in the great respect accorded President Kennedy a sanction for self-criticism and encounter. Studies made by my students at Brandeis University of the opinion of Catholic instructors and students at Catholic and non-Catholic universities in the Boston area revealed that Kennedy spoke to their needs and aspirations as Catholics to a considerable extent. In praising him, they said repeatedly that the President represented the ecumenical conviction that, as one of them put it, "truth can be found in many places." Kennedy spoke for them, they maintained, in implicitly attacking the ghetto mentality that had separated Catholics from their fellow Americans. Because Kennedy was a culture-hero—millions mourning him watched his funeral on television and knew that Mass was said in the White House for the first time in history—Catholics could be more self-confident than at any time since the Revolution.

For many non-Catholics, John F. Kennedy made it clear that Catholicism was not incompatible with freedom. He maintained his own position on social and political questions in the face of strong opposition in the episcopacy, making the doctrine of papal (usually read by non-Catholics as priestly or episcopal) infallibility seem as irrelevant to the issue of personal freedom as Al Smith always said it was. Actually, the Catholic Church was still authoritarian, as even the new breed acknowledged in submitting to its doctrines and rituals, in the sense that the source of authority given to the bishops and the Pope is God. Logically, America's culture-religion and the Roman Catholic Church were as uncongenial as ever. In reality, John F. Kennedy revealed the extent to which personal freedom for Catholics is consistent with their view of loyalty to an authoritarian Church.

Evidence of such freedom abounded everywhere in the 1960's. Studies showed that at least 30 percent of married Catholics in the United States practiced birth control. There were no violent Catholic protests against the allocation of antipoverty funds for birth control or even against the more activist proposals being studied by the United States Senate. An increasing number of Catholics challenged the desirability of parochial schools, and in 1962 the St. Louis archdiocese placed a ban on the building of schools and recommended that parents vote for bond issues to expand the public school system. Although movies and books were much more explicit on sex in the 1960's than they were in the 1940's, Catholic pressure for censorship slackened considerably, and hundreds of thousands of Catholics paid scant attention to the censorship of books and motion pictures by the NODL.

CATHOLIC ADAPTATION

Did this mean that American Catholicism was somehow less Catholic than that of Italy, France, or the Philippines? Clearly, it was different. Wherever the Church has gone, each national culture has stamped its values on Catholicism. Only because Europe has gone through the agony of the Protestant Reformation do we find in France and Germany profound dogmatic and speculative theological discussion. The colonial style of Catholicism in Latin America was essentially pre-sixteenth-century Catholicism imposed primarily by the sword and mission on top of Indian and Malayan folk religions which were adaptable. Catholicism in those countries shows the effects of Spanish Catholicism prior to the Council of Trent (1545–63) and the convulsions of the Reformation. It has produced an anticlerical tradition in reaction to medieval Catholicism comparable to Europe's but virtually no sophisticated theological thought.

The conditions of the Church in America have been radically different from those found in Europe or in colonial outposts. In the United States, Catholicism has been a minority religion in an overwhelmingly Protestant but pluralistic society held together by a culture-religion inspired by the dogma of eighteenth-century liberalism emphasizing the possibilities of human nature; in addition, Catholicism in America has been the religion of immigrants, particularly the Irish who came from the northernmost corner of Europe where they had been relatively untouched by the influence of the Enlightenment, and where religion had been their major defense against English oppression.

These two factors account for the recurring tension within American Catholicism between the forces of encounter and separatism. Most immigrants wanted to become Americans and remain Catholics too. They wanted to share the promise of a new Jerusalem without repudiating altogether the traditions of the old country and the authority of their Church. From a European point of view, reconciliation was impossible. Even the most brilliant of all European observers on American life, Alexis de Tocqueville, predicted in the 1830's that either all Americans would become Catholic or Catholic Americans would abandon their religion. It is easy to excuse de Tocqueville's mistake. No one before or since has better understood the tendencies and implications of democracy in America; it was not democracy which de Tocqueville saw as uncongenial to Catholicism, it was the emphasis in America's culture-religion on personal independence. It has been the genius of American history to defy even de Tocqueville's logic. Catholics such as England, Ireland, and Gibbons saw that Catholicism could flourish under these new and peculiar conditions, but it is not surprising that Rome and even many priests and parishioners had a difficult time understanding their attitudes.

To the extent that adaptation to the culture-religion is crucial to the Americanization process and to the degree that the culture-religion represents a transmogrified Protestantism, the character of American Catholics has been affected by the psychological implications of Protestant principles. This was what the controversy over Americanism in the Church at the turn of the century was about as it applied to Americans. Because the errors Pope Leo XIII condemned were stated as hypothetical positions, it was possible for American Catholic leaders to disassociate themselves explicitly from the heresies under attack, and to act as if they applied to Europeans only. Had the Pope named names and cases, a schism might have followed. Instead, the Church in America continued to produce men who were loyal to it, but whose actions and stated convictions often seemed to illustrate the condemned heresies. Finally, Pope John and the Second Vatican Council—without explicitly rejecting the utterance of any previous Pope—endorsed doctrines associated sixty years before with the errors of Americanism.

History confounded the logic not just of de Tocqueville and the clerics of nineteenth-century Rome but of self-appointed spokesmen for America's culture-religion. To see American Catholicism, as Blanshard did in the late 1940's, primarily in terms of unrefuted encyclicals and canon laws produced in the European enviroment was to miss the point of the uniqueness of the American experience. Logically, one can still find much in Catholic dogma and law which would justify the destruction of American civil liberties, but in history experience usually triumphs over logic, and that probably has been more true in the United States of America, whose people have defied tradition and exalted experience, than elsewhere. American Catholics have been gripped by the experience of American history, shaped and transformed by it, while, in the main, remaining true to the Church. They have been able to drink deeply of the wine of freedom and prosper within the Church of Rome.

CHANGES IN ROME

By the middle of the twentieth century, the meaning of the history of American Catholicism had penetrated a resilient Church under the leadership of Pope John. A large measure of American separatism in the past could be attributed to the usually strident defensiveness of the Vatican under attack from spreading Jacobinism in Europe. As long as Rome felt under siege, the principles embodied in America's culture-religion seemed threatening. By the middle of the twentieth century, the Church itself lived in an increasingly modern and pluralistic world requiring *aggiornamento* (updating) and *avvicinamento* (neighborliness with other creeds and faiths). Archbishop Carroll had faced the need for *aggiornamento* and *avvicinamento* in the United States more than 150 years before. His approach did not always prevail in America, but by the 1960's it was once again rising, and not just in America, but in Rome too.

So strongly had the idea of individual choice and commitment become identified with American life that the ecumenical council's declaration on religious liberty was commonly called the "American Schema." The declaration was a victory for the idea of freedom which transcends national inspiration, but it had a special meaning in the United States, where personal freedom and religious freedom have been most deeply rooted in its culture-religion. The chief author of the American Schema was Father John Courtney Murray, and its most powerful support came from American bishops, against key figures in the Roman Curia, Spanish bishops, and southern Italian prelates, whose European experience in church-state relations made it difficult for them to accept the American emphasis on rights of conscience.

In previous papal encyclicals and other expressions of Catholic theology, religious liberty was something to be tolerated in the interests of civic peace. There were no rights of conscience to be recognized when they conflicted with the one, true Church which, whenever possible, was to be favored over other religions. It was this overarching position in Roman Catholicism which millions of American Catholics had repudiated, but which had been a source of sharp embarrassment to Al Smith and John F. Kennedy in their campaigns for the presidency.

For two decades before the Vatican Council, John Courtney Murray had been attempting to work out a formula to give theological justification for the traditional American view of church-state relations and religious liberty. In his writings, which were often steeped in American history, Murray argued that it was impossible to separate religious freedom from civil freedom and that persons in error have rights which must be respected by church and state no less than those who embrace truth.

Murray's views were frequently challenged in America and Rome. In 1950, when he argued with Father Francis Connell and Monsignor Joseph Fenton of the Catholic University in the *American Ecclesiastical Review,* he received an admonition from the Jesuit authorities in Rome, who insisted that all his future writings on the subject of religious liberty be cleared. Only after Pope John abandoned the hermetic policy designed to protect Catholics from the contamination of error, were the characteristically American Catholic views on church-state and religious liberty able to prevail.

American bishops had fought against the doctrine of papal infallibility promulgated by the First Vatican Council in 1870 and for the schema on religious liberty issued by the Second Vatican Council in 1965 not because they had given long theological study and debate to issues involved (with the exception of a few individuals like Father Murray), but because they had a pronounced American view of the issues. When theological questions have had secular implications in their own country, members of the American hierarchy have been vitally interested. When theological questions central to the Church's teachings on faith and morals are decided—such as the Pope's encyclical letter in September, 1965, reaffirming the doctrine of the Eucharist (Jesus Christ's real presence in the bread and wine of the Mass)—European theologians become deeply involved but the Church in America seems hardly to notice. What was seen in this case as a setback to the progressives in Europe, for whom strictly theological questions are often burning issues, appeared almost irrelevant in the United States. The lay and clerical leaders of European Catholicism often seem primarily interested in theological matters which may have practical consequences; in America, Catholic spokesmen are preeminently concerned with practical questions, such as church-state relations or birth control, which sometimes have theological implications. Like Protestant Americans, church leaders have been doers—administrators, builders, and missionaries—rather than theologians.

RELIGION IN AMERICA

If the test of religiosity in any society is theological preoccupation backed by sectarian intensity, then Americans have failed ever since they stopped hanging heretics in the seventeenth century. Both European and Oriental critics of religious life in America find it wanting. The Europeans stress the absence of sectarian convictions; Asians observe the absence of mysticism. Both point out that religious life in the United States is social and practical, although they often fail to notice the intensity of commitment which Americans make to their culture-religion and the extent to which its principles have infused sectarian religious life.

From Tom Paine, who explained that he wrote his *Age of Reason* to preserve "true theology" from the destruction of the French Revolution, through the Second Great Awakening, when Protestant ministers were imbued with Jeffersonian and Jacksonian ideals, to the post-Kennedy writings of Callahan and Novak, Americans—more than any other people in history—have believed in the capacity of man to fulfill the will of God. To the Puritans, the Arminian heresy lay primarily in its optimistic judgments of man's capacity to choose goodness. This too was the essence of St. Augustine's criticisms against Pelagius and of the orthodox Catholic judgment on what came to be known as the heresy of Pelagianism. One can quarrel with Jeffersonian optimism as being shallow and mischievous without denying that it is at the heart of the American culture-religion or failing to see that it is grounded in metaphysical presuppositions.

Several spokesmen for traditional Protestantism, Catholicism, and Judaism have complained of the pervasive Arminianism-Pelagianism (without calling it that) of America's culture-religion as an insufficient explanation of and an inadequate weapon to deal with the complexly tragic questions of human existence. They have seen the backlash of frustrated utopian Arminian-Pelagian dreams result in vigilantism or isolationism; but the most penetrating of critics have not failed to see that Americans, as much as any modern nation, have been true believers. Their culture-religion has had its prophets (Emerson), philosophers (Jefferson), poets (Whitman), and heroes, including John F. Kennedy.

Oliver Wendell Holmes once said, "We are the Romans of the modern world . . . a great assimilating people," but he also said that we are all tattooed in our cradle with the beliefs of our tribe. In America, the beliefs of many tribes have been tolerated and even welcomed. The Buddhists in Hawaii prosper; Mormons in Utah thrive; Jews in New York flourish; and forty million Catholics win increased respect and recognition. The price has been acceptance of other religions as having equally valid rights, the minimization of forms and rituals, considerable indifference to theology, and endorsement of a humanistic culture-religion which emphasizes man's capacity for choice based on experience.

America is the meeting ground where different cultures encounter each other, and in the process of confrontation, the characteristics of some of them persist and influence the others; but not all cultures are equally influential. Americans, including Catholics, have been enveloped by the dominant values of our culture-religion. Immigrants have been permitted to continue their traditions with respect to food, music, and art, and to have their own newspapers, languages, and churches. In the process of encounter, they change the customs of their hosts, as Catholics did in promoting the celebration of Christmas in the United States, but they are acculturated to the fundamentals of Americanism. No metaphor yet invented describes the process: neither a melting pot, pressure cooker, nor rainbow.

The dominant value of American culture is personal independence—the right and ability to choose without external restraint—and American Catholics, while not expecting their children to show as much independence as Protestants or Jews and not valuing intellectual autonomy above obedience as much as non-Catholics, have embraced that value to a considerable extent. Although the 1958 study referred to above revealed that a significantly higher proportion of Jews and Protestants than Catholics valued intellectual autonomy above obedience in the raising of children, perhaps the most remarkable finding was the degree to which American Catholics did choose intellectual autonomy. Some 70 percent of the upper-middle-class white Catholics, 63 percent of those in the lower-middle class, and even 51 percent in the upper-working-class Catholic group preferred the value of autonomy. While a significantly higher proportion of Protestants than Catholics believed they had the right to challenge what their church teaches, a surprising 67 percent of active Catolic laymen also asserted that right. The studies, made by sociologist Gerhard Lenski in Detroit, while revealing that many Catholics were still tattooed with the beliefs of their tribe, showed also the assimilative power of America's culture-religion.

Lenski's most startling finding was that third-generation Catholics were in many respects more typically Catholic than their parents and grandparents. Middle-class Catholics, for example, showed a smaller proportion of the third generation committed to the principle of intellectual autonomy than in the first and second generations. From such statistics, Lenski concluded that the nation would become more Catholic in many ways, including a declining emphasis on intellectual independence, a slowing rate of material progress, rising birth rates, a narrowing of the latitude for the exercise of the right of free speech, and increased restraints on Sunday business, divorce, and possibly birth control.

The opposite has happened in every respect since the book was published in 1961, indicating that either the concept of intellectual autonomy has a much more complex meaning to middle-class third-generation Catholics than it had to their parents or grandparents or Catholics in the working classes, or that John F. Kennedy and the Second Vatican Council have stimulated profoundly the tendencies toward autonomy which did exist among Catholics of all generations, especially those with more education. This particular finding by Lenski was contradicted implicitly by two other sociological studies published in 1964 and 1965, and based on later surveys than the one made in Detroit. One of them, by Father Joseph H. Fichter, found the older generation conservative (as measured by views on public policy questions) and less critical of the Church than younger parishioners. The other, by Father Andrew Greeley, showed on the basis of a large sample of college graduates in 1961 that Catholic anti-intellectualism had sharply declined by the early 1960's. Statistics aside, by 1966 an increasing number of younger Catholics tended to prize their personal independence and believed as much as Protestants and Jews that spiritual self-direction was indispensable to genuine religious commitment. They insisted, as Gary MacEoin put it in *New Challenges to American Catholics,* that "the Church must be a society of freedom."

The process of Americanization or adaptation to the culture-religion of America is often deplored by respected religious leaders such as Reinhold Niebuhr, Robert McAfee Brown, Father Gustave Weigel, and Rabbi Will Herberg. Even when they grant that the blunting of sectarian differences helps to promote vital unity in a pluralistic society, they sometimes see the process as compromising traditions and practices long associated with deep concern for the ultimate questions of human existence. Americans are charged not just with merging their transcendental concerns with those of the secular culture, but as lacking in spiritual or religious concerns.

There is no question that religion has often been subsumed by national patriotism in America, but it is doubtful if transcendental religion was more of a check on the worldly goals of sixteenth-century Catholic Spain or is currently more of a test of the national foreign policy of Moslem Pakistan than it has been in the United States. By valuing personal independence, Americans may burden themselves with vicious status competition and deep psychological isolation, but they have not been prevented from recognizing the claims of individual conscience. Probably no religious group so well exemplifies traditional American values as the Quakers, who have given a higher proportion of conscientious objectors to participation in American wars than any other group.

The accusation that spiritual life in America is often banal, and religious commitment often superficial because the culture-religion has blurred sectarian differences, can be analyzed only in terms of some standard of spirituality and religious commitment. If ritual is an important index of spiritual life, then Americans are not as spiritual as Filipinos or Colombians. If the passive virtues of obedience, piety, and austerity are the primary measures of transcendental concern, then most Hindus and Buddhists are far more religious than Americans. If theological preoccupation is the test, the Germans and French are certainly more religious. The obvious and more traditional indexes of religiosity indicate a decline in America in recent decades. Studies show that per capita contributions to Protestant churches over the past twenty-five years have been declining. The ratio of clergymen to the general population in the past hundred years has gone down, the number of church seats available in proportion to the population has declined, and even reports of church attendance by the Gallup poll show a drop over the past twenty years. Among Protestants there is probably less doctrinal orthodoxy and devotionalism than at any time since the Revolution.

Yet it was only a few decades ago that ministers and priests were congratulating themselves on the so-called "religious revival" in America. Then, climbing church attendance may have been little more than a function of suburbanization with its demand for a church-centered social life. In retrospect, it seems to me that no genuine religious revival could have permitted the vigilantism of McCarthy, the platitudes of Eisenhower, and the moralisms of Dulles. By contrast, the marching nuns, priests, and rabbis in Selma, Alabama, the extraordinary emphasis on renewal in Protestant churches, the accelerated activity in evangelical sects such as the Jehovah's Witnesses or the Seventh-day Adventists, and the deep soul-searching reported by group leaders, psychiatrists, and college teachers indicate that religion is far more a vital force in the 1960's than it was in the two previous decades.

But these developments have been accompanied by a rising agnosticism and widespread assumption that religion is less a force than it used to be. Studies have shown that a higher percentage of college students in the 1960's professed agnosticism than in the 1950's, and that there were proportionately more agnostics in college in the 1950's than in 1913. A 1965 Gallup poll revealed that the percentage of Americans who see religion as losing influence had more than tripled since 1957. But do statistics that show that 52 percent of the college students believe that religious influence is losing ground actually demonstrate that religion is losing ground? Or do they signify a deepening awareness of the vulnerability of the human condition and a profound feeling of dissatisfaction with the answers provided by sectarian religion to questions of ultimate concern?

The growing opposition to automated faith and the commitment to the value of personal choice rather than militating against religion may be a prelude to a deeper, more complex spirituality than Americans have known before. Paul Tillich's assertion that salvation can be located in "the courage to be" has been embraced by new-breed Catholics, Jews, Protestants, agnostics, and atheists on college campuses all over the country. His definition of religion as "ultimate concern" is not only compatible with a culture which emphasizes personal responsibility for choice but which has been called the most secular civilization in a secular age.

Secularism—which is characterized by neutrality of the state with respect to religion, tolerant attitudes toward religious differences, and an assessment of men in terms of how they function—is incompatible with extreme sectarianism; but it is not necessarily antagonistic to profound and complex religious commitment unless one defines religion in purely sectarian terms. Many Catholic and some Protestant writers have equated secular religion with materalism, assuming that the advance of secularism would mean the corruption of spiritual values, but Protestant theologian Harvey Cox has argued that secularism should be welcomed by believing Christians and Jews precisely because it makes possible a greater range of freedom and responsibility for man. It tests his spiritual resources more sharply and disturbingly than they have been challenged before.

Secularism makes war on parochialism, but not necessarily on religion. Are Jews more religious if they insist on their chosenness to live according to the moral law? Are Catholics more religious if they maintain that nonbelievers are eternally damned? Are Protestants more religious if they hold to a belief in the predestination of the elect? Parochialism says not just "Here I stand," but "There you must stand." It is often a defensive reaction to fear that puts up walls and signs that read: "Be careful," "Whites only," "No Irish need apply."

AN ECUMENICAL MAN

John F. Kennedy represented an antithetical approach to parochialism in human affairs. For him, life was not to be feared but affirmed. Experience was not to be avoided but courted. Cardinal Cushing has quoted the President as saying, "We must esteem other religious faiths" (not tolerate, but "esteem"). Kennedy had the capacity to expose himself to differences, even to reach out to understand them, and yet remain true to his own convictions. He wanted it absolutely clear that he was against religious extremism and intolerance from whatever source. When he talked to the United Nations in September, 1963, just two months before his death, he protested that human rights "are not respected when a Buddhist priest is driven from his pagoda," a not very subtle reference to alleged Catholic persecution of Buddhists in Vietnam. Then, to make it clear that no group is immune from the fault of intolerance, religious or racial, he pointed out that human rights are attacked "when a synagogue is shut down, when a Protestant church cannot open a mission [something Protestants have complained against Catholics in Latin America for years], when a cardinal is forced into hiding, or when a crowded church service is bombed [as had happened recently to a Negro church in Alabama]."

Kennedy's broad ecumenism—his desire for encounter with others—was not incompatible with a deepening sense of ultimate concern or growing identification with Catholicism. For Kennedy, as he told the students and faculty of Boston College in April, 1963, the importance of Pope John and his farsighted encyclicals was that "we are learning to talk the language of progress and peace across the barriers of sect and creed." Following the Pope's death, Kennedy pointed out that while John had been "the chosen leader of world Catholicism, ... his concern for the human spirit transcended all boundaries of belief or geography." Three weeks later, the President told the Irish Parliament: "The supreme reality of our time is our indivisibility as children of God and our common vulnerability on this planet . . . we must remember there are no permanent enemies." Because that was Pope John's belief too, Kennedy was able to say, after reading Pope John's remarkable encyclical *Pacem in terris:* "As a Catholic I am proud of it; and as an American I have learned from it." Pope John had made Kennedy proud to be a Catholic exactly because John himself was not prideful. Kennedy praised *Pacem in terris* but pointed out to his Catholic audience that it was not uniquely Catholic and "that it closely matches notable expressions of convictions and aspirations from churchmen of other faiths, as in recent documents of the World Council of Churches, and from outstanding world citizens with no ecclesiastical standing."

Only a few weeks before he died, John F. Kennedy spoke to the Protestant Council of New York City. In this speech, Kennedy went beyond not only his sectarian origins but the culture-religion of Americanism too. Although he saw the mission of Americans as the promotion of the family of man, he did not define progress in terms of the spread of American values. He pointed out that most of the world knew nothing about free enterprise, due process of law, or the Australian ballot, and asserted that the family of man could accept differences of ideology, politics, and economics and transcend differences of race and religion. He reminded his audience that most members of the family are not white and most of them are not Christian, but all of them share the desire to survive in dignity. Warning that the family of man could not survive a nuclear war or endure the growing gap between the rich and the poor, he hoped that man would prevail, not just Catholicism, or America, or even political freedom or personal independence, as Americans have known them, but man. To judge from the worldwide reaction to Kennedy's death, this secular President from a secular country spoke to the spiritual needs of men everywhere.
· This man who wore his religion so lightly communicated his sense of ultimate concern.

The culture-religion of America can be faulted on many grounds. At its worst, it has been no less ethnocentric than any other religion, and even more intolerant than the absorptive, flexible philosophies and religions of the East. By its insistence on personal independence, it has often inhibited mutuality and love in personal relationships. It has helped to promote a kind of competitiveness and loneliness unknown to the more traditional cultures of Asia. It has torn at traditions, burdening Americans, especially Protestants, with the need to find meaning from one's naked existence rather than as a member of a family, tribe, church, or historic community. The response of Americans often has been a weak, other-directed conformism to the values of the Rotary and to the standards of the marketplace, or an avoidance of a crisis of personal decision, but there also has been the response of Lincoln and Kennedy.

If Americans have lived with alienation longer than most people, it is mainly because they are a nation of uprooted Europeans and Asians held together partly by the customs and loyalties of their subcultures but also by a commitment to a culture-religion which in its emphasis on independence often confines them, in de Tocqueville's words, to the solitude of their own hearts. Americans took from Luther and Calvin those Protestant principles which had the most meaning for their unique historical experience. Whatever in the new theology of Protestantism promoted self-sufficiency was grasped before the turn of the eighteenth century. Protestantism thus became both a result and a cause of psychic isolation. For Luther, a representative of the new breed of his time, there was one way to know God's word: "Thou must thyself decide. Thy life is at stake. Therefore must God say unto thee in thy heart, 'This is God's word,' else it is still undecided."

Until the election of John F. Kennedy, the Catholic Church, more than any other single institution, and Catholics more than any other group of Americans, were viewed as hostile to the American insistence on personal independence. Kennedy was President for less than three years and the Roman Catholic Church still asserts its claim to truth through authoritative spokesmen commissioned by God beginning with the Pope of Rome. Yet the Church both in America and the world has embraced the value of individual choice long associated with the civilization of North America. It is a powerful and explosive value, creating technology which expands the aesthetic and intellectual dimensions of human personality and builds friendships across traditional barriers, but which also destroys traditions which have enabled men for centuries to find themselves in others and in nature. It is a dangerous value which has often led to pride, willfulness, and hatred; but it is a value which can also lead to commitments to love God and to care for man, as well as self-centeredness devoid of either. It is a value which may be muted or even radically altered with the passage of time as Americans encounter Asians, Latin Americans, and Africans in mutually enriching relationships. But it is the value of our time and culture, of Protestants and Jews, and increasingly of Catholics, Western Europeans, and peoples in large cities everywhere, forcing them to think with Luther that "everyone must do his own believing as he will have to do his own dying." Or was it John F. Kennedy who said that?

NOTES

Chapter 1. A City upon a Hill

I am indebted to many students of the history of Protestantism in America. Notable is William W. Sweet. His book, *The Story of Religion in America*, New York, Harper & Brothers, 1930, is as fine an introduction as can be found anywhere. He shows a keen appreciation of Americanism as a culture-religion. Other books by Sweet which were helpful are: *Religion on the American Frontier*, Vol. I, *The Baptists, 1783–1830*, New York, Cooper Square Publishers, 1931; *The American Churches: An Interpretation*, New York, Abingdon-Cokesbury Press, 1947; and *Religion in Colonial America*, New York, Cooper Square Publishers, 1949. Another fine short introduction on which I relied considerably is Winthrop S. Hudson, *American Protestantism*, Chicago, University of Chicago Press, 1961.

An extremely useful source for me was Thomas C. Hall, *The Religious Background of American Culture*, New York, Frederick Ungar Publishing Co., 1930. Hall provides an excellent bibliography, which he brought up to date in 1958 in the second edition. I relied on him for an interpretation of the significance of John Wycliff and his relationship to the dissenting Protestant tradition which was transplanted to the United States from England. There were several other books which were helpful in developing my understanding of the special qualities of Protestantism in the United States. They include: Ernest S. Bates, *American Faith*, New York, W. W. Norton & Company, 1940; Jerald C. Brauer, *Protestantism in America: A Narrative History*, Philadelphia, Westminster Press, 1953; Elmer T. Clark, *The Small Sects in America—Historical, Theological, and Psychological Backgrounds*, rev. ed., Nashville, Tenn., Abingdon Press, 1949; Joseph R. Haroutunian, *Piety Versus Moralism: The Passing of the New England Theology*, Hamden, Conn., Shoe String Press, 1932; Charles H. Hopkins, *The Rise of the Social Gospel in American Protestantism, 1865–1915*, New Haven, Conn., Yale University Press, 1940; Charles Roy Keller, *The Second Great Awakening in Connecticut*, New Haven, Conn., Yale University Press, 1942; G. Adolph Koch, *Republican Re-*

ligion: The American Revolution and the Cult of Reason, New York, Henry Holt & Company, 1933; John Moffatt Mecklin, *The Story of American Dissent,* New York, Harcourt, Brace & Company, 1934; Helmut Richard Niebuhr, *The Social Sources of Denominationalism,* New York, Henry Holt & Co., 1929; and Liston Pope, *Millhands and Preachers,* New Haven, Conn., Yale University Press, 1942.

The best known and probably the best treatment of the social and religious revolution in seventeenth-century England may be found in G. P. Gooch, *The History of English Democratic Ideas in the Seventeenth Century,* London, Cambridge University Press, 1898. Also important is Canon Henson, *English Religion in the Seventeenth Century,* London, 1903, and Theodore Calvin Pease, *The Leveller Movement,* Washington, D.C., American Historical Association, 1916.

No one has contributed more to my understanding of puritanism in America than Perry Miller. See his *Orthodoxy in Massachusetts, 1630–50,* Cambridge, Mass., Harvard University Press, 1933; *The New England Mind,* Vol. I, *The Seventeenth Century,* New York, The Macmillan Company, 1939; *Roger Williams: His Contribution to the American Tradition,* Indianapolis, Bobbs-Merrill Company, 1953; and *The New England Mind: From Colony to Province,* Cambridge, Mass., Harvard University Press, 1953. An excellent sourcebook edited by Miller is the *American Puritans,* New York, Harper & Brothers, 1953.

An extremely good article by Miller entitled "From the Covenant to the Revival" appeared in *The Shaping of the American Religion,* Vol. 1, edited by James Ward Smith and A. Leland Jamison, Princeton, N.J., Princeton University Press, 1961. I am particularly indebted to that article for my emphasis on the fusion of American and Protestant messianism during the Revolutionary War.

Other useful books on Puritanism in America include: G. B. Taphan, *The Puritans in Power,* Cambridge, Harvard University Press, 1913; William Haller, *Liberty and Reformation in the Puritan Revolution,* New York, Columbia University Press, 1955; Ralph B. Perry, *Puritanism and Democracy,* New York, Vanguard Press, 1944; and George Malcolm Stephenson, *The Puritan Heritage,* New York, The Macmillan Company, 1952.

For significant books on the formative period of American values and character, Louis Booker Wright is especially helpful. See his *The Atlantic Frontier: Colonial American Civilization, 1607–1763,* New York, Alfred A. Knopf, 1947; and—which for me was particularly useful—*Cultural Life of the American Colonies, 1607–1763,* New York, Harper & Brothers, 1957. I also recommend Daniel Boorstin, *Americans,* Vol. I, *The Colonial Experience,* New York, Random House, 1958; Merle Curti, *The Growth of American Thought,* New York, Harper & Brothers, 1943; Marcus Cunliff, *The Nation Takes Shape: 1789–1837,* Chicago, University of Chicago Press, 1958; Russel Nye, *The Cultural Life of the New Nation, 1776–1830,* New York, Harper & Brothers, 1960; Clinton Rossiter, *Seedtime of the Republic,* New York, Harcourt, Brace & Company, 1953; and Max Savelle, *Seeds of Liberty,* New York, Alfred A. Knopf, 1948. I leaned considerably on Nye, who provides an excellent survey of the writings of Jefferson, Franklin, Washington, Adams, and Hamilton, for my interpretation of the doctrine of progress at the time of the revolution and the years following.

My material on John Winthrop comes from John Winthrop, "A Model of Christian Charity," *Collections of the Massachusetts Historical Society,* third series, Vol. VII, Boston, Massachusetts Historical Society, 1838, and from Winthrop's own journal, John Winthrop, *The History of New England from 1630–1649,* edited by James Savage, Boston, Little, Brown and Company, 1853. The discussion from William Bradford is from his own *History of the Plymouth Plantation,* Boston, Little, Brown, and Company, 1859.

The Frederick Jackson Turner material comes from two of his major articles: "The Significance of the Frontier in American History," *American Historical Association, Annual Report,* 2, Washington, 1894, and "The Problem of the West," *Atlantic Monthly,* Vol. LXXVIII, September, 1898.

All of the material on the movement of settlers from Watertown to Sudbury to Marlboro comes from Sumner Chilton Powell, *Puritan Village,* Middletown, Conn., Wesleyan University Press, 1963. The report of the Colonial Board of Trade comes from *Calendar of State Papers, Colonial Series, American and West Indies, May 15, 1696–October 31, 1697,* edited by J. W. Fortescque, London, 1904.

Two interpretations on the importance of abundance and open land for understanding American character on which I placed considerable reliance are: Henry Nash Smith, *Virgin Land,* Cambridge, Mass., Harvard University Press, 1950; and David M. Potter, *People of Plenty,* Chicago, University of Chicago Press, 1954. It was from Smith that I took my emphasis on the rising expectations of the Kentuckian and Virginian who look at bountiful nature in America.

I have learned a great deal in understanding American values and character by reading the comments of foreign visitors and immigrants. A partial summation of views which have bearing on this book may be found in a superb study of American character by Seymour Martin Lipset in Part 2 of the *First New Nation,* New York, Basic Books, Inc., 1963.

On the shift from state church to the separation of church and state, there are two excellent short books which were useful to me: Evarts B. Greene, *Religion and the State,* Ithaca, N.Y., Cornell University Press, 1941, and Franklin Hamlin Littell, *From State Church to Pluralism,* Garden City, N.Y., Doubleday & Company, 1962. Greene's book has a superb bibliography and Littell's book brings major themes of the story up to date.

I am strongly indebted to the classic book by Max Weber, *The Protestant Ethic and the Spirit of Capitalism,* translated by Talcott Parsons, New York, Charles Scribner's Sons, 1958, for my emphasis on the interrelationships between religious and social ideas. First published in German in 1920, Weber's seminal thesis that Calvinism is the major source of capitalism has been qualified and criticized ever since, but it is always taken seriously. I have also been instructed and inspired by one of his major critics and supporters, Richard Henry Tawney, in his *Religion and the Rise of Capitalism,* New York, Harcourt, Brace & Company, 1926.

An important book which lends support to certain of Weber's ideas is David McClelland, *The Achieving Society,* Princeton, N.J., D. Van Nostrand Company, 1961. Another book, which bears out the brilliance of many of Weber's insights and gives support to my emphasis on a correlation between Protestantism and the values of personal independence and achievement, is a recent sociological inquiry by Gerhard Lenski, *The Religious Factor,* Garden City, N.Y., Doubleday & Company, 1961. Lenski presents a variety of data linking self-reliance and independence to Protestantism.

Chapter 2. DEFENDING THE CITY

An important source for understanding the impact of the Reformation inheritance on Protestant reactions to Catholics is Mary Augustina Ray, *American Opinion of Roman Catholicism in the Eighteenth Century,* New York, Columbia University Press, 1936.

Another major source for this chapter is Ray Allen Billington, *The Protestant Crusade, 1800–1860: A Study of the Origins of American Nativism,* New York, Rinehart & Company, 1938. Billington has an extensive bibliography of primary sources including pamphlets and newspapers. He is particularly good on Know-Nothingism and nativism generally, although he exaggerates the extent of the more violent and vitriolic manifestations of anti-Catholicism.

To better understand the clash of cultures represented by the Brahmins and the Irish of New England, see Barbara Miller Solomon, *Ancestors and Immigrants: A Changing New England Tradition,* Cambridge, Mass., Harvard University Press, 1956. Mrs. Solomon also has excellent notes.

I made considerable use also of Oscar Handlin, *Boston's Immigrants, 1790–1865,* Cambridge, Mass., Harvard University Press, 1941, an extremely careful and detailed history of the developing clash between the two cultures in the city of Boston. The two historians referred to as disputing the extent to which prominent citizens of Boston shared responsibility for destruction of the Ursuline Convent are Billington and Handlin. Billington infers from the evidence a much clearer responsibility for Boston's leading citizens. Handlin stresses the isolated causes and effects of the burning of the convent and the lower-class character of the mob.

A broad history that provides a rich understanding of the Anglo-Saxon nativist response to Catholics and others is John Higham, *Strangers in the Land,* New Brunswick, N.J., Rutgers University Press, 1955. While I relied on Billington for much general nineteenth-century material, I used Handlin as a source for Boston and Higham and several of the primary sources which he lists for my later nineteenth-century material on nativism, the APA, and the Ku Klux Klan.

For those who would like to see a Catholic historian's version of Protestant reaction to Catholicism and Catholics in America, I suggest Theodore Maynard, *The Story of American Catholicism,* 2 vols., New York, The Macmillan Company, 1941.

For an excellent recent interpretation of the pervasiveness of anti-Catholicism in the Evangelical as well as the older Calvinist sects, see Seymour Martin Lipset, "Religion and Politics in American History," in *Religious*

Conflict in America: Studies of the Problem Beyond Bigotry, edited by Earl Raab, Garden City, N.Y., Doubleday & Company, 1964.

The authority on the persecution of Quakers is Richard Price Hallowell, *The Pioneer Quakers,* Boston, Houghton Mifflin Company, 1887.

The important quotation from Herman Melville on an American Eden comes from his book, *Redburn, His First Voyage,* New York, A. & C. Boni, 1924.

The long quotation from de Crèvecoeur can be found in any unabridged edition. An excellent recent one is (J. Hector St. John) de Crèvecoeur, *Letters from an American Farmer,* with a foreword by Albert E. Stone, Jr., New York, Signet Classics, 1963.

For material from de Tocqueville, I used Alexis de Tocqueville, *Democracy in America,* the Henry Reeve text revised by Francis Bowen, New York, Vintage Books, 1954.

The long quotation from John Jay is from the *Federalists Papers.* I used the edition edited by Roy P. Fairchild, Garden City, N.Y., Doubleday & Company, 1961.

For the 1928 election I relied mainly on Edmund A. Moore, *A Catholic Runs for President,* New York, The Ronald Press Company, 1956.

Chapter 3. HOPE AND FEAR

Of the several histories of Catholicism in America that I read, the most useful was Theodore Maynard, *The Story of American Catholics,* 2 vols., New York, The Macmillan Company, 1941. Maynard's book has an excellent bibliography through 1941. Maynard is very Catholic in his interpretations of social and political conflict, which makes his work all the more valuable to me in trying to empathize with Catholic reactions to Protestantism and Americanism. Earlier histories which are helpful include: Thomas D'Arcy McGee, *The Catholic History of North America,* Boston, P. Donahoe, 1855; and John Gilmary Shea, *History of the Catholic Church in the United States,* 4 vols., New York, J. G. Shea, 1886–1892. In checking names, dates, and meetings, I often relied on the *Catholic Encyclopedia,* edited by C. G. Herbermann *et al.,* 15 vols., New York, 1907–1912, and *Catholic Builders of the Nation,* edited by Constantine Edward McGuire, 5 vols., Boston, Continental Press, 1923.

In gaining a better understanding of the spirit, philosophy, and theology of Catholicism, I found two books particularly helpful: Karl Adam, *The Spirit of Catholicism*—I used the translation of Justice McCann, O.S.B., in the Image Books edition of 1954, although the book was first published in New York, 1935; and Ronald Knox, *The Belief of Catholics*—I used the Image Books edition, 1958, although the book was first published in New York, 1927.

The Catholic historian upon whom I relied the most is John Tracy Ellis, particularly his *American Catholicism,* Chicago, University of Chicago Press, 1956, and also *The Formative Years of the Catholic University of America,* Washington, D.C., The Catholic University of America Press, 1946, and *The*

Life of James Cardinal Gibbons, Archbishop of Baltimore, 1834–1921, 2 vols., Milwaukee, Bruce Publishing Co., 1952. Extremely useful to me was Ellis' *Perspectives in American Catholicism*, Baltimore, Helicon Press, 1963. Ellis writes clearly, and although his main interest is biography, he always manages to communicate a great deal of history. An extensive bibliography on the Church in America may be found at the end of this book.

On the early period of American Catholic history, see John Gilmary Shea, *The Catholic Church in Colonial Days*, New York, J. G. Shea, 1888, and *Life and Times of Archbishop Carroll*, New York, J. G. Shea, 1888. Also useful is Kate Mason Rowland, *Life of Charles Carroll of Carrollton, 1737–1832, with His Correspondence and Public Papers*, 2 vols., New York, G. P. Putnam's Sons, 1898. A leading historian of the period was Peter Guilday, whose major books were *The Life and Times of John Carroll*, 2 vols., New York, The Encyclopedia Press, 1922, and *The Life and Times of John England*, 2 vols., New York, The American Press, 1927.

For an understanding of liberal Catholicism, there are two books that I found especially helpful. First, Robert D. Cross, *The Emergence of Liberal Catholicism in America*, Cambridge, Mass., Harvard University Press, 1958. It is an extremely well-written and comprehensive account of the struggle between the liberals and the conservatives in the Church in America, with an extensive bibliography of primary and secondary sources. Cross has gone into much greater detail than I have been able to do on nearly all of the major issues of the nineteenth-century struggle. His chapters on education and the emergence of the Americanizers are superb. The other book, although smaller, is also superb. It is Daniel Callahan, *The Mind of the Catholic Layman*, New York, Charles Scribner's Sons, 1963. While Cross is not a Catholic, Callahan is, and his book profits rather than suffers from the special emphases and insights which he can give from the point of view of liberal Catholics. I relied particularly on his excellent analysis of trusteeism. Callahan also has a good, selective bibliography.

My major source for understanding the Americanist controversy was an excellent volume by Thomas T. McAvoy, *The Americanist Heresy in Roman Catholicism, 1895–1900*, South Bend, Ind., University of Notre Dame Press, 1963. McAvoy uses primary sources liberally, although some of the most important documents have never been released by the Vatican. His book suffers because of the absence of a bibliography and for those who wish to follow the Americanist controversy further, the following are useful: Henry J. Browne, *The Catholic Church and the Knights of Labor*, Catholic University Studies in American Church History, Vol. 38, Washington, D.C., The Catholic University of America Press, 1949; John Tracy Ellis, *John Lancaster Spalding*, Milwaukee, Bruce Publishing Co., 1961—this is not as important a work as his biography of Gibbons, but it is useful; Mary Evangela Henthorne, *The Career of the Right Reverend John Lancaster Spalding, Bishop of Peoria, as President of the Irish Catholic Colonization Association of the United States, 1879–1892*, Urbana, Ill., University of Illinois, 1932; Vincent F. Holden, *The Early Years of Isaac Thomas Hecker, 1819–1844*, Washington, D.C., The Catholic University of America Press, 1939; Fergus Macdonald, *The Catholic Church and the Secret Societies in the United States*, New York, The U.S. Catholic

Historical Society, 1946; Theodore Maynard, *Orestes Brownson, Yankee, Radical, Catholic,* New York, The Macmillan Company, 1943; J. H. Moynihan, *The Life of Archbishop John Ireland,* New York, Harper & Brothers, 1953; Arthur M. Schlesinger, Jr., *Orestes A. Brownson,* Boston, Little, Brown, and Company, 1939; Allen Sinclair Will, *Life of James Cardinal Gibbons,* 2 vols., New York, John Murphy Company, 1911. An exceptionally valuable source book of primary materials focusing on an issue which is often at the heart of the progressive-conservative struggle within the Church in America is *American Catholicism and the Intellectual Ideal,* edited by Frank L. Christ and Gerard E. Sherry, New York, Appleton-Century-Crofts, 1961.

For those who wish to read more on the question of Catholics and Negroes in the nineteenth century, see John C. Murphy, *An Analysis of the Attitudes of American Catholics Toward the Immigrant and the Negro, 1825–1925,* Washington, D.C., The Catholic University of America Press, 1940; Madeline H. Rice, *American Catholic Opinion in the Slavery Controversy,* New York, Columbia University Press, 1944; and Florence E. Gibson, *The Attitudes of the New York Irish Toward State and National Affairs, 1848–1892,* New York, Columbia University Press, 1951.

For those who wish to follow the German controversy further and to find out more about non-Irish Catholic groups see: Colman J. Barry, *The Catholic Church and German Americans,* Milwaukee, Bruce Publishing Company, 1953; Joseph Edward Ciesluk, *National Parishes in the United States,* Washington, D.C., The Catholic University of America Press, 1947; and Thomas T. McAvoy, *Roman Catholicism and the American Way of Life,* South Bend, Ind., University of Notre Dame Press, 1960. The last is a collection of essays which includes material on Italian and Polish as well as German and Irish Catholics.

I relied on several histories concerning the Irish. Oscar Handlin, *Boston's Immigrants,* Cambridge, Mass., Harvard University Press, 1938, was helpful. A useful early history is John Francis Maguire, *The Irish in America,* New York, Longmans, Green & Co., 1868. Carl Wittke, *The Irish in America,* Baton Rouge, La., Louisiana University Press, 1956, provides an excellent bibliography of works and articles and many unpublished theses and dissertations. A somewhat better written and more analytical book is William B. Shannon, *The American Irish,* New York, The Macmillan Company, 1963. Although it does not have a general bibliography and its notes are much less extensive than Wittke's, its topical approach is extremely well done. There are particularly superb portraits of Cardinal Gibbons, Al Smith, and James Curley as well as an excellent chapter on Tammany Hall. George Potter, *To the Golden Door: The Story of the Irish in Ireland and America,* Boston, Little, Brown and Company, 1960, is another helpful survey.

On the background to Irish immigration, nothing is better than Cecil Woodham-Smith, *The Great Hunger, Ireland, 1845–1849,* New York, Harper & Row, 1962. Also helpful is Stephen Byrne, *Irish Emigration to the United States,* New York, Catholic Publication Society, 1873, and William Forbes Adams, *Ireland and Irish Emigration to the New World from 1815 to the Famine,* New Haven, Yale University Press, 1932.

On the Irish and Catholics in politics through the election of Herbert

Hoover, I used Berton Dulce and Edward J. Richter, *Religion and the Presidency*, New York, The Macmillan Company, 1962; Edmund A. Moore, *A Catholic Runs for President*, New York, Ronald Press Co., 1956; James Michael Curley, *I'd Do It Again*, Englewood Cliffs, N.J., Prentice-Hall, 1957; R. V. Peel and T. C. Donelly, *The 1928 Campaign*, New York, R. R. Smith, 1931; and Oscar Handlin, *Al Smith and His America*, Boston, Little, Brown and Company, 1958.

The quote from Archbishop John Hughes on converting Americans to Catholicism comes from his own book, *The Decline of Protestantism and Its Cause*, New York, E. Dunigan & Brother, 1850.

Chapter 4. DEEPENING TENSIONS

Father Coughlin and Senator McCarthy are covered in many recent histories on the Roosevelt and Truman periods, but there are particularly good chapters in William V. Shannon, *The American Irish*, New York, The Macmillan Company, 1964. There are many books on McCarthy and one biography of Coughlin, but none of them add much to the essential facts in Shannon's interpretative essays.

To understand the mood and the quality of the liberal attacks on Catholicism in this period, I relied on America's foremost critic, Paul Blanshard, and his principal work, *American Freedom and Catholic Power*, Boston, Beacon Press, 1949. Blanshard employs extensive documentation, particularly in this book, and has a large and useful general bibliography, consisting overwhelmingly of Catholic sources. Also helpful were his other books: *Communism, Democracy, and Catholic Power*, Boston, Beacon Press, 1951; *The Irish and Catholic Power: An American Interpretation*, Boston, Beacon Press, 1953; *The Right to Read: The Battle Against Censorship*, Boston, Beacon Press, 1955; and *God and Man in Washington*, Boston, Beacon Press, 1960, to which I refer several times in the latter part of this chapter.

The quotation from James B. Conant comes from his own book, *Education and Liberty*, Cambridge, Mass., Harvard University Press, 1953.

The three quotations on a graduated system of power, a church whose leader assumes the title of Prince, and the potential threat of the Catholic Church come respectively from Marcus Bach, *Report to Protestants*, Indianapolis, Bobbs-Merrill Company, 1948; Winfred Ernest Garrison, *A Protestant Manifesto*, New York, Abingdon-Cokesbury Press, 1952; and V. Ogden Vogt, *Cult and Culture*, New York, The Macmillan Company, 1951.

One Catholic writer who takes much the same view as Blanshard is Thomas Sugrue, *A Catholic Speaks His Mind on America's Religious Conflict*, New York, Harper and Brothers, 1951. A much more sympathetic Catholic interpretation but also sharing many of the criticisms of the liberal non-Catholics at the time is Thomas F. O'Dea, *American Catholic Dilemma*, New York, Sheed & Ward, 1958. The lay Catholic journal, *Commonweal*, made a comparable effort to understand criticisms of Catholics from a non-Catholic point of view. The quotation from James O'Garrick is typical and comes from the *Commonweal* for May 30, 1958.

Father John Courtney Murray, S.J., defended the Catholic point of view in a series of lofty articles on Church and state in the 1940's and 1950's. For a full analysis of his writings, see Thomas T. Love, *John Courtney Murray: Contemporary Church-State Theory,* New York, Doubleday & Company, 1965. Murray was in the forefront of attempts to raise the Protestant or Americanist vs. Catholic controversy to the level of rational discussion. In this he received considerable assistance from Gustave Weigel, S.J., whose trenchant writings won the respect of many non-Catholics. One Weigel book which I found particularly helpful is *An American Dialogue,* New York, Doubleday & Company, 1960, by Father Weigel and Protestant critic Robert McAfee Brown. On a comparable plane of excellence were a series of pamphlets published by the Fund for the Republic in the late 1950's. See *Religion and the Free Society,* 1958; *Religion and the School,* 1959; and *The Churches and the Public,* 1960. These pamphlets emphasize the importance of clear, effective communication in symposia with Protestant, Catholic, and Jewish participants, who, to a remarkable degree, fulfill that objective set by themselves.

Of particular importance to me in understanding the tensions of this period is Kenneth Wilson Underwood, *Protestant and Catholic: Religious and Social Interaction in an Industrial City,* Boston, Beacon Press, 1957. A comparable earlier book, not nearly as impressive as Underwood's but helpful nonetheless, is Elin L. Anderson, *We Americans: The Study of Cleavage in an American City,* Cambridge, Mass., Harvard University Press, 1937. My report of the Sanger incident is taken directly from Underwood.

W. Lloyd Warner and his colleagues are also helpful in illuminating the sociological bases for Catholic–non-Catholic conflict. See W. Lloyd Warner and Leo Srole, *Social Systems of American Ethnic Groups,* New Haven, Conn., Yale University Press, 1945. This material and other works by Warner appear in a one-volume, abridged edition entitled *Yankee City* by W. Lloyd Warner, J. O. Low, Paul S. Lunt, and Leo Srole, New Haven, Conn., Yale University Press, 1963.

Significant Catholic rebuttals to Blanshard came from James Milton O'Neill in two volumes: *Religion and Education Under the Constitution,* New York, Harper & Brothers, 1949, and particularly, *Catholicism and American Freedom,* New York, Harper & Brothers, 1952. O'Neill and O'Dea generally spoke for the encounter point of view, although O'Dea was considerably more self-critical. Defensive parochialism was advanced in John A. Ryan and Francis Joseph Boland, *Catholic Principles of Politics,* New York, The Macmillan Company, 1940.

Other answers to the non-Catholic critics of which I made considerable use include: Walter J. Ong, S.J., *American Catholic Crossroads: Religious-Secular Encounters in the Modern World,* New York, The Macmillan Company, 1959, and John Joseph Kane, *Catholic-Protestant Conflicts in America,* Chicago, Henry Regnery Co., 1955. Kane's chapter on the origins of Catholic separatism in America gives the Catholic point of view in defending the historical inevitability of separatism. It is from Kane that I took my material on the changing anti-Catholic content of the nondenominational Protestant magazine, *Christian Century.*

Chapter 5. NOT THE CATHOLIC CANDIDATE

The early paragraphs in this chapter on presidential availability and the growing importance of personality politics in the 1950's essentially rest on my own interpretation of American political history. One extremely important source book is the *American Voter* by Angus Campbell, Phillip E. Converse, Warren E. Miller, and Donald E. Stokes, New York, published by John Wiley & Sons, Inc., 1960, which draws primarily on the results of election surveys carried out by the Survey Research Center at the University of Michigan in 1952 and 1956.

In trying to understand Kennedy's earlier years in politics, I relied considerably on James MacGregor Burns, *John Kennedy: A Political Profile,* New York, Harcourt, Brace & Company, 1960. Also helpful were two magnificent presidential biographies, Theodore C. Sorensen, *Kennedy,* New York, Harper & Row, 1965, and Arthur M. Schlesinger, Jr., *A Thousand Days: John F. Kennedy in the White House,* Boston, Houghton Mifflin Company, 1965. Sorensen is somewhat more interested and closer to the Catholic aspects of Kennedy's quest for the Presidency, but both biographies are helpful in understanding Kennedy and the campaign. I relied also on Theodore H. White, *The Making of the President, 1960,* New York, Atheneum Publishers, 1960. White's book has been justly praised for its scope and intensity in dealing with the campaign; he also seems to have an especially keen and sensitive appreciation of Kennedy.

On Kennedy's upbringing and school days, Burns was helpful. Particularly useful was Richard J. Whalen, *The Founding Father: The Story of Joseph P. Kennedy,* New York, New American Library, 1964, a superb treatment of the Kennedy family and the forces which influenced its members.

In digging deeply into the religious aspects of the 1960 campaign, I read many Catholic and Protestant periodicals, referred to in the body of the chapter; but I did not attempt to duplicate the labors of Sister Patricia Barrett in her *Religious Liberty and the American Presidency,* New York, Herder and Herder, 1963, a short but fact-packed analysis of anti-Catholicism in the 1960 campaign. At the conclusion of her essay, Sister Barrett lists all the campaign pieces that deal with the issue and provides her readers with an extensive bibliography of scholarly articles and journalistic accounts concerning the religious factor in the 1960 campaign. Also helpful were a fine series of essays by Monsignor Francis Lally, *The Catholic Church in a Changing America,* Boston, Little, Brown and Company, 1962, and the last several chapters of Berton Dulce and Edward J. Richter, *Religion and the Presidency,* New York, The Macmillan Company, 1962. For a helpful analysis of Catholic voting behavior, see John Harold Fenton, *The Catholic Vote,* New Orleans, Hauser Press, 1960. Much useful information can also be found in *Religion and Politics,* edited by Peter H. Odegard, Dobbs Ferry, N.Y., Oceana Publications, Inc., 1960.

Chapter 6. PROMISES TO KEEP

The early material dealing with the nature of the Presidency, culture-heroes, and presidential heroes is based on my own interpretation of American culture and presidential history.

My paragraphs on the earlier Kennedy rely to a considerable extent on James MacGregor Burns, *John F. Kennedy: A Political Profile,* New York, Harcourt, Brace and Company, 1960, and Richard Whalen, *The Founding Father: The Story of Joseph P. Kennedy,* New York, New American Library, 1964. On Kennedy as a Catholic and Kennedy in the White House, I leaned heavily on Theodore Sorensen, *Kennedy,* New York, Harper & Row, 1965, and Arthur Schlesinger, Jr., *A Thousand Days: John F. Kennedy in the White House,* Boston, Houghton Mifflin Company, 1965, but much of the interpretation is my own. Also helpful was a biography by Hugh Sidey, *John F. Kennedy: President,* New York, Atheneum Publishers, 1963. Kennedy's words come from many sources including his collected speeches, especially John F. Kennedy, *The Burden and the Glory,* edited by Allan Nevins, New York, Harper & Row, 1964, and *Kennedy and the Press: The News Conferences,* edited and annotated by Harold W. Chase and Allen H. Lerman, with an introduction by Pierre Salinger, New York, Crowell-Collier Press, 1965.

On Kennedy's religious views see *The Faith of JFK,* edited by T. S. Settel, introduction by Richard Cardinal Cushing, New York, E. P. Dutton & Co., 1965, a compilation of Kennedy's utterances which bear upon his religious convictions, and *Religious Views of President John F. Kennedy in His Own Words,* compiled by the Reverend Nicholas A. Schneider, St. Louis, B. Herder Book Co., 1965, a similar collection with remarkably little overlapping. The Schneider book focuses on addresses and state papers while the Settel volume concentrates on quotations from the Bible, poetry, and excerpts from speeches.

On the nationwide outpouring of grief in response to Kennedy's assassination, I found the following instructive: *A Tribute to John F. Kennedy,* edited by Pierre Salinger and Sander Vanocur, foreword by Theodore Sorensen and dedication by Lyndon B. Johnson, New York, Atheneum Publishers, 1965; *A Man Named John F. Kennedy: Sermons on His Assassination,* edited by Charles J. Stewart and Bruce Kendall, Glen Rock, N.J., Paulist Press, 1964; and *The Trumpet Summons Us . . . John F. Kennedy, a Compilation of Editorials, Columns and Poems,* by Sister M. Bernadette Schmidt, New York, Vantage Press, Inc., 1964.

For those who wish to pursue further my interpretation of the affinity of the culture-religion for certain aspects of Pelagianism—discussed in the last pages of this chapter—see Adolf von Harnack, *History of Dogma,* Vol. 5, pp. 188–201, translated from the third German edition by Neil Buchanan, New York, Dover Publications, 1961. The interpretation is entirely my own.

Chapter 7. THE VALUE OF OUR TIME

To follow up my discussion of the clash of Catholic and non-Catholic psychological styles, readers may want to look at *American Catholics: A Protestant-Jewish View,* edited by Philip Scharper, with afterword by Gustave Weigel, S.J., New York, Sheed & Ward, 1959. Although some of the writing in this book may seem outdated by post-Vatican Council ecumenism, the six essays by Protestants and Jews are extremely helpful in revealing how Catholics were perceived by others in the 1950's. The article by Robert McAfee Brown, "The Issues Which Divide Us," was particularly useful to me as a concise and typical interpretation of points of view shared by many Protestants. Along the same lines, *An American Dialogue,* by Robert McAfee Brown and Gustave Weigel, S.J., New York, Doubleday & Company, 1960, is insightful and stimulating. See also *Religious Conflict in America,* edited by Earl Raab, New York, Doubleday & Company, 1964.

For fuller citations on the "New Breed" type of books mentioned in the text and others like them, see: Donald J. Thorman, *The Emerging Layman,* New York, Doubleday and Company, 1962; Daniel Callahan, *The Mind of a Catholic Layman,* New York, Charles Scribner's Sons, 1963; Daniel Callahan, *Honesty in the Church,* New York, Charles Scribner's Sons, 1965; *Generation of the Third Eye,* edited by Daniel Callahan, New York, Sheed & Ward, 1965; Michael Novak, *A New Generation: American and Catholic,* New York, Herder & Herder, 1964; Michael Novak, *The Open Church: Vatican II, Act II,* New York, The Macmillan Company, 1964; Michael Novak, *The Experience of Marriage,* New York, The Macmillan Company, 1964; *Objections to Roman Catholicism,* edited by Michael de la Bedoyere, Philadelphia, J. B. Lippincott Co., 1965; Mary Perkins Ryan, *Are Parochial Schools the Answer?,* New York, Holt, Rinehart & Winston, 1964; and Gary MacEoin, *New Challenges to American Catholics,* New York, P. J. Kenedy & Sons, 1965.

The hardest hitting self-criticism I have read (not discussed in the text of my chapter) is Frank Getlein, *The Trouble with Catholics,* Baltimore, Helicon Press, 1964.

Aside from polemical, historical, and philosophical argument, there has been a substantial volume of scholarly writing by Catholics on social questions. Of special value to me has been the work of sociologist Father Andrew Greeley: *The Church and the Suburbs,* New York, Paulist Press, 1959; *Religion and Career,* New York, Sheed & Ward, 1963; and *The Education of American Catholics,* written with Peter G. Rossi, Chicago, Aldine Publishing Company, 1966. Also helpful to me in the preparation of this chapter were the Reverend Joseph H. Fichter, *Priest and People,* New York, Sheed & Ward, 1965, and John B. Donovan, *The Academic Man in the Catholic College,* New York, Sheed & Ward, 1964. Extensive and useful bibliographies of Catholic writings on social issues appear in *The Social Conscience of a Catholic,* edited by the Reverend Everett J. P. Morgan, S.J., Milwaukee, Marquette University Press, 1964.

Helpful in underpinning my understanding of the relationship of Americanism to sectarian religion in the United States were Robin M. Williams, Jr.,

American Society: A Sociological Interpretation, New York, Alfred A. Knopf, 1951, pp. 315–51; Roy F. Nichols, *Religion and American Democracy,* Baton Rouge, La., Louisiana State University Press, 1959; and "Religion and the American Way of Life," by William Lee Miller, in *Religion and the Free Society,* a pamphlet published by the Fund for the Republic, 1958.

Lenski's work referred to in the text comes from Gerhard Lenski, *The Religious Factor,* New York, Doubleday & Company, 1961. The two sociological studies referred to as being critical of certain of Lenski's findings are Joseph H. Fichter, *ibid.,* and Andrew M. Greeley, *Religion and Career,* New York, Sheed & Ward, 1963.

Two important books emphasizing and welcoming tendencies toward making the Church more secular and more human, both written by religious men, one Protestant and the other Catholic, are: Harvey Cox, *The Secular City,* New York, The Macmillan Company, 1965, and Father William H. DuBay, *The Human Church,* New York, Doubleday & Company, 1966. Although aspects of both books have been sharply criticized, it is clear that in essentials the messages they communicate spoke to some of the same tendencies and convictions within John F. Kennedy.

A judicious assessment of the effect of Kennedy's election on new directions of the Catholic Church can be found in Francis J. Lally, *The Catholic Church in a Changing America,* Boston, Little, Brown and Company, 1962.

INDEX